Aneurin Bevan:
Cautious Rebel

Aneurin Bevan: Cautious Rebel

by

Mark M. Krug

Thomas Yoseloff
New York · London

THOMAS YOSELOFF, Publisher
11 East 36th Street
New York 16, N. Y.

THOMAS YOSELOFF, LTD.
123 New Bond Street
London W.1, England

Printed in the United States of America

Acknowledgments

The author is indebted to Professor Charles L. Mowat of the University of Wales, formerly of the University of Chicago, for his valuable suggestions and counsel. Grateful appreciation is due to Professors Herman Finer and A. L. Burt of the University of Chicago, who read the manuscript and offered important suggestions.

Most of all, the author is deeply grateful to Professor C. William Vogel of the University of Cincinnati. Without his friendly guidance, stimulation, and encouragement, especially in the initial stages, this book would not have been written.

TO RUTH, ELYSE AND ORAH

Contents

Aneurin Bevan:
Cautious Rebel

ᴄ᷉1᷍ᴄ Introduction

THE PASSING away of Aneurin Bevan at the age of sixty-two on July 6, 1960, evoked a general expression of mourning and sorrow in Great Britain and in the world. Queen Elizabeth II sent a message of condolence to the widow, Premier Khrushchev of the Soviet Union expressed his deep regret at the news, and Prime Minister Nehru of India mourned the death of "a great and very lovable man."

Prime Minister Harold Macmillan expressed profound sorrow at the "loss of a real personal friend and a great courageous fighter for what he believed to be right." Hugh Gaitskell, the Leader of the Labour Party, stated that Bevan's death was "a most grievous loss to our party, to Parliament, to Britain and indeed to the world."

And yet only a few months before, in March 1959, Macmillan looked straight at Bevan who sat on the Front Opposition Bench and said, "I feel sorry for him as he gropes about, abandoned by his old friends and colleagues —a shorn Samson surrounded by a bevy of prim and aging Delilahs." It is difficult to imagine that even during the recent years of their collaboration, Gaitskell had forgotten that Bevan called him a "dessicated calculating machine" or that Bevan had forgiven Gaitskell for his efforts to have him expelled from the Labour Party.

11

While there is no reason to doubt that the expressions of profound sorrow at Bevan's death voiced by Earl Attlee and Lord Morrison were sincere, it may be recalled that both Clement Attlee and Herbert Morrison voted in 1939 to expel Bevan from the Labour Party, and in 1955 led an attack on Bevan which resulted in his expulsion from the Parliamentary Labour Party. An editorial in the *Times* of London stated that Bevan's death "left Labour immeasurably poorer" and other British newspapers representing all shades of political opinion carried warm editorial tributes to the Labour Party's Foreign Minister in its "Shadow Cabinet."

And yet only five years ago, the *Spectator* called Bevan "the cancer in the Labour Party" and the *Times* of London and other newspapers called on the Labour Party leaders to still the rebellious voice of Aneurin Bevan.

American newspapers led by *The New York Times,* which in an editorial paid tribute to the "outrageously attractive . . . Aneurin Bevan," were on the whole quite generous in appraising the career of the departed British labor leader. But it should be borne in mind that for many years no foreign statesman of an allied or an uncommitted nation, with the possible exception of Krishna Menon of India, was as feared and distrusted by the American press and American public opinion as was Bevan. At the time of Bevan's appointment in 1956 as the Labour Party's spokesman on foreign affairs, scores of editorials appeared in American newspapers and magazines warning that his assumption of the office as Britain's Foreign Secretary would result in British appeasement of the Soviet Union and mark an end to the Anglo-American alliance. Bevan, well aware of his unpopularity in America, made light of the fears he aroused in the United States and the pro-American (London) *Economist* wrote, "Mr. Bevan's appointment as shadow

Foreign Secretary should not frighten the country . . . he has it in him to be a more thoughtful Ernest Bevin." There were many who knew Bevan well who asserted that Mr. Khrushchev's joy at Bevan's appointment as Foreign Secretary in case of Labour Party's victory at the general election would be quite short-lived.

Bevan's death while still only the Deputy Leader of Her Majesty's Opposition made it impossible to ascertain whether the fears or the hopes engendered by Bevan's political aspirations would have been realized. But the assessment of Aneurin Bevan's long, fascinating, and color-ful political career, while difficult, should prove to be in-teresting as well as instructive. The rise, the influence, and the magnetism of this flamboyant, fiery-tongued Welshman, who was besides Winston Churchill a commanding figure in the British Parliament, provide an important lesson in the complicated structure of British politics. The complexity of Bevan's personality coupled with the turbulence of his career and the hatred and the affection which he so easily aroused among his foes and friends render a clear estimate of the man quite difficult. Perhaps the ensuing survey of his political development will prove useful in putting the life and accomplishments of Aneurin Bevan in a clearer perspective.

∾II∾ The South Wales coal field

ANEURIN BEVAN began his life in the South Wales coal field. The memory of the bitter boyhood days never left him and became an influence of major importance in his subsequent career. It was his practice to refer in the House of Commons to the experiences of his childhood. His frequent emotional outbursts against mine owners and "capitalists" can be traced, in a large measure, to the poverty and deprivation which he experienced in his youth and to the long and bitter labor disputes, characteristic of the region, in which he participated through his union and political activities. Bevan was a Welshman, and his personality and his unique political career can be fully understood only against the background of the South Wales coal region, the history of Wales, and the recognized characteristics of the proud sons of that British principality.

Scholars, both Welsh and English, do not agree on the depth of the differences separating Englishmen from Welshmen. The leaders of the small but vocal Welsh Nationalist Party, which was founded in 1925 and which demands a Dominion status for Wales, maintain that the differences are sharp and unbridgeable. Malcolm Thomson, the official biographer of David Lloyd George, wrote:

Very many English people think of the Welsh as a kind of provincial English; a bit peculiar in their way perhaps, and with a

14

local dialect to which they cling rather perversely, but essentially a part of the English nation. That is an utterly mistaken conception. In race and perhaps even more in long-sustained tradition and social and cultural outlook the Welsh are a separate people, differing sharply and indeed antagonistically from their English neighbors.[1]

David Williams, professor of Welsh history at the University College of Wales, acknowledged in 1950 that there was still a divergence of opinion among Welshmen on the desirability of the union with England which took place in 1536. In addition, he wrote,

The Anglicans and dissenters of the seventeenth and eighteenth centuries still have their protagonists. This is even more true of the landowners and their tenants, the industrialists and their workmen, whose struggles form such important aspects of the history of Wales in the eighteenth and the nineteenth centuries.[2]

There are also those who advocate a measure of autonomy for Wales and those who oppose it. Sir Frederick Rees, Vice Chancellor of the University of Wales, takes a moderate and therefore probably a more acceptable position on the Welsh-English relationship. The two and a half million Welshmen inhabit a small country, he said in 1945, which has no well-marked boundary with its powerful English neighbor, with a population of close to 36 million. The Welsh have the right to claim to be the original inhabitants of Britain, having invaded the island six or seven centuries before the English did. Rees pointed out that in spite of all attempts to assimilate and amalgamate the Welsh and the English, the Welsh people continue to have a separate national identity. The English ascribe this separateness to sheer cussedness, and some Welsh nationalists to the enduring characteristics of the Welsh nationality. Be it as it may, Sir Frederick wisely concluded that ". . . we need not quarrel about words. The fact remains that a distinction can be drawn between England and Wales." [3]

The Anglo-Norman conquest of Wales culminated in the defeat of the Welsh in Gwynedd by Edward I at the end of the thirteenth century; this was a closing event to a process of conquest which had lasted for over two centuries. But even then the conquest was neither complete nor secure. The Welsh, driven to the mountains and forests of North Wales, were unconquered in spirit. They continued to speak Welsh and kept Welsh customs and mores. The violence done to the old structure and way of life by the conquerors produced a series of small and large revolts, the most serious of which was the uprising led by Owen Glyn Owr in the first decade of the fifteenth century. A considerable measure of peace and stability came to Wales after the victory of Henry Tudor at Bosworth. Henry's grandfather, Owen Tudor, was of pure Welsh descent and the King himself was brought up by a Welsh nurse and spent the first fourteen years of his life in Wales. During his reign, Henry VII repealed several of the restrictive acts against the Welsh people. These concessions prepared the ground for the Union of England and Wales, which came in the reign of Henry VIII in 1536. The long course of the conquest, the influx of English troops and officials, and most of all the establishment of English settlements brought into Wales English influences and the English language, especially in North Wales and in the valleys of South Wales. But ". . . throughout the Tudor period, while English was spoken in the market towns of Wales, it can safely be assumed that the countryside remained almost entirely Welsh in speech." [4] Although the number of Welshmen who speak Welsh is declining, the Welsh language is still today the strongest cohesive factor of the Welsh people. In 1951, 29 per cent of the population spoke Welsh. Welsh is the lan-

guage of the home and of the primary schools in the rural
communities of North and West Wales, and English is
spoken in the industrial South Wales.[5]

While the English effort of conquest and assimilation was
resisted by Wales as a united national unit, the region has
always suffered from sectionalism. The differences between
North and South Wales and between the eastern and
western parts of Wales are deep-rooted. The latter are
particularly pronounced. Western Wales, preponderantly
rural and in a large proportion Welsh speaking, stretches
from Anglesey to the English border of Pembrokeshire,
while Eastern Wales, mostly English speaking, includes the
populous industrial areas from the northeastern coast to the
Bristol Channel. The line between the two parts runs somewhere from Rhyl to Swansea. One Welsh editor gloomily,
and probably with a great measure of exaggeration, predicted that unless the two halves of Wales get together,
"Western Wales will nurse its grievances and shrink with
each generation; Eastern Wales, left to itself, will drift
off to England." [6]

South Wales is largely one big coal field extending
roughly over 11,000 square miles. It extends from the Bristol
Channel over the counties of Monmouth, Glamorgan,
Brecknock, and Carmarthen. The dominant feature of the
entire region is the Pennant Plateau, which covers almost
the entire coal field and is divided into the valleys of the
eastern, western, and central sections. The division is based
on the river system of the region. There is a succession of
small colliery towns in the valleys of Monmouth, Sirhowey,
Taff, Rhymney, and Rhondda. The proximity of the region
to the Bristol Channel exposes it to the southwest winds,
which bring a great deal of moisture and rain. The climate,
however, is on the whole mild and equable. The coal field
lies across South Wales and is shaped like an elongated

oval. The proximity of the coal deposits to the sea and to the deep transverse valleys was the most important factor in their early exploitation.

The South Wales coal is basically of three varieties: anthracite coal in Pembrokeshire and on the Swansea and Carmarthen bays, and steam and bituminous coal in the eastern parts, including Glamorganshire and Monmouthshire.[7] The South Wales coal has "a lower average volatile content and higher calorific value than those in the English coalfield. . . ."[8]

[It is] pre-eminently suitable for steam raising . . . [and] coke production. It was this quality of the Welsh coal and abundance of iron ore deposits that brought an iron industry into South Wales by the second half of the eighteenth century. The Seven Year War and the American War increased the demand for iron and the discovery of a method of smelting iron by coke made by Abraham Darby at Coalbrookdale and improved by his successors, caused iron manufacturers to build foundries in proximity to coal-mining centers. In the course of a relatively short period of time, through the influx of English capital and English enterprisers, iron works and coal mining companies dotted the landscape of South Wales. Among the larger ones were the Plymouth Works, the Llanishen Works, the Abernant Works, the Tredegar Works, and the Ebbw Vale Works. The iron works were concentrated in a stretch of land eighteen miles long from Hirwau to Blaenavon. It is significant that with the exception of Thomas Sear's, the iron works were owned by Englishmen and were built by English capital. The same was true of most of the larger coal mines. Among them were Chauncey Townsend's collieries at Llamlet and Charles Raby's mines at Llanelly.[9]

Almost simultaneously, the great demand for copper and brass goods brought about the establishment of copper-smelting works. Labor was relatively cheap in South Wales, and since three tons of coal were needed to smelt one ton of copper, it was obviously economical to have the copper works right on the coal field. By the first half of the nineteenth century, South Wales became the greatest iron-producing region in the world and enjoyed a virtual world monopoly in the manufacture of tin plate.[10] The industrial growth brought the development of roads, turnpikes, and canals. Neither the turnpikes nor the canals were efficient for commercial transportation.

The Industrial Revolution in Wales, which came with much greater speed and impact than its counterpart in England, rapidly increased the population of Wales. This growth was caused by an increase in the native population and by immigration of workers from England and Ireland. The population of Wales in 1750 was 480,000 but rose to 673,000 in 1801.

In time mine owners began to mine coal not only for the iron and copper industry but also for export. New mines were opened, and first the canals and then the railways were used to bring the coal to the docks of Cardiff, Newport, and Swansea for export. Soon the coal industry was as important to Wales as the older iron and copper industries. The ownership of the mines was largely in the hands of English companies that owned the iron, copper, and steel works. The giant Ebbw Vale Steel, Iron and Coal Company, for instance, manufactured iron bars, steel rails, and tin plates, and mined coal for the local industry and for export.

It seems important to stress that since South Wales had no industrial tradition, the development of coal mining and coal export depended almost completely upon the influx of capital and enterprise from England. The workers and the miners were mostly simple Welsh country folk, while the owners were English outsiders, often living in London and exercising control through managers and agents. Consequently, ". . . in no other coalfield was the difference between master and man so clearly emphasized." [11] Much of Bevan's vehement animosity toward the mine owners can be explained against this industrial background of South Wales.

The rapid process of industrialization in Wales brought far-reaching and even revolutionary changes. "The social consequences," writes Williams, "which everywhere followed industrialism were, on this account, greatly intensified in Wales." [12] The rapid transformation from an agricultural area into a highly industrialized one and a great influx of population created serious social tensions. Between the 1801 census and the fifth census of 1841 the population of Monmouthshire increased by 117 per cent, and by 1861 the counties of Glamorgan and Monmouth had become predominantly industrial. In Monmouthshire 31,041 persons were employed in industry and 13,855 in agriculture. [13] In spite of large-scale emigration of Welshmen to Canada, Australia, South Africa, the United States, and even Russia, the population of Glamorganshire increased between 1861 and 1889 from 317,752 to 511,283. [14] The discovery of new processes for the manufacture of steel, the discovery of ore mines in the United States, and the 1890 McKinley Act which imposed a tariff duty on imported tin plates caused a decline in the Welsh iron and tin plate industry. This decline was gradually offset by an increase in coal mining, but the transition did not come without periods of depression and unemployment. To this one must add the animosity between the Irish and the Welsh workers and, much more important, the growing animosity between the English owners of mines and factories and the workers, and between the English and Welsh squirearchy and the Welsh tenants. All these factors caused unrest and tension in the coal field. Housing conditions were bad, and there was a great deal of overcrowding, with several families living together in one modest cottage.[15] The mines were located at the bottom of narrow valleys, and proper drainage and sanitation were impossible. Working hours were long, and work in the mines, which lacked safety devices and arrangements, was dangerous, especially for women and children. The pay was low and the cost of living high, especially because of the high prices charged in the truck or company food shops. No wonder, therefore, that there was a succession of riots: the Tredegar riots of 1816, the Merthyr riots of 1831, the Denbighshire riots of 1830, and the Chartist uprisings of 1838, 1843, and 1848. The profound discontent of the Welsh peasantry exploded in the 1830's in the famous Rebecca riots in West Wales and partly in North and South Wales. Thousands of peasants attacked turnpike toll gates to protest excessive tolls, increased church rates and tithes, and the harsh operation of the Poor Law of 1834.

The miners of South Wales, yet unorganized, were called upon not to fight for better wages but to resist efforts of the mine owners to reduce their earnings. "It is significant," writes Williams, "that, at least until 1871, not a single strike of any importance whatsoever was caused by a demand for increased wages; strikes were invariably attempts to resist reduction in wages." [16] The miners soon came to realize that they must organize for the protection of their rights, and after several local unions were established, the Amalgamated Association of Miners came into being in 1869. Another miners union was established by William Abraham (better known as Mabren), which took the name of the Cambrian Miners' Association. The mine owners countered by organizing the Monmouthshire and South Wales Coal Owners Association under the leadership of William Thomas Lewis. The miners went on a first major strike in 1871, demanding a 10-per-cent increase in wages; after six months of a partial shutdown of the mines they were defeated.[17] But the defeat brought forth a demand for greater unity, and seven unions, including the Amalgamated Association of Miners and the Cambrian Miners' Association, united into the South Wales Miners Federation, which soon became affiliated with the Miners Federation of Great Britain. The unity brought immediate results in the election in 1900 of Keir Hardie, who had already in 1893 founded the Independent Labour Party, to Parliament. In 1912 the militant South Wales Federation joined its parent body in a general strike of miners that eventually led to the award of about four shillings and sixpence per day as a minimum wage.

~III~   Bevan and Welsh Nationalism

IN THE second half of the nineteenth century the cleavage and antagonism between the Welsh miners and ironworkers and their English employers and managers, the gap between the tenant farmers and the anglicized Welsh gentry, became aggravated by a religious controversy—the struggle for the disestablishment of the Anglican Church of Wales and the freeing of the schools from church control.

In the eighteenth century the majority of the Welsh people had become Calvinistic Methodists, as part of the evangelistic movement in England of Wesley and White-field. The Methodist revival resulted in the establishment of Nonconformist chapels where fiery sermons on salvation were delivered in Welsh by Welsh preachers. Many Welsh union leaders and M.P.'s received their initial instruction and inspiration in effective oratory, in which many of them excelled, from listening to the weekly sermons in the chapels. The chapels soon became socio-religious centers by sponsoring week-night prayer and study meetings and by the establishment of schools where the children were taught the Bible in the Welsh translation made by William Morgan in 1588. The number of chapels grew rapidly. The 1851 census showed that the Anglican Church had 1,180 places of worship in Wales, as compared with 2,769 Nonconformist chapels. In addition, a literary revival of native art, folklore, and literature in the nineteenth century accentuated the differences between the Anglophile gentry and the mass of the people. The Welsh landowners, mine owners, nobles, and officials were English in their education, language, and spirit, and faithful members of the Established Church, while the common people were proud of their national and literary traditions and Nonconformism. Nonconformity became the strongest link between rural and industrial Wales. Among miners in the coal field, the Nonconformists outnumbered the Anglicans three to one. By 1906, a royal commission estimated that 74 per cent of the members of the Protestant churches of Wales were Nonconformist.[1] Thus the religious, economic, social, and linguistic cleavage between the small upper class and the people was a characteristic feature of Welsh society by the first decade of the twentieth century. As one writer puts it,

When the Welsh woke up to new awareness of themselves, they felt themselves foreigners in their own land. Two communities inhabited the country; one strongly conservative, allied with and exerting the powers of government, rules the destinies of the workers, controlling the security and well-being of farmer and peasant through ownership of the land and its resources.[2]

The people became increasingly unhappy with the imposed payment of church rates and tithes to the Anglican Church and with the church control of the education of their children. The parish schools were not only under control of a minority church but were also poorly housed and, in the main, staffed by incompetent teachers. From 1869, when the act to disestablish the Irish Church became law, the Welsh people fought for the disestablishment and the disendowment of the Anglican Church and for the establishment of a free school system. The drive for a new independent network of schools received its greatest impetus from the publication of the "Blue Books" in 1847. The report was prepared by three commissioners appointed to inquire into the status of education in Wales following the Rebecca riots. The Blue Books did contain some valid evaluation of Welsh education, and the commissioners made no attempt to whitewash the church schools. They were highly critical of their housing, teachers, and curriculum. One of the commissioners did not hesitate to put his finger on the root of the problem. He wrote, "The wealthy classes who contribute towards education belong to the Established Church; the poor who are to be educated are Dissenters. The former will not aid in supporting neutral schools; the latter withhold their children from such as require conformity to the Established Church." [3] The Blue Books, however, also contained insulting statements concerning the alleged immorality of Welsh women (significantly attributed to the week-night services) and a harsh condemnation of the Welsh language as a barrier to the moral progress of the principality. The Welsh never forgot or forgave the insults, and their leaders often recalled the treachery of the Blue Books.

The leadership in the movement for disestablishment and for Welsh schools was undertaken in 1890 by the most illustrious son of Wales, David Lloyd George, who in that year was elected Member of Parliament for Caernarvon Boroughs after defeating a Tory squire. Lloyd George's victory signified the increasing determination of Welshmen to seek redress of their grievances in Parliament through the election of Liberals. In election after election they delighted in administering defeats to the Tory candidates, who were as a rule supported by the Welsh gentry, the industrialists, and the Anglican Church. After World War I and the decline of the Liberals, Wales became and remains until this day a stronghold of the Labour Party.

Immediately after his election, Lloyd George decided to gain national prominence by giving expression to Welsh nationalist demands. He demanded "a free religion and a free people in a free land." [4] In a later speech delivered in London, in a typical fiery and emotional style of Welsh oratory, he declared that

The spiritual wants of the Welsh people are attended to by Non-Conformity. The Non-Conformist chapels are crowded but the churches of the Establishment are forsaken in every rural district of Wales. It is the same old story—it is not the people who do the work who receive the pay.[5]

Lloyd George and other Liberal M.P.'s began a vigorous campaign for the passage of a Welsh disestablishment act and for freeing of the educational system in Wales from church control. When in 1902 Parliament passed the Education Act, which empowered the counties to establish schools under a local school authority but also allowed the churches to retain their tax-supported "voluntary" schools, Welsh nationalists started the so-called "Welsh Revolt." Led by Lloyd George, they took control of the county councils which established a considerable number of schools supported by the counties and the Government. The disestablishment of the Anglican Church took longer to achieve; it was not completed until 1920.

The struggle for Welsh national aspirations continued, if in a somewhat abortive fashion, during the childhood and youth of Aneurin Bevan, who was born in November 1897. Its background and motivations and the economic struggle of the miners for a measure of job security and decent wages greatly influenced his political thinking. The Tory landed gentry and aristocracy, which included the mine owners, were the object of Bevan's enmity and a favorite target of his frequent and barbed attacks. He never tired of denouncing the rich Tory mine owners who from their spacious homes and estates on the hills ruled the lives and exploited the labor of the miners living in small cottages in the grimy mining towns in the valleys. His biting oratory, full of ridicule of the heartless Tory squires, seldom failed to arouse his Ebbw Vale constituents to a pitch of enthusiasm. He delighted and stirred them to cheers for their "Nyrin."

There is little in the long record of Bevan's speeches in Parliament and on meeting platforms to indicate that he was ever very much preoccupied with the struggle against the Anglican Church in Wales. Religious upbringing and religious issues apparently played little role in Bevan's life. He did not speak Welsh and his concern with Welsh problems and national aspirations was never as strongly pronounced as Lloyd George's in the early years of the latter's political career. Bevan was a proud Welshman; he loved Wales and particularly the South Wales coal field, but his primary concern and interest lay in his determination to force British governments to provide a better deal for the workingmen and to assure employment and protection from sickness and disability for the common people of England, Wales, and Scotland. He never had any difficulty in accepting the official policy of the Labour Party, which is not in favor of any degree of Welsh self-government.

In October 1944, the Welsh members of Parliament succeeded in getting a day set aside in the House of Commons for the discussion of the problems of Wales. Bevan listened to his countrymen expound the glories of Wales and the special needs of their constituents and then made a speech that annoyed the Welshmen but delighted the rest of the House. He denouncd the whole idea of the

Welsh Day and declared that Welsh problems are identical
with those of the entire country.

My colleagues, all of them Members of the Miners Federation
of Great Britain, have no special solution for the "Welsh" coal
industry which is not a solution for the whole mining industry
of Great Britain . . . why should we deceive the people by this
deplorable humbug that there is anything like a Welsh mining
problem. . . . Our problem is to get enough political leverage
to secure attention to our difficulties. Look where we have got
to-day—if you take this technique as a way of drawing attention to Wales. The English are not listening to us, nor have the
Welsh been listening to us most of the day. As a means of directing public attention upon particularly Welsh problems, it is
a farce.[6]

His Welsh colleagues were distressed by his speech but
they acknowledged his influence and his power by electing
him in December 1944 chairman of the Welsh Parliamentary Party. Lady Megan Lloyd George, the daughter of the
Prime Minister, and herself and M.P., remarked upon the
election, "I do not think that a saddle has ever been put on
this bucking broncho of ours before, and I am looking forward to seeing him try to keep others in order." [7]

In 1946 Aneurin Bevan was awarded the degree of Doctor of Laws, *honoris causa*, by the University of Wales. But
neither the degree nor the election to the chairmanship
changed his conviction that the deliverance of Wales, and
especially of the coal field, would come not by a Welsh victory but by a British Socialist Government. While Bevan
has never followed the temptation to use Welsh nationalism
as a means of enhancing his political career—a temptation
to which Lloyd George so willingly and so skillfully suc-
cumbed—his character and personality were profoundly
affected by the general characteristics ascribed to all Welshmen. What are these characteristics?

As with all generalizations concerning peoples and nations, one must be careful when making any categorical assertions. Some generalizations can, however, be made, especially if they are suggested by Welshmen. Thus one Welsh writer maintains that Welshmen are ". . . a more emotional, temperamental, excitable people than the English. . . ." [8] The Welsh certainly possess a special gift for storytelling; they are much less reserved and more talkative than the English, and their representatives in the British Parliament have fully confirmed the long-held opinion that Welsh politicians have a natural flair for oratory which tends to be emotional and picturesque. The history of the militant Welsh miners' unions confirms the impression that the Welsh like a good fight often for fight's sake. There are few things that Bevan liked better than the intricate talking duels of a negotiating table, and even his enemies conceded that he had a special gift for difficult negotiations. The generations of miners have developed some unique characteristics, and it is possible, in a limited way, to speak of a typical South Wales miner. One author says:

The South Wales collier is a type quite of his own. Short, dark, sturdy, quick-tempered, friendly and generous to the point of extravagance. . . . He is intelligent and impatient, qualities that make him the first to advocate any improvement for the benefit of mineworkers and the first to go on strike to obtain it. Fundamentally he is a true democrat, believing with all his heart in freedom for others as well as for himself. . . . He has a rare gift of imagination, a lyrical sense which finds its spontaneous outlet in poetry and in singing. . . . His special brand of humor has a sardonic flavor.[9]

This generalized picture of a South Wales miner fits Bevan very well. There is, however, one characteristic of the Welsh miner which is difficult to reconcile with Bevan's zest for life and his natural gaiety and good humor, namely, the acceptance, in a spirit of stoic resignation, of disaster, disease, and death as natural phenomena. The Welsh folk poetry abounds in themes of death and gloom. Typical is this beautiful poem:

> One night as I lay on my bed,
> And sleep on fleeting foot had fled,
> Because, no doubt, my mind was heavy
> With concern for my last journey.
>
> I got me up and called for water,
> That I might wash, and so feel better;
> But before I wet my eyes so dim,
> There was Death on the bowl's rim.
>
> I went to church that I might pray,
> Thinking sure he'd keep away;
> But before I got on to my feet,
> There sat Death upon my seat.
>
> Then to sea I rowed a boat,
> Thinking surely Death can't float;
> But before I reached the deep,
> Death was captain of the ship.[10]

~IV~ Bevan's early Parliamentary career

THE GENERAL conditions in the South Wales coal field at the end of World War I, when Bevan was a youth of twenty-one, were improved as far as living and working conditions were concerned but greatly worsened as far as the employment situation was concerned. We get a comprehensive picture of the region from the Report of the South Wales Regional Survey Committee, which was appointed by the Ministry of Health and published its findings in 1921.[1] The committee found that South Wales had about 480 collieries in the coal field, employing about 260,000 men with an output of 47,500,000 tons. In 1913 the coal output was 56,830,000.[2] The drop in coal production was attributed primarily to the facts that warships began to use oil instead of coal and that Holland and Poland greatly increased the output of their coal mines. Some of the mines were large, employing over two thousand men, and most of them were situated on the floors of the valleys, with only a relatively few being located on the sides of the hills. Of the large number of iron and steel works only those of Dowlais, Tredegar, Ebbw Vale, and Blaenarvon remained on the coal field. Others either closed or moved to other sections of Wales or England. Only a small number

of local ore was mined, but the production of steel remained quite considerable. In 1918 South Wales produced
2,057,907 tons of steel as compared to the 9,591,478 tons
produced by the United Kingdom. There were 382 tin plate
mills which produced in 1919 about 260,000 tons of tin
plate, thus assuring for South Wales a virtual monopoly in
that field of production in Great Britain.

The committee reported that "In most of the valleys coal-
mining is the principal and usually almost the sole industry
of importance. The restricted range of choice results in the
fact that the whole of the male members of a family usually
resort to mining as their life occupation." [3] The miners are
devoted to the South Wales Miners Federation and "although they often refer to the organization in harsh terms,
their belief in it as a means of securing their economic eman-
cipation is deep-rooted." [4]

The committee found the birth rate in South Wales considerably higher than that of all English counties and the
death rate quite comparable to that of other industrial re-
gions. The housing conditions were greatly improved; the
report states that, "As compared with the older coal field,
it may be stated that the amount of unsanitary housing accommodation in South Wales is relatively small." [5] The cottages of the miners were small, with a parlor or kitchen and
three bedrooms on the first floor. Very few houses, however, had bathrooms or a hot-water supply. The report also
noted that most cottages were built without adequate site
planning and consequently had only a limited amount of
sunshine and were exposed to cold northerly winds.[6] A
great change had also occurred in the home ownership.
While in the latter decades of the nineteenth century miners' homes were owned by the mine companies, the committee estimated that in 1920 80 per cent of the homes and
cottages were owned by the miners.

Into this environment Aneurin Bevan was born, in Tredegar in November 1897, and here he spent his childhood
years. The improvements in housing which the Survey Committee found in 1921 were still a long way off. When
Aneurin was born, miner's families occupied many houses
in Tredegar which were formerly stables for the Tredegar
Iron and Coal Company horses. Other houses were built
on the sides of the coal tips—tips made up of stone, shale,
and other refuse from the mines and dumped at the surface
in close proximity to the collieries. Iron Street and Iron Row
were long the streets of slums of Tredegar. The town had
more imposing public buildings, including the old church
with galleries and horse-box pews where the gospel of "God
bless our masters and their dear relations, and keep the rest
of us in our proper stations" was regularly preached. Bevan's
family had a sturdy five-room cottage home, but the harsh
facts of the miners' life were impressed upon him very early
in his life. One can get a good picture of life in a mining
town and the people in it from a story entitled "A Welsh
Mining Village" which appeared in *The Welsh Review* in
1946. In its basic and very perceptive features the story is
undoubtedly descriptive of Tredegar in Bevan's youth, in
spite of a considerable lapse of time.

. . . the days are mostly behind a screen of slow rains. . . .
While the air becomes oily, the roofs and roads glossy, the river
fuller and noisier, men bite their pipes and . . . enjoy as always,
a talk for talk's sake. . . . Life here [is] mostly grey, but there
is also a drop of gold in it. . . . What happens today to one
happens tomorrow to another. Therefore there is sincere concern in each other's lives. . . . Men need each other if only to
talk to—or just to make the heart easier . . . thus men listen
with heavy concentration, and share feelings, laughter and tears.
. . . Birth and death are faced as a matter of fact, the first without too much fuss and the other without too much gloom. . . .

Emotion replaces sentimentality, the quality of voice replaces the choice of smart words. . . . Even underground men [are] falling naturally into oratory. . . .[7]

Bevan's parents had had a small sheep farm, but they had to sell out and move into the poverty and squalor of semi-industrial Tredegar, where his father, David, went to work in the mines. Aneurin was one of thirteen children, five of whom died in childhood. His was a very modest home, where poverty and sickness were no strangers. He attended the Mixed and Infants School in Sirhowy, but had to leave at thirteen to work in the mines to supplement the meager wages of his father. Shortly thereafter his father died in Aneurin's arms of pneumoconiosis, a coal-dust disease to which miners' lungs are subject. In an autobiographical sketch Bevan bitterly comments that no compensation was paid to his family because the illness was not, at that time, considered an industrial disease.[8] During his early years as a Member of Parliament, Bevan devoted strenuous efforts to assure the miners and their families of adequate medical service and compensation for occupational diseases.

Bevan threw himself wholeheartedly into union activities, and the Miners Federation soon recognized his potential value. At the age of nineteen he was made chairman of a miners' local with a membership of four thousand. He became an active and popular union leader and was clearly destined for bigger things, but was severely handicapped by an embarrassing stammer which made public speaking a painful experience. He decided to correct it and sought the advice of Walter Conway, the chairman of the South Wales Medical Society. Bevan told him that he was despondent because of his stammer, and Conway gave him advice which, as Bevan said later in his life, was the best he had ever received. He told him, "You stammer in speech because you falter in thought. If you can't say it, you don't know it." [9] Bevan later testified that he had never forgotten Conway's diagnosis of his trouble. He decided to talk less often in public and to devote a great deal of his time to acquiring more knowledge. "I spent hours in our workman's library," he wrote, "every week, reading industrial history, sociology and philosophy." [10]

The test came when, as president of his miners' lodge (the local unit of the union), the young Bevan led a delegation to meet with the representative of the mine owners to negotiate a new contract. To avoid stammering he studied thoroughly all the facts and figures pertaining to the mine situation and the contract negotiations. He emerged from the ordeal with flying colors, was effective and persuasive, did not stammer, and his delegation won a small wage increase. "For me," he related, "it was a double triumph." [11]

But Bevan noticed that during the negotiations the mine owner's representative mentioned things Bevan did not know and quoted from the works of two great English philosophers, John Stuart Mill and Jeremy Bentham. Bevan felt humiliated that his knowledge in areas outside of mining was so limited and it annoyed him that his opponent "kept me walking up to the frontiers of my knowledge." [12] He discovered that a truly cultured and educated person must learn around and beyond his immediate subject and interest. This he decided to do. With utmost dedication and determination Bevan decided to educate himself in philosophy, geography, and even art. He saw in art, with which he was soon on familiar terms, an expression of man's longings and dreams, and a reflection of the various stages of civilization. "Where can you see," he asked, "the conditions of working people in the eighteenth century better than in the drawings of Hogarth and Rowlandson? Where better judge the effect of war on people than in Goya's art?" [13]

He was soon sent to London at the expense of the union

to attend the Central Labour College. He studied and read avidly and became a Socialist largely through the influence of the works of two American Socialist leaders, Eugene V. Debs and Daniel de Leon.[14] He read Marx, but quite early in his studies came to the conclusion that "classic Marxism consistently understated the role of political democracy with a fully developed franchise." [15] This concise statement contains the core of Bevan's rejection of Communism with its inherent contempt for political freedom and free elections.

Upon his return to South Wales, Bevan became a miners' agent, but could no get work in the mines because the mine owners blacklisted him. He earned his livelihood for three years as a day laborer on road building. Bevan vividly recalls his poverty-stricken Monmouthshire district of the thirties: "In part of Monmouthshire whole townships were idle for years. The poverty was appalling and the outlook black to the point of despair. . . . Idle looms, deserted pits and silent steelworks mocked at the claims of capitalist economies." [16] This experience of hopeless poverty had a profound influence on Bevan's political philosophy. It throws a light on his uncompromising hatred of capitalism and his abiding Socialist faith.

One of his friends attempted to persuade him to emigrate with him to Australia, but Bevan told him: "David, I hate to see you leave us, but if this is how you feel about it, then you must go and I wish you all the luck in the world. For myself, *I am going to stay here and fight* it out. . . . I can't bear the thought of seeing them win over us. . . ." [17] He had never ceased fighting.

Then came the turbulent and bitter days of the General Strike. The origins of this memorable strike can be traced to the decision of the British Government of Stanley Baldwin on April 28, 1925, to return to the gold standard. The new British monetary policy, which was announced by Winston Churchill, then Chancellor of the Exchequer, resulted in an in increase in the cost of British goods and consequently made the export of British products, and especially coal, more difficult. The mine owners felt that the only way to produce cheaper coal which could compete in the export markets would be to increase working hours and to reduce wages. The miners, led by the militant A. J. Cook, rejected these demands and blamed the sickness of the coal industry on the unwillingness of the mine owners to introduce modern and efficient machinery, to close unproductive mines, and to eliminate the senseless competition among a large number of individually owned mines. They demanded the nationalization of the coal industry. The conflict was averted at the last minute by an offer of the Government to provide a subvention to avert a reduction in wages.

In the meantime, a royal commission under the chairmanship of Sir Herbert Samuel studied the entire coal industry. Both the miners and the owners rejected the proposals of the commission, and in 1926 the mine owners terminated the miners' contracts in order to rehire their working forces at lower wages. The Miners Federation threatened a strike and the mediation efforts of the Government collapsed. The General Council of the Trades Union Congress gave full support to the miners and called for a General Strike on midnight of May 3. The strike was only partly successful because of the efficient measures taken by the Government to assure essential transportation and supplies for the nation. It also became clear that the basically moderate and patriotic trade union leaders were alarmed at the far-reaching implications of a General Strike.[18]

They were not prepared and had made no plans to meet the concerted attack of the central government and the bitter criticism of the nation's press. The labor leaders,

basically respectful of authority and quite content with the
established social order, shuddered at being called "bolsheviks" and "revolutionaries." The strike could have been successful only if its leaders had been ready to give it a revolutionary character. This they were completely unwilling to
do. "Had the menaced nation seen, as I had just seen," wrote
David Low, "the batch of scared trade union rabbits scut-
tering up Downing Street, hats in hands, to implore the
Prime Minister to make the mine-owners negotiate, they
would have appreciated Jix's [the Home Secretary, Sir William Johnson-Hicks] egregious absurdity." [19]

When Sir Herbert Samuel offered a prospect of renewal
of negotiations, the Trades Union Council called off the
strike on May 12. The miners, with Cook as their uncompromising leader, decided to continue the strike to the bitter end, which came when starvation drove them back to
the pits. Bevan strenuously opposed any suggestion of compromise or surrender. The situation in South Wales and in
other mining areas was charged with hate and desperation.
Aneurin Bevan was one of the leaders of the strike, and he
never forgot the bitterness and the hopelessness of those
days of strife and hate. He testified that during the General
Strike he was a delegate to all the miners' conferences and
negotiating meetings and spent a great deal of time in the
company of A. J. Cook, the national secretary of the Miners
Federation. He defended Cook against the charges of extremism. While he conceded that Cook lacked negotiating
skill, he paid tribute to him for being "passionately devoted
to the miners, and he burned himself out in a flame of protest against unjust conditions imposed on his people." [20]
Finally, the exhaustion of union funds and the hunger of the
miners' families forced the Federation to order the men
back to the mines on terms laid down by the mine owners.
This was a painful and humiliating defeat that Bevan re-

membered all his life. Of the collapse of the strike he wrote: "The British governing class was determined to crush their [the miners'] resistance at whatever cost. And the cost was high. We are still paying it." [21] After the strike he again suffered many years of unemployment as the price of his union activities.[22]

The General Strike marked the end of one epoch in the history of the British Labour movement and the beginning of another. British labor leaders realized that the full mobilization of the workers' power in a General Strike was unsuitable for them because it could not be reconciled with their adherence to political democracy. They became convinced that improvement in the lot of the workers would be attained through the growing power and influence of the Labour Party in Parliament. In the words of a Labour Party historian: "The General Strike represents a decisive watershed . . . the trade unions moved increasingly towards a more constructive industrial policy, and the Socialist movement as a whole, despite the clamor in the Communist wing, set itself to work for advance exclusively through constitutional political means." [23]

Aneurin Bevan drew his own conclusions from the new situation, and in June 1929 he stood for Parliament from the Ebbw Vale constituency in South Wales and was elected at the age of thirty-two. He rallied the solid support of the miners and their families, who continued to give him substantial majorities in all subsequent elections. The affection of his constituents did not waver even when Bevan was in deep trouble with the leadership of the Labour Party and the nation's press.

In 1939, after the Labour Party expelled Bevan and withdrew its blessing and support of him, his miners gave him a vote of confidence by electing him to the House of Commons by a large majority. The South Wales miners looked upon Bevan as one of their own and gave him steadfast and loyal support. They were fully cognizant and appreciative of the utmost devotion to their welfare that was the most characteristic feature of Bevan's Parliamentary service. Aneurin Bevan, as Hansard conclusively proves, was a superbly effective fighter for better working conditions for the British miners. He was always in the forefront of all efforts to improve the lot of the miners, and he never allowed the many political battles in which he so often engaged to distract him from looking after the interests of his constituents and of his home district. A miner, Bevan's constituent, once told an American correspondent, "Look man, Nyrin tells them, see, what it's like in the mines. He's for us and our people. He's always thinking about us, fighting for us, see." [24] The pictures of poverty and degradation in his home district were always vivid in Bevan's consciousness. A contemporary eyewitness related after a visit to Britain's depressed areas, "I had never seen real poverty and degradation before. Ugh, the places crawled. I was filled with rage and disgust, rather than pity at the blind stupidity that allowed such things to be." [25]

As an obscure backbencher in the Labour Party, Bevan supported the Labour Government of Ramsay MacDonald but fought for the improvement of the Coal Mines Bill of 1929 and repeatedly urged larger benefits for the unemployed from the Unemployment Insurance Fund. He found it difficult to adjust himself to the age-honored niceties of the British Parliament. His initial appearance on the floor of the House of Commons was marred by an unfortunate incident. To avoid any possibility of the reappearance of his stammer, Bevan devoted many days to the preparation of his maiden speech and delivered it smoothly but with a great deal of fire and polemic. He was the Welsh coal miner who came to give these high-born gentlemen a piece of his mind. It is the custom of the House that the next Member who rises offers the congratulations and best wishes of Parliament to the new Member. In Bevan's case this was not done, and years later Bevan wrote that "in my case the courtesy was unintentionally neglected." [26] Winston Churchill, as Bevan recalled, quickly noted the oversight and came over to him and said, "I liked your speech. It was spontaneous, like a debater in rebuttal." [27]

In spite of the difficulties, by tenacious efforts he soon overcame his stammer, and was later generally regarded as the best speaker and debater in the House of Commons with the exception of Winston Churchill, who did not hesitate on several occasions to praise the oratorical talents of his bitterest critic.

The General Election of 1929 gave the Labour Party the largest number of seats, and Ramsay MacDonald formed the second Labour Government in British history. But the Labour rule was shaky because it needed the support of the fifty-nine Liberal M.P.'s, with Lloyd George exploiting to the fullest his possession of the balance of power. The elections were fought on the central issue of unemployment and the worsening economic situation. There were a million unemployed who were receiving unemployment payments but clamored for work instead of public charity. The blight and the degradation of the depressed areas were increasing and the restlessness and hopelessness of their growing populations became a matter of grave concern even in the councils of the Tories.

It soon became clear that MacDonald's Government had no concrete and effective plans for fighting unemployment. In October 1929 the situation worsened, following the Wall Street stock market crash which plunged the United States into the worst depression in its history. The depression had disastrous effects on world trade and on British economy.

Unemployment rose to two million, and inadequate measures of the Government to initiate public works did not succeed even in alleviating the grave situation.

Aneurin Bevan, while generally supporting the Government, was growing increasingly impatient with the ineffectiveness of the Government in eradicating unemployment, getting a constructive program to deal with the depressed areas, and improving the lot of the British workers, particularly of the coal miners. He neither liked nor approved the obvious determination of the Labour ministers—particularly of J. H. Thomas, MacDonald, and Philip Snowden—to adopt the traditional dress and manners of British statesmen and play down their adherence to Socialist principles. His strong speeches urging effective measures to deal with unemployment and calling for vigorous Government intervention in the coal crisis were gaining respect and recognition for the young Welshman. He was thorough in preparing the data for his speeches and his delivery was steadily improving. The Tory opposition was soon to feel the stings of his sallies and invectives, and even his friends were not spared his wrath when in Bevan's opinion they gave offense to his strong Socialist convictions.

When the Labour Government asked in a coal mines bill to reduce the working hours of the miners and regulate the production and the sale of coal, Bevan gave his full support to the measure, which he considered inadequate but at least a step in the right direction. To his chagrin, Lloyd George, his respected and admired countryman, attacked the measure because of its provision for a levy on home-sold coal and led the Liberals in voting against the Government. MacDonald survived by a majority of eight votes.

Outraged by this show of Liberal–Tory cooperation, Aneurin Bevan delivered a slashing attack on Lloyd George and Winston Churchill as being "in a temporary re-alliance, which may be carried right through to the division lobby in their capacity as joint executioners." [28] In a display of emotional oratory which later became his trademark in the House of Commons, Bevan bitterly denounced his illustrious fellow Welshman. "Better to have slightly dearer coal than cheaper colliers," he cried.

. . . We say that you cannot get from the already dry veins of the miners new blood to revivify the industry. Their veins are already shrunken white, and we are asking you to be, for once, decent to the miners . . . not to use all your Parliamentary skill, all your rhetoric, in an act of pure demogogy to expose the mining community of this country to another few years of misery.[29]

Veteran Parliamentary correspondents later reported that Lloyd George was very uneasy during Bevan's speech. He was seen listening intently and crossing and recrossing his legs, a sure sign of his unhappiness. When he got up to reply, Lloyd George expressed his sincere regret "to have fallen foul of a young countryman of mine, for whom I have a great deal of admiration." [30]

Bevan did not wait long to attack the Government of his own party. On November 4, 1930, he rose and assailed Herbert Morrison, the Minister of Transport, for lack of effective action to help the two million unemployed in the country. This speech marks the beginning of Bevan's long career as an irrepressible rebel. He said:

This is the first time that I have spoken critically of the Government on the floor of this House, but I submit there is a case to answer, and that Parliament has a right to expect an answer from the Government. You cannot leave 2,000,000 unemployed all the while. We, who have not been in the House for very long, have been listening to the speeches of the elder statesmen with quite a deal of hopelessness and despair.[31]

The resignation of Ramsay MacDonald in August 1931 and his defection from the Labour Party by the formation of the National Government made Bevan's task as an outspoken critic of the Government much easier. Great Britain was in the throes of a severe economic crisis, and Mac-Donald's Government found it necessary to increase taxes and reduce the costs of social services. His openly declared inability to cope with the critical economic situation was widely interpreted as a confession of bankruptcy of the socialist program. The Labour Party's morale was shattered and sinking lower.[32] But Bevan was undaunted and castigated MacDonald by the use of the personal invective for which he later became famous and feared in the House of Commons. He repeatedly accused MacDonald of substituting beautiful gestures (in speaking) for actions in combating unemployment and poverty.

In 1931 MacDonald got the royal consent to the dissolution of the Parliament, and the ensuing General Election brought a crushing defeat to the Labour Party. The Labourites elected only 46 members as compared to 287 in the previous Parliament. The reasons for this debacle were mainly the general failure of the domestic program of MacDonald's Socialist Government, the growing economic crisis, and the blow to the Labour Party's prestige by the "betrayal" of MacDonald and Philip Snowden.[33]

Bevan survived the debacle and returned to the House to continue his fight for more effective measures to combat the growing unemployment. Clement Attlee, never fond of Bevan, testified that Bevan upon his return to Parliament made "a series of brilliant speeches on the problem of depressed areas and on the unemployment regulations." [34] As the depression continued, the Parliamentary Labour Party grew more and more restive. Many of the younger backbenchers believed that the official leaders of the Party were too moderate and conciliatory. They formed a more radical group under the leadership of Sir Oswald Mosley, who at that time was a member of the Labour Party. In December 1929 the group published a manifesto attacking the Government's policies on fighting unemployment. The signers included A. J. Cook, Aneurin Bevan, and John Strachey.[35] Bevan shunned Mosley after the latter was expelled from the Labour Party on March 10, 1931, and became his bitter enemy when Mosley formed the British Fascist Union.

In the period between 1931 and 1936, Bevan rarely spoke in the House on foreign affairs matters—he continued to press for a greater effort to eliminate or at least diminish unemployment. Bevan told the Parliament that almost half of the adult population in his constituency was unemployed. "Colliery owners in my district," he said, "are employing boys of 14 and keep them at the underground work until the age of 20 and then throw them out of work." [36] Bevan demanded help for the depressed areas, and particularly for South Wales, in the form of public works and greater unemployment compensation. He gradually grew exasperated with what he considered the inadequate measures taken by the National Government of Stanley Baldwin to deal with the situation. In the language which later became known as "Bevanese" he told Baldwin and his ministers, "If you go on this way much longer, you will be digging your own graves and I hope that you dig them deeply enough." [37]

The rarity of Bevan's utterances on foreign affairs was probably not an indication of his lack of interest in external relations, but because he was completely absorbed in the task of fighting for measures which would alleviate the misery of unemployment. His concern with foreign affairs was sharpened by the international crisis brought about by Mussolini's ruthless invasion of Abyssinia and the inability of the League of Nations to stop the aggression. The inva-

sion brought a division of opinion within the Labour Party
between the pacifists led by the Party leader, George Lansbury, and the Ernest Bevin faction, which believed that
Great Britain should rearm and give effective support to the
collective security policy of the League of Nations even at
the risk of war. The issue was fought out at the Thirty-fifth
Annual Conference of the Labour Party, held in Brighton.
The great majority voted for full support of League of Nations sanctions against Italy, but not before Bevin, a powerful leader of the Transport Workers, using his characteristic
blunt language forced Lansbury's resignation by telling the
delegates that "this conference ought not to continue to be
put in a position of watching Lansbury cart his conscience
around from conference to conference asking to be told
what to do with it." [38]

Bevan supported, both at the Labour Party conference
and in the House of Commons, an effective security system
for the League of Nations, and demanded from the British
Government effective steps to stop Mussolini's and Hitler's
aggressive plans. He was disgusted with Baldwin's Government for having done nothing, or very little, to alleviate the
curse of unemployment, bad housing, and ill health.

In one of his occasional scathing outbursts, which made
Bevan hated and feared by many, he told the House of
Commons, "It is no use my going on. I cannot move the
Hon. Members to pity. It is impossible. There is only one
thing left, that is hate. I believe more in hate than in pity
myself. . . . There never was a ruling class in the whole
history so stupid as you are." [39]

~ V ~ The "United Front" Campaign

THE DETERIORATING international situation in 1935 and 1936, caused by the growing menace of Fascism and Nazism, caused Bevan to devote an increasing amount of his time and activity to foreign affairs. He was deeply troubled by the mouting evidence that the Nationalists were gaining the upper hand over the Republicans in Spain, largely because of the help received from Italy and Germany. Like many rank and file members of the Labour Party, he was convinced that British Socialists did not do enough to help Republican Spain and erred in condoning England's policy of neutrality, which in fact denied men and arms to the Republican cause. The march of Adolf Hitler into the Rhineland while the League of Nations looked on helplessly was to Bevan and to the left wing of the Labour Party additional proof that only a government elected and supported by all workers parties and relying on broad support would be able to avert war. In this struggle for a United Front, Bevan followed the lead of Sir Stafford Cripps, a brilliant although somewhat austere and aloof Socialist barrister.

The Socialist League, of which Cripps was the leader, published early in 1936 a proposal for a United Front to include all working-class parties—namely the Labour Party, the Independent Labour Party, and the British Communist Party.[1] The League maintained that such a United Front was the only way to assure a Socialist victory in the Parliamentary elections and to elect a government capable of stopping the expansion of Fascism and averting the outbreak of war. The Independent Labour Party and the Communists promptly declared their readiness to join a United Front. Only two Labour M.P.'s endorsed the Cripps proposal—Aneurin Bevan and George Strauss. Others in the group included Harold Laski, John Strachey, Victor Gollancz, and G. D. H. Cole. The United Front issue was not new to the Labour Party. It was thoroughly discussed and fought out at the Thirty-fourth Annual Conference, held in Southport in October 1934. The National Executive Committee had recommended to the conference that disciplinary action be taken against any member of the Labour Party who associated himself in any United Front activity with members of the Communist Party.[2]

Aneurin Bevan strongly attacked the position of the National Executive Committee, and stated that, while he was not a member of the proscribed organizations, he had appeared on the same platform with Communists "in carrying out Labour propaganda." He charged that many of the activities in which he and others were engaged in association with the Communists would not have been necessary "were it not for the inertia, lack of enterprise, and insipidity of the Executive. . . . These activities are being frowned upon because they bring into bold relief the incapacity of the Party leadership in the face of the situation."[3]

The delegates took notice of the bold speaker, and the Party leaders—who were in no mood to tolerate rebels—took steps to silence him. His credentials as a delegate were challenged, and it was brought out that he was only a substitute delegate, with the right to speak but not to vote. Ernest Bevin rebuked Bevan and told him, "No, in this Conference, Aneurin Bevan, you are not going to get the flattery of the gossip columns that you get in London, you are not going to get flattery, you are going to get facts." [4] The motion to censure the Executive, which had Bevan's support, received a bare 89,000 votes against 1,820,000.

The Thirty-fifth Labour Conference in Brighton, held in October 1935, overwhelmingly defeated a United Front resolution and by a great majority rejected the affiliation of the Communist Party. The only large union that supported Cripps and Bevan was the Miners Federation. To be sure, Cripps and Bevan[5] and others in the group had misgivings about joining hands with the Communists, but declared themselves ready to take this step because they viewed their cooperation as essential to the working of a "United Front." [6]

The leaders of the Labour Party—Attlee, Bevin, Morrison, and the secretary of the Trades Union Congress, Sir Walter Citrine—were unalterably opposed to a United Front. With much wisdom and foresight, they maintained that the Communists were inherently incapable of working in a democratic coalition and would eventually attempt to dominate and exploit the United Front for their own ends. Attlee and particularly Morrison, who was known as "Labour's Apostle to the Middle Class," were convinced that if the Labour Party were to win in the 1939 elections, it would have to gain a substantial measure of support from the middle class voters, who would be instantly alienated by a Socialist–Communist alliance. They too were proved to be eminently correct in their position, because the analysis of the vote in the 1945 General Election showed that without middle class support the Labour Party would have gone down to defeat.

The national Executive Committee of the Labour Party

stated in a preconference resolution that no Party member was allowed to associate with people or parties "who do not believe in democracy." [7] The leaders of the Party also pointed out that anything done to encourage the Communists would provoke the growth of British Fascism, which had been gaining strength under the leadership of Sir Oswald Mosley. The Transport House leaders felt that by fighting Communism they were also fighting Fascism.

In March 1937 the National Executive Committee announced that membership in the Socialist League would henceforth be incompatible with membership in the Labour Party. Members of the Socialist League were now faced with a choice of either leaving the League or the Party. They prudently dissolved the organization and remained in the Party. They began, however, a systematic countrywide campaign for a United Front and made an effort to appeal to the rank and file members over the heads of the leaders. Many meetings were called at which Cripps and Bevan appeared on the same platform with the British Communist leaders Harry Pollitt and William Gallacher. The slogan adopted for these meetings was a fiery one: "United Front of the Workers Class to Fight Fascism and War." [8]

In the 1937 elections to the London County Council, the Communist Party suported Labour Party candidates, who won handsomely. The Communists claimed a large share of credit for the victory, although their support had been unequivocally rejected by the secretary of the London Labour Party, Herbert Morrison. The generally despised British Communists were becoming respectable through the well-intentioned but quite misguided efforts of Cripps and Bevan.

The joint meetings with the Communists were an open challenge flung by Cripps and Bevan at the Party leadership, and thus served to highlight another aspect of their rebellion, namely the growing dissatisfaction of a substantial part of the Labour Party with the domination of the Party by the trade unions. The block voting, quite similar to the proxy voting in large American industrial corporations, allowed the Trades Union Congress with approximately three million votes to dominate the Party Conferences and defeat any opposition. By 1935, says one observer, a pattern had been established in the Labour Party by which "the moderate intellectuals [Attlee and Morrison] ran the Labour Party, supported by the great trade unions [Bevin and Citrine]." [9] Cripps and Bevan, whose support came from the Constituent Labour Parties, representing a maximum of a third of the voting strength at Party conventions, yearned for change in leadership. Cripps wrote in 1936, "I am afraid the Labour Party leadership at the present time is extremely unsatisfactory. It is both hesitant and weak. . . ." Bevan fully shared Cripps' views and aired them frequently in the *Tribune*, which he and Cripps founded in 1937 and edited with Bevan's wife, Jennie Lee, like himself a left-wing Labour Member of Parliament.

During the vigorous campaign there occurred an incident worthy of mention because it illuminates one aspect of the unique but attractive mores of British political life. Cripps was refused the use of the Albert Hall for a United Front meeting and wrote to the trustees of the Hall, among them Winston Churchill, asking their intervention in rescinding the order. Churchill in his inimitable way castigated Cripps and his group for working with the Communists. "You are," he wrote, "working in political association with the Communists at the present time. And it has always been the rule whenever they have the power, forcibly to suppress all opinions but their own." [10] To this Cripps answered with a sharp letter condemning Churchill's refusal to intervene and accusing him of being more eager to fight Communists than

to protect the principle of free speech.[11] Three years later,
Churchill made Sir Stafford Britain's Ambassador to the
Kremlin.[12]

The time had come when the Labour Party Executive decided on a showdown and issued, on January 12, 1937, "an
Appeal to the Movement," in which it sharply condemned
the advocates of the United Front and pointed out that two
Party conferences had defeated by overwhelming majorities
proposals in favor of Communist Party affiliation and pro-
motion of a United Front. The Executive, therefore, urged
"all our members to place the party loyalty in the forefront
of their political activities." [13]

Five days later, on January 17, 1937, the United Front
supporters, including the leaders of the Independent Labour Party and the Communists, answered the Executive
and issued a "Unity Manifesto." The manifesto was strong
and far-reaching. It called for unity of the workers against
"Fascism, Reaction and War," and using typical Communist
jargon denounced Baldwin's Government as a "tool of British Capitalism and Imperialism." It further stated, "To save
the peoples of the world, the working class must mobilize
. . . for the maintenance of peace, for the defense of the
Soviet Union and its fight of peace." [14] The Unity Manifesto was obviously more the work of Pollitt and Gallacher,
the leaders of the British Communist Party, than of Cripps
and Bevan. In stressing the defense of the Soviet Union,
the Communists were already using the United Front for
their own aims. In line with the views of Sir Stafford Cripps,
the manifesto denounced the rearmament of Great Britain
as imperialist warmongering. Cripps was wrong but consistent. During the great debate, at the Thirty-fifth Annual Conference, on applying the economic sanctions against Italy
after the invasion of Abyssinia, Cripps bitterly opposed
sanctions as leading to war and denounced the League of

Nations as an "International Burglars' Union."[15] Cripps resigned from the National Executive in protest against the Labour Party's support of the enforcement of the principle of collective security by the League of Nations.

Bevan in his characteristically individualistic fashion did not support Cripps' and Lansbury's pacifist position at the Thirty-fifth Conference, and his speeches and votes in the House gave every indication that he supported sanctions against the Fascist aggressors. It seems, however, that his eagerness to see a United Front established outweighed his disagreement with Cripps on the issues of sanctions, the League of Nations, and collective security.

The leaders of the Labour Party reacted to the Manifesto with forthright vigor. The Labour Executive announced that any member of the Labour Party who appeared jointly on a platform of any meeting with the Communists would be automatically expelled. Cripps and Bevan respected the directive and discontinued the joint meetings, pending consideration of the entire question of the United Front at the Annual Labour Party Conference. But they made every effort to enlist the support of the rank and file members for their cause. While claims made at the time that a poll of the entire Party membership would show a majority for Cripps[16] can well be discounted, the movement did attract considerable support, particularly among the younger members in the Constituent Labour Parties and the universities.

The 1937 Annual Labour Party Conference once again overwhelmingly defeated all proposals for a United Front and fully endorsed the decisions of the Executive Committee. However, a long overdue reform, which allowed the Constituent Labour Parties to elect directly members of the National Executive Committee, and which was passed at the 1938 Conference, resulted in the election of Sir Stafford

Cripps and Harold Laski to the Executive. Thus, while the campaign of Cripps and Bevan for a United Front was a failure, their fight for a greater measure of democracy within the Labour Party was a partial success.

In the House of Commons Cripps and Bevan, with the full blessing of the Party, joined hands in a slashing attack on the "nonintervention" policy pursued by the British Government in the Spanish Civil War. They also bitterly denounced Chamberlain's Munich agreement of September 1938. It should be said that Cripps and Bevan were hardly entitled to criticize Chamberlain's appeasement, because the Unity Manifesto, which they had signed only a year before, declared with a remarkable degree of political blindness "its opposition to the re-armament program of the National Government." [17]

How Cripps and Bevan expected Chamberlain to stand up against Hitler without considerable military strength behind him is not easy to explain. The inconsistency between the demand for armed intervention in Spain—an active resistance to Fascist expansion—and the desperate clinging to outdated pacifist slogans must be considered one of the weakest points of Cripps' and Bevan's United Front campaign. The argument often used by Cripps to explain this inconsistent position—his unwillingness to trust Chamberlain even with a revolver—cannot outweigh the damage to the security and the very survival of the free countries of Europe caused by this ill-considered policy. Bevan's support of Cripps' pacifism was also completely inconsistent with his attacks in the House of Commons on Baldwin's Government in 1935 for failing to stop Mussolini's and Hitler's aggressions.

On January 9, 1939, Cripps addressed to the Labour Executive a memorandum which urged the Labour Party to come out "boldly as the leader of a combined opposition to the National Government" and adopt a "positive policy of peace by collective action with France, Russia and the United States." [18] The memorandum further urged a United Front of the Labour Party with the Liberals and the Communists. Cripps sent out the memorandum to the press and to all Constituent Labour Parties. The Labour Executive rejected the memorandum by a vote of thirteen to three and faced Cripps with an ultimatum to cease the campaign or face expulsion. He refused and his expulsion followed in April 1939. Aneurin Bevan and G. R. Strauss, M.P., announced their full support of Cripps, and were likewise expelled after due warning.

Cripps, Bevan, and their supporters took the issue again to the Labour Party members all over the country and received a substantial measure of support, less for the United Front idea than as "martyrs of the dictatorial tactics of the National Committee." [19] Richard Crossman, then a young Socialist intellectual and later Bevan's colleague and supporter in the House of Commons, gravely warned, "If the Executive Committee refused to take this line [of compromise] and prefers to come to heel whenever Mr. Bevin cracks his whip, not only will they insure that Mr. Chamberlain remains in power, but they will prepare the ground for a Fascist leader of the future." [20] An editorial in the influential Labour weekly, the *New Statesman and Nation*, also decried the "steamroller tactics of the Executive" and called for a compromise solution.[21]

In spite of the voices calling for a compromise and conciliation, the 1939 Annual Conference meeting in Southport, after allowing Cripps to defend his views, affirmed the expulsion by a majority of 2,100,000 to 402,000. Cripps did not return to the Labour Party until February 1945; but Aneurin Bevan, who throughout his turbulent and rebellious career was always careful to stay within the Labour Party

and never considered a secession, gave the Executive the
requested assurances to abide by Party discipline and returned to the fold in October 1939. His expulsion had lasted
only a few months. Significantly, he never admitted,
in light of subsequent history, how wrong he was during this
period of his life.

Bevan was ready to carry his rebellion against the Party
and its leadership only to a certain length. Always a realist
in politics, he retreated and compromised when it became
clear to him that further resistance to the majority would
be useless and might result in a permanent disassociation
from the Labour Party. This last eventuality Bevan was
very careful to avoid throughout his tempestuous career. In
times of crisis in the Party fortunes, and especially in the
periods immediately prior to a General Election, Bevan was
ready to compromise and accept watered-down resolutions
and policies for the sake of a united front to be presented
by the Labour Party to the British electorate. Hugh Dalton
astutely observes in his memoirs: "The Scarborough Conference [of 1931] was an affair of quasi-unanimities. (So it always is when the Labour Party is facing an immediate election. So it was twenty years later, again in Scarborough, in
1951)." [22]

∞VI∞ Troublesome backbencher during World War II

WHEN THE Labour Party made it clear that it would not enter a Government headed by Neville Chamberlain, Winston Churchill formed a Coalition Government. Clement Attlee and his colleagues agreed to enter the Government after the National Executive Committee and then the Labour Party Conference agreed that the Labour Party should join a coalition Government to bring about a victory and a just peace.[1] Attlee accepted the post of Lord Privy Seal and Deputy Prime Minister, and others given high posts were Ernest Bevin, Herbert Morrison, Arthur Greenwood, and Hugh Dalton.

Bevan within the Party and Cripps from outside bitterly complained that the Labour Party should have set important programmatic conditions before entering the coalition. They vindictively insisted that the "men of Munich"—including Neville Chamberlain, Lord Lloyd, and Sir John Simon—must be dropped from the Government.[2] Their objections were brushed aside. The British Labour Party, leaders and members alike, was united in its determination to submerge Party differences for the defense of the homeland and the defeat of Hitler's Germany. Ernest Bevin paternally advised his friends, "I do not want you to get worried too

57

much about every individual that may be in the Government. We could not stop to decide the issue." [3] Attlee and Bevin were convinced that the national interest required the acceptance of Churchill's leadership, both in foreign and domestic affairs.

Critical days lay ahead for Bevan in the House of Commons, where he was a rather obscure and isolated member of Parliament. The leaders of his Party were allies of the Tories in the Government and bound by the principle of collective responsibility and solidarity in the cabinet. In the general structure of the British Parliament backbenchers, as a rule, exert little influence even on the policies of their own parties. Policies and positions on important issues of the Parliamentary Labour Party are decided by a small group of leaders, usually the Executive Committee, known as the Shadow Cabinet. All Labour members meet about once in two weeks for general discussion, but there is no voting on issues except on very rare occasions, and even when a consensus of opinion is reached the Party leaders do not feel bound by it. The opportunities to deliver an extended speech in the House of Commons are quite limited for a backbencher, because speeches on behalf of the three major political parties are assigned in conferences of the three chief whips. The decision on what matters are discussed in the House of Commons is theoretically decided by a vote of the Members, but in practice the agenda is determined by the Leader of the House, who is usually the Prime Minister and who, as a rule, consults with the Leader of the Opposition. An individual member of Parliament, if he wishes to speak on his own, addresses the Speaker and must "catch the Speaker's eye." [4]

Faced with these realities, Bevan had an alternative of either becoming a relatively quiet and well-disciplined member of his Party, supporting the Government and es-

pecially his own representatives in it, or of embarking on
an independent course of action and becoming a "rebel,"
always keeping in mind the necessity of staying within the
limits of minimum propriety in order not to risk expulsion.
This was a difficult and perilous course to follow, especially
in wartime. But Aneurin Bevan succeeded in following it
with tenacity and quite an astonishing degree of success.
Within five years he became known and widely acknowledged as the best orator in the House of Commons (with
the exception of Winston Churchill), a veritable thorn in
the flesh of the Prime Minister and the Labour ministers,
and a leader of a sizable group of followers inside and outside of Parliament.

The record of Parliamentary debates discloses an increasing amount of attention given by ministers and Members
of Parliament to the views of the Member for Ebbw Vale.
When Winston Churchill, who was more often than not a
match for the fiery Welshman, lost his temper on one occasion, Bevan exploited this temporary weakness by crying
with mock humility: "The Prime Minister lost his temper,
not over one of his ministers . . . but with the poor, simple
backbencher Member of Parliament." [5]

Many of his unwary Conservative and Labour colleagues
were made to suffer the sting of Bevan's quick and lashing
tongue. When interrupted by a comparatively new Member,
he told the House, "He is one of those irresponsible people
who know that he never will be elected to the House again
and does not care what he says." [6] Observing that Churchill
was talking to one of the Conservative whips while he was
addressing the House, Bevan assured Churchill that by listening to him he would learn immeasurably more than he
could ever learn from any of his Party officials. On another
occasion, Bevan gave vent to his spleen by making fun of
Churchill's occasional predilection for wearing uniforms.

Bevan begged the Prime Minister to recognize that he was a civilian head of a civilian government and "not go parading around in ridiculous uniforms." [7] Bevan did not show a much greater consideration for the Labour ministers. We have the testimony of the patient and forbearing Attlee that Bevan was indeed a heavy cross for him to bear.[8] His style of debating became increasingly sharp. When a member interrupted his speech with the word "puerile," Bevan paused, and looking straight at him, said, "Let the Hon. Member suppress himself. After all, a weak engine ought not to need such strong brakes." [9] Once when Churchill was leaving the House during Bevan's address, he paused and said, "Ah! As I see the right Hon. Gentleman is about to leave the House, I think of what Shakespeare said: 'What private anxieties we have yet know not!' " [10]

In spite of the infamous Hitler-Stalin pact of August 1939, which was fully endorsed and supported by the British Communist press, Bevan took Herbert Morrison to task for closing down the London *Daily Worker* in January 1941. In the months preceding Hitler's attack on the Soviet Union, the British Communists conducted a vicious antiwar campaign calling on British workers to sabotage the war effort. A month after the outbreak of the war, the *Daily Worker* wrote: "The Communist party which has always stood in the forefront of the struggle for peace and against Fascism, declares the continuance of this war not in the interests of the people of Britain, France and Germany. . . . This war is a fight between imperialist powers." [11] In February 1940 the organ of the Communist party declared: "The British people have no quarrel with the German people. Our quarrel is with those in high places in our own country, who dragged us into this cruel and unjust war." [12] On January 10, 1941, the Communist Party held a "People's Convention for a People's Peace" in London; in effect, this meeting urged capitulation to Hitler through a negotiated peace.

Shortly after the People's Convention, the Home Secretary, Herbert Morrison, suspended the *Daily Worker* on the grounds of incitement to treason and sabotage. Aneurin Bevan immediately moved a resolution in the House that expressed unmeasured condemnation of the antiwar propaganda conducted by the *Daily Worker* but opposed the suppression of the paper by the Home Office. The Communists, said Bevan, were a small and detested minority but should be permitted to spout their propaganda. Fredom of press and assembly must be upheld even in time of war.[13]

The resolution was on its face a statement of high principle, but was implicitly a censure of Morrison. The Home Secretary rose not only to oppose the motion, but to relieve himself of a few things he apparently had wanted to say for some time to the House about Mr. Bevan. "My Hon. Friend, Member for Ebbw Vale," he said,

is very strong on the point of democracy. He and I with great friendship, have often differed in the Labour Party and he and I enjoy an argument. My Hon. Friend and I have had great experience of Labour Party democracy. If I wanted to find one distinguished member of the party, who more than any other, has set aside the democratic decisions of the majority of his colleagues, I think I should choose my Hon. Friend the Member of Ebbw Vale. Therefore, his democracy is rather skin-deep. He speaks of democracy for himself and not so much for the other fellow.[14]

When the division came on his motion, Bevan found himself completely isolated. Only six Members, among them the two Communists, stood with him. Three hundred and twenty-three Members voted against the motion.

It did not take long for Bevan to become increasingly unhappy with the National Coalition Government. He wanted either to participate actively in the vital tasks of prosecuting the war for Britain's survival or engage in constructive opposition to prod the Government into more effective actions intended to bring about a speedy victory and to pass legislation aimed at improving the lot of the British workers in general and miners in particular. He would have probably preferred the latter role.

The deadly peril in which Britain found itself, the growing threat of Nazi invasion of the British Isles, the great prestige of Churchill as a war leader of an embattled nation and of the Western world, made Bevan's position as the Government's relentless critic quite difficult. The difficulty was compounded by the presence of Labour ministers in Churchill's Cabinet. Furthermore, Attlee, Bevin, and Greenwood, all members of the War Cabinet, made no secret of their admiration for the Prime Minister and loyally called upon the Labour Party to submerge its differences with the Tories in a united patriotic effort in an hour of grave national peril. Bevan profoundly disagreed with the position taken by his leaders. He too wanted to see a complete victory over the Nazis, but felt that the united war effort in which British labor and trade unions wholeheartedly and unstintingly participated was an opportune time to transform Britain into a welfare state, based on Socialist planning, the state ownership of basic industries, and far-reaching social legislation. While he recognized Churchill's greatness as a war leader, he distrusted many of his Conservative ministers and ambassadors, including Lord Halifax, Sir Samuel Hoare, and Lord Lloyd; in his opinion, these men could not be relied upon to work for a true alliance of all democratic and Socialist groups and parties in the free world and in Nazi-subjugated Europe.

After the German attack on Russia, Bevan became convinced that the blind hatred of Communism and the Soviet

Union by many Tory leaders was preventing a closer alliance and cooperation of Britain and the Soviets. The Labour Party must, he felt, free itself from the shackles and restraints of its wartime alliance with the Conservatives and go into opposition fighting for a victory over the Nazis in close collaboration with the Russians and for the realization of Socialist principles and objectives.

Prevented from speaking his mind on the floor of the House of Commons, Bevan used the pages of the *Tribune,* of which he was a director, to publish fiery articles attacking the Government and the Labour ministers.

In January 1941, less than a year after the establishment of Churchill's War Ministry, Bevan addressed some plain words to the Labour Party. "We might as well say it quite frankly," he wrote, "that on the domestic front, that is on the organization of the nation's economic war effort, Mr. Churchill's administration does not differ from Mr. Chamberlain's. Labour has brought about no change of importance on the economic front." [15] Continuing this rather irresponsible attack Bevan demanded that the Labour ministers press for the ". . . nationalization of the railroads. If Labour insisted upon it," he added, "if Labour demands that railways be nationalized as an essential step towards the successful prosecution of the war, no vested interests would dare raise any objection. Why don't Mr. Greenwood, Mr. Attlee and Mr. Bevan insist upon it? In God's name, what stops them?" [16]

The Labour ministers ignored Bevan's demagogic tack. To attempt to nationalize the railways in the midst of the war, at the height of the Battle of Britain, would have been sheer folly. To add insult to injury, Bevan warned that unless the Labour ministers mended their ways, the British Labour movement would by "next Whitsun" withdraw its support of Labour participation in the War Government.

A week later Bevan again warned the Labour ministers to remain true to Socialist principles or lose the support of the British working class.[17] on February 7, 1941, in a dramatic article entitled "Choose How To Live or Die," Bevan called for the end of the political truce. "The Labour leadership," he wrote, "has accepted the deadly doctrine that it is disloyalty to the Labour Ministers to attack the Government's policy." [18] This policy, he continued, drives many members of the Labour Party to support Communist causes because they must have the freedom to criticize the Tories, even in wartime. With characteristic courage, Bevan expressed doubts whether Winston Churchill, in spite of his gifts of eloquence and leadership, could provide "social inspiration and political insight from which to expect a strategy of victory." [19] He concluded his article by demanding freedom of action for the Labour M.P.'s to speak their minds in Parliament and for the Labour groups to conduct political agitation. Later in February Bevan returned to his demand for the nationalization of the railways. He also urged that all harbors and all means of commercial transport be declared to be under public ownership and demanded that the Labour Members in the House of Commons should be free to express their opinions and to vote in accordance with the wishes of their constituents.[20] He soon made this demand even stronger. The restraints of the coalition lay heavy on this fiery Parliamentary orator. In a remarkable declaration which was fully reflective of his strong admiration and respect for the British Parliament, Bevan proclaimed the doctrine that members of Parliament owe their primary allegiance not to their parties, but to their constituents and to the country as a whole. "Individual members of Parliament," he wrote,

should be free to express in open discussion what they consider is in the interest of their constituents and of the country. Party discipline should end at the point where it impinges upon Parliamentary liberty. It is dangerous for British democracy to allow Ministers of the Crown to believe that they need no longer face the possibility of hostile criticism in the House of Commons. War demands supreme exertions and many sacrifices, but there is one sacrifice that war should never ask the nation to make, and that is to give up the prize for which alone the war is being fought.[21]

This was a lofty, sound, and well-formulated credo of a Britisher dedicated to the best traditions of English democracy. It was only a pity that it appeared in a series of articles written by Bevan for the *Tribune,* whose main characteristics were poor writing, occasional clear political demagoguery, and often downright irresponsibility. Thus, only a month after this splendid expression of his democratic beliefs, Aneurin Bevan demanded that the Government expropriate all lands in Britain whose owners did not put them under cultivation. Using harsh terms, Bevan asked, "With these things being so, what prevents the nation from taking over idle acres? I will give the only answer that I can think of, lack of political guts on the part of the leaders of Labour." [22] One wonders what, besides the heavy preoccupation with war duties, prevented Attlee, Morrison, and Bevin from striking back at their fellow Party member who was so mercilessly and so unjustly attacking them from the rear. It might be that they decided to ignore Bevan's attacks out of conviction that he represented, at that time, a small and insignificant minority in the Labour Party. The call of the *Tribune* for the 1941 Labour Party Conference held in London to order the Parliamentary Labour Party to give freedom of expression and vote to all Labour M.P.'s went to a crushing defeat. The Party leadership, aided by the trade union bosses, had the conference under complete control and Bevan was little heard from. Unconcerned by his lack of success at the conference, Bevan returned to the House of Commons and urged that all public schools (the term given in England to private schools) be closed in the interests of the war and in order to abolish "class privilege." The proposal was received with dismay not only by the Conservatives but also on the Labour benches, where many M.P.'s were proud graduates of distinguished private schools. Even the Speaker of the House who seldom, if ever, expresses an opinion on an issue under discussion, heatedly interrupted to tell Bevan that his proposal made no sense.

After the German invasion of Russia in June 1941, Bevan became the most persistent spokesman for the second front idea in the House of Commons. He repeatedly pleaded and demanded that the Western Allies open a second front in Western Europe to relieve the German pressure on Russia and assure the ultimate defeat of Hitler. Immediately after the Nazis attacked Russia, Bevan wrote: "Every thinking man and woman in Great Britain is asking today what can be done by us to assist the Soviet Union." [23] He demanded that the R.A.F. coordinate its attacks with the movements of the Soviet armies and that British units organize diversionary raids to relieve the pressure on the Soviets. Bevan maintained, and with some justification, that there was considerable public sentiment for a second front in Britain. But in keeping with his violent dislike and distrust of the Tories, he accused Churchill and his Government of a "negative, passive attitude to the Russian campaign." [24]

The Government, Bevan charged, was not ready to take any risks for Russia because some of its members hated the Soviet Union and Communism as much as they hated Hitler and Nazism. He was particularly distrustful of former collaborators of Neville Chamberlain, including Lord Halifax, Sir John Simon, and Lord Lloyd. He declared that "the time has come to throw out the old, jaded, tired Ministers who have been associated with disastrous policies." [25]

William Gallacher, the Communist, speaking after Bevan, asked him a question that undoubtedly many of his Labour colleagues were eager to have answered. Gallacher agreed with Bevan on the desirability of a second front, but wanted to know how Bevan could still remain in the Labour Party after his attack on the Government, in which Labour had "a number of distinguished representatives in the War Cabinet." [26]

Anthony Eden, the Foreign Secretary, told Bevan that military actions undertaken by Great Britain would be dictated by the best interests of the nation and not by prejudices against any country fighting a common foe. Unconvinced, Bevan shortly returned to the attack, charging that "many people are beginning to feel that the Government is as much out of touch with the real feelings of the country as was the Administration of Mr. Chamberlain's. There is a feeling that the Soviet Union is not being taken into full consultation and cooperation." [27]

While the *Tribune* in a series of editorials bluntly accused Churchill and the Labour ministers of not wanting to make an all-out effort to help the Soviet Union, Bevan and his close associates embarked on a tour of the country and spoke to packed and aroused meetings on the imperative necessity of a second front. Returning to London, Bevan reported that "the country is ahead of the House of Commons and the House of Commons is ahead of the Government" [28] on the issue of help to the Russians and on the realization of Socialist objectives. "The policy of the Government," he continued, "should be revised and Labour should insist that in the new policy the principles of socialism should begin to receive recognition." [29] Angered by the refusal of the Government to be pushed into hasty military action, Bevan resorted to threats and intimidation. He warned that following the defeat of Russia "there will be an intense anger and an irresistible demand for a change in the personnel and policies of the Government." [30] In an open defiance of his Party's leaders, he denounced Clement Attlee and Arthur Greenwood for allegedly following blindly the policies of Winston Churchill. The rebellious Bevan demanded the removal of Lord Halifax as Britain's Ambassador to Washington and urged that "the Labour Members of the Government show little more resilience than their Tory colleagues." [31] The articles attacking the Government and the Labour ministers appeared week after week in the *Tribune* and bore the signatures of Bevan, Harold J. Laski, and G. R. Strauss.

However, even in the long months of bitter attacks on the British Government on the issue of the second front, which closely paralleled the line adopted by the Communist parties in England and in America, Bevan reiterated his faith in Western democracy. In an article entitled "Hope and New Strength," he proclaimed his personal credo in a moving and memorable passage:

For democracy is a new arrival on the stage of history. It is only a short time since ordinary men and women have enjoyed even the partial right to shape the policies that govern their countries. . . . And yet in that short time mankind has made more progress in the sciences, in the arts, in literature than was made in the ten thousand years that preceded it.[32]

A few months later Bevan described a vision of his perfect society which would take from Russia the idea of subordination of economic activities to the state but which would also guard against sacrificing the principles of personal choice, of personal liberty, and personal freedoms of all its individuals. "Without planned economic organization," he wrote,

liberty cannot live. But planned economic organization alone does not preserve liberty. The society of the future must bring forth both conceptions. It is because the Soviet Union has made such massive contributions towards the one, and democratic society towards the other, that in their common cooperation, as much as in their immediate common sacrifice, lies the possibility of conducting a society in which it is safe to be free.[33]

Bevan stubbornly continued to clamor for a second front, and in the fall of 1942 declared in the House of Commons that the Germans would have been beaten if the British Government had had the "guts to open a Second Front."[34] The leaders of the Labour Party promptly disassociated themselves from this point of view. On September 9, 1942, Bevan told a protesting House that the "Prime Minister's continuation in office is a major national disaster."[35] Addressing himself to the Labour benches, Bevan added, "It is no use for men in the Trades Union Congress to make adulatory speeches about the Prime Minister because these speeches do not represent the feelings of the men in the workshops."[36]

Bevan was obviously unhappy over the respect and even affection felt and often expressed by Attlee and Bevin for Churchill. The Labour Members told Bevan on many occasions that the wartime Government was theirs as well as the Tories'.[37] It is axiomatic that Attlee's and Bevin's evaluation of the role played by Winston Churchill and his place in the hearts of the British people during the memorable days of the Battle for Britain was more accurate than that of Aneurin Bevan.

Yet this immoderate line was a political asset, as Bevan was well aware. The steadfast loyalty shown him by the miners of his district can be explained by his readiness to fight for what he considered their due even against great odds. Bevan thundered throughout the war for greater social security benefits for the workers. He was apt to fly into an emotional outburst at any opposition to substantial compensation to injured miners. Such a dispute brought him, in 1943, into a bitter conflict with Herbert Morrison when the latter, after weeks of negotiating with the Trades Union Congress and the Employers Confederation and his Labour and Tory colleagues in the Government, brought in a compromise Workman's Compensation Bill. Bevan's attack on Morrison for allegedly selling out to the Tories was so violent that Morrison, the veteran of Parliamentary battles, pleaded for support and bitterly said that "there ought to be a whole crowd of people in the dock with me for having endorsed it." [38]

Aroused to intense anger by Morrison's refusal to accept an amendment to increase the benefits for injured miners, Bevan fulminated a dire threat. If the amendment was lost and the bill withdrawn, he said, "If that cowardly thing were ever done, if the Home Secretary sank to such despicable depths as to withhold the increase [in compensation] for the married men, I would stump the coal fields and get the men out on strike in a fortnight." [39] There were cries of "shame" from all sides of the House.

Less than a year later, Bevan clashed with the tough Ernest Bevin and started a row which almost ended in his expulsion from the Labour Party. Once again the root of the controversy was Nye Bevan's complete identification with what he considered the best interests of the miners. In April 1944, before the Easter recess of the House of Commons, Ernest Bevin, in his capacity as Minister of Labour, promulgated and put into effect an Anti-Strike Defence Regulation which provided a five-year prison term for strikers and strike fomenters in vital industries. The action was taken to put a stop to a number of serious miners' strikes incited and organized, the Government charged, by a "group of irresponsible Trotskyites." The Communists, it should be remembered, were not in favor of strikes because the Russians were also at war and they needed British war supplies. Bevin told the House that the regulation, which was distasteful to him and his Labour colleagues in the Government, was put into effect with the full approval of the Trades Union Congress and reflected the sentiments of the men and women in uniform who were deeply aroused by strikes and stoppages in important defense industries.

But Bevan was not persuaded by these arguments. He moved that the regulation be annulled, and bitterly charged Bevin with inciting the nation's press to undertake a "campaign of calumny against the miners." [40] If strikes had occurred, he charged, they were a direct result of incompetence and bungling by the Labour Ministry. The law was a whim and a caprice, and while the General Council of the Trade Unions at the top might support this bill, "the workers at the bottom oppose it." [41] Thus Bevan openly challenged Party discipline and made a serious attempt to undermine the official leadership of his Party. This the patient and long-suffering Labour leaders could not countenance. Arthur Greenwood told Bevan that he had made an antiunion speech "the like of which I have never heard from the most die-hard Tory." [42] Bevin, shaking with rage, called one of Bevan's statements a lie and withdrew the word only when directly ordered to do so by the Speaker.

While only twenty-three M.P.'s voted for Bevan's motion, his actual support was considerable because over seventy Labour members abstained, obviously agreeing with his position, but unwilling to flout Party discipline. The Parliamentary Labour Party was called into session to deal with

Bevan's flagrant breach of Party rules and discipline, and a motion was made to "withdraw the whip from him." Faced with expulsion, Bevan refused to recant or retreat and again denounced the antistrike regulation. In the debate on the expulsion motion several Labourites, including Tom Driberg and Sidney Silverman, warmly defended Bevan's behavior. While the leaders of the P.L.P. had a great majority ready to sanction expulsion, they decided not to press for a vote, and a compromise was worked out which deferred the issue. They may have reasoned that the generally unpopular and distasteful antistrike regulation was not a proper issue on which to bring Bevan's insubordination to a showdown, or there might have been some doubts in their minds, carefully fostered by Bevan's supporters, as to whether the forthcoming Annual Conference of the Labour Party would endorse the expulsion. At any rate, Bevan emerged from this dangerous crisis with the "new status of a leader of the left in the Labour Party." [43]

The influential *New Statesman and Nation* proclaimed editorially that Aneurin Bevan "is almost the only prominent spokesman of the unrest and dissatisfaction manifest inside the Party and the Unions." [44] The editorial further advised Bevan not to leave the Labour Party and not to form a splinter group. It reminded him that all such small groups, like the Independent Labour Party and the Communists, remained weak and powerless. There is every reason to believe that for Nye Bevan such advice was entirely superfluous. He skated at times on thin ice in his encounters with the Party leaders, but was at all times careful to assure himself a line to retreat. Bevan already had his goal clearly in mind. He was determined to gain power and leadership in the Labour Party, and would never be satisfied with the minor distinction that belonged to the leader of a small splinter group. As after his expulsion during the United

Front controversy, Bevan was again ready to make concessions to the Party leadership in order to remain inside the Labour Party.

As the war was drawing to a victorious close, Bevan sensed the gradual disenchantment with Winston Churchill's Government on the part of a growing section of the British population. He saw that the British workers were becoming restless and unhappy with wartime restrictions, ceilings on wages, and the curtailment of social services. Bevan decided to exploit this feeling and assumed the leadership of a frontal attack on the Coalition Government. Using the first occasion of a vote of confidence, he told the House on August 2, 1944, "I will be quite frank. . . . I have no confidence in the Prime Minister . . . and in the Government's conduct of war. . . . I shall not find myself embarrassed by voting against the Government." [45] When the vote came, the Bevanite faction, amorphous and heterogeneous, was able to gather forty-three votes. By December 1944, Aneurin Bevan began calling for the dissolution of the Coalition Government.[46] The participation of the Labour ministers in the Government, he maintained, had weakened the Party. In total disregard of his repeated attacks on the coalition idea, Bevan told the *Tribune* readers that he has "all along" held that Labour's participation in the Coalition Government during the war was justified and even imperative, but now he asked: "Has not the time come for Labour to regain its freedom and set itself at the head of the British people in their march to the new world?" [47] He was eager for the Labour Party to go into vigorous opposition and do away with the restraints that the Labour leadership had imposed on him in the House of Commons. With uncanny political insight he sensed that the majority of Britishers, in spite of their abiding love and admiration for Winston Churchill as a great war leader, were not convinced that he and the Conservative Party should be entrusted with the tremendous tasks of postwar reconstruction. "I have all along taken the view that too much political value was attached to Mr. Churchill's personal ascendancy in the country." [48] He counseled the Labour Party to leave the coalition, select the proper issues and slogans, and prepare for the forthcoming General Elections.

Almost overnight the *Tribune,* under Bevan's direction, adopted a mild and conciliatory tone toward Bevin, Morrison, and Attlee. The Welshman was obviously ready to get back into the good graces of the Party leaders to assure for himself a post in the Government in case of a Labour victory at the polls. Such a victory over Churchill and the Tories, Bevan concluded, could come only by a United Front of the Labour Party, the Communists, the Independent Labour Party, and the Commonwealth Party. Bevan had obviously forgotten his unfortunate experience with the United Front idea that he advocated in the thirties under the leadership of Stafford Cripps. "Our main task will be to construct," he wrote, "a People's Government through the instrumentality of what I have called a coalition of the Left." [49] The election would have, he maintained, considerable results not only for Great Britain but for the entire free world. "Labour needs," he continued,

an emotional drive based on the clear distinction of "we" and "they" [the Conservatives]. . . . The Labour Party should be ready to come to terms with all those sections and parties that can be properly described as belonging to the "we". . . . The details of their respective programs are less important than the fact that, in the mind of the mass of people, they belong to the same emotional grouping.[50]

While the meaning of these ill-considered and at best mistakenly naive suggestions was quite clear, Bevan cautiously refrained from naming the Communists as the allies he had in mind. However, the *Tribune* editorially threw caution to the winds and, undoubtedly with Bevan's approval, published a front-page editorial on December 15, 1944, entitled "The Issue Before Labour." "The need for the moment," the editorial stated,

is to combine all the forces of progressive [*sic!*] opinion in the country into a mighty punch directed against the Tories at the General Election. The Progressives must be prevented from fighting each other. The I.L.P., the Communists, Common Wealth and the Independent Liberals, all will strive to secure parliamentary representation. In the name of the common sense who can be expected to gain from that situation but the Tories? [51]

Fortunately for the best interests of the free world, the leaders of the Labour Party used their good common sense and unhesitatingly rejected any and all appeals for collaboration with the Communists. The National Executive Committee of the Labour Party branded the Communists "as purveyors of hate, even when they pose as Socialists." [52] The Labour Party Conference overwhelmingly approved the decision of the National Executive Committee, and Aneurin Bevan shrewdly surrendered without a fight. He had no desire to fight for a lost cause and endanger his standing in the Labour Party's hierarchy. Instead, he used his considerable oratorical powers to bring the delegates to their feet cheering his impassioned plea for faith in Socialism and his call that "the Socialist representatives in the Government should use their influence more and leave to the Tories to do their own dirty work." [53]

At the Labour Party Conference in Blackpool in May, 1945, Bevan completely abandoned his advocacy of the United Front and instead loyally joined the party and the trade union leaders in a call for complete unity within the Labour Party toward victory in the General Election called by Churchill. He gave his full approval to the Party's middle-of-the-road platform, contained in a pamphlet entitled *Let Us Face the Future,* and joined the leaders in expressing full confidence in the ability of the Labour Party to win the elections without the "help" of the Communists. Bevan became once again the loyal and faithful Party member and worked hard to improve his relations with Attlee, Bevin, and Morrison. As if touched by a magic wand, the *Tribune* abandoned its attacks on the leadership and called for unity and harmony. The editorials hinted broadly that Bevan should be given a high Party post and be included in any future Labour Government.

The pre-election Labour Party Conference in Blackpool was all light and sunshine. Bevan's supporters loyally joined in an ovation for Herbert Morrison and Ernest Bevin and voted for the policy recommendations of the National Executive Committee. Bevan was elected to the Executive Committee by 418,000 votes, as compared to Emanuel Shinwell's and Harold Laski's 430,000 votes. Herbert Morrison got 424,000. The Welsh rebel had obviously made substantial inroads in the Constituent Labour Parties. The conference concentrated its fire on the Conservatives, and Bevan, of course, outdid his colleagues in denouncing the Tories. He called for the "complete political extinction of the Tory Party for twenty-five years." [54]

During the years of war and Coalition Government, Aneurin Bevan won notoriety by his fiery parliamentary encounters with Winston Churchill. The British and the American press seemed to be fascinated by these duels. In spite of Churchill's position as Prime Minister, his great and proven oratorical talents and debating ability, enhanced by a rich and varied experience in the House of Commons, he was not the consistent winner in these encounters. Bevan often achieved a draw and sometimes became the acknowledged winner. While they often used harsh language against each other, there is reason to suspect that they enjoyed the clashes and gradually developed a respect, if not an affection, for each other. It is rather astonishing to contemplate that in spite of the enormous differences in background between Churchill the aristocrat, and Bevan the Welsh pit boy, they had many things in common. Both were powerfully built men who loved and enjoyed life—including good conversation, good food, and good drink. Both had had a speech impediment in their youth which they overcame by strenuous efforts, in time becoming very effective orators. Churchill and Bevan shared a deep and profound love for the British Parliament and its free-wheeling debates and truly democratic procedures. Both were nonconformists, ready and eager to rebel against their respective parties, although Bevan had a much stronger sense of Party regularity and, unlike Churchill, never even contemplated the risks attendant on secession from his Party. Both, however, were fully capable of standing alone against all comers regardless of the momentary unpopularity of their positions.

A story which has appeared repeatedly in British publications, while probably apocryphal, is significant because it provides a rather accurate picture of the less attractive features of Bevan's personality, his bravado and a brutal frankness that often borders on rudeness. The story relates that sometime in the thirties, when Churchill was ostracized by his Party for attacking the Conservative Government for not rearming, and Bevan was on the verge of expulsion from the Labour Party for advocating the United Front, they had dinner together and Churchill suggested that he and Bevan join in forming an opposition to the

Government. Bevan allegedly answered, "What use would I have for a lieutenant who has turned on so many of his party leaders?" [55]

In spite of interesting points of similarity there was an unbridgeable gulf between Churchill, an English squire, a firm believer in capitalist free enterprise, convinced of the basic righteousness of British imperialism, and Bevan, a dedicated Socialist who conceived his life's task to be the return to the British workers of their birthright. He was determined to secure for them a better life, which, he passionately believed, they were robbed by the privileged classes. Thus the clash between Churchill and Bevan was inevitable. In appraising the conduct of the war, Bevan told the House in 1941, "The Government has conceived the war wrongly from the start and no one has more misconceived it than the Prime Minister himself." In answer, Churchill told Bevan, "You sir, are nothing more than a slave to scurrility." [56] On another occasion in the days of the Battle of Britain, Churchill, stung by Bevan's needling in those critical hours, called him "a merchant of disloyalty," to which Bevan replied, "Better than being a wholesaler of disaster." [57] When it was announced once in the House that Bevan was indisposed, Churchill was heard to mutter, "Nothing trivial, I trust." Among the epithets they thrust at each other were such gems as Churchill's calling Bevan "this gamin from some Welsh gutter" and Bevan's referring to his opponent as "a man suffering from petrified adolescence." [58] These were hard and searing words, and the clashes in Parliament were at times awesome to behold. But such is the nature and tradition of British politics that had Churchill not retired from active politics before Bevan's death, the possibility of his eventual collaboration with and support of Aneurin Bevan could not have been excluded.

Some years later Bevan gave his considered opinion of

Winston Churchill, which quite obviously contains both enough half-truths to make it sound objective and enough exaggeration to attract attention, but is nevertheless greatly distorted and unfair. Bevan said that he always looked upon Churchill

as more of an artist than an intellectual. . . . He is not a great orator because careful preparation beforehand is not the way oratory is produced. He is really not equipped with a wide knowledge of affairs [*sic!*]. . . . In peacetime Mr. Churchill has never shown he has a sufficient intimate, or wide enough grasp of economics and finance to justify the term "greatness." His most endearing quality is his mental generosity.[59]

It is indeed a pity that Bevan had too little mental generosity to see and concede that Churchill is one of the few very great men that history has produced, his admitted ignorance of economics notwithstanding. Bevan, however, acknowledged one facet of Churchill's genius. He told the House in a preface to an unrestrained attack on Churchill: "I freely admit that the right Hon. Gentleman is the most articulate Englishman that has ever lived. He has a gift of language, both in speech and in writing, and many of his spoken and written contributions are adornments of the English language." [60]

~VII~ Minister of Health and Housing

THE LABOUR PARTY, having submerged for the moment its internal differences, agreed on a platform to be presented to the nation in the General Election scheduled for July 1945. The platform, entitled "Let Us Face the Future," a relatively short one of some 5,000 words, was adopted without opposition at the forty-fourth Annual Conference of the Party held in Blackpool, in May 1945. The manifesto proposed the nationalization of the Bank of England and of the coal, fuel, power, transport, and iron and steel industries. The Party also pledged itself to a substantial expansion of social services, especially in the field of health and housing. The foreign policy statement was mild and moderate, pledging the Party to work for peace and the international comity of nations. Bevan did not hesitate to vote for this relatively mild platform, as did the trade union leaders whose moderation and lack of "true Socialist faith" he so often and so bitterly criticized. Bevan, with his practical political acumen, agreed with Bevin, Attlee, and Citrine that the Labour Party had a chance to win in the election only with a middle-of-the-road "New Dealish" program. He was ready in 1945, as he would be ready several times in the future, to compromise and

conciliate in order to safeguard the best interests of the
Party and preserve his status in it. At the 1945 Conference
Bevan, with his shrewd sense of political realism, raised the
issues of 1935 and concentrated on angry attacks against
Churchill and the Conservatives. He told the conference
that Britain needed a new Industrial Revolution. "Labour,"
he said, "goes into the elections with bitter and angry passion because of what the people had to endure under the
Tories." [1] This time the leaders of the Party did not wince
at Bevan's sharp tongue. They beamed and approved.
Bevan's proven oratorical talents and his ability to arouse
enthusiasm with his slashing attacks on the Conservatives
were of great value to the Labour Party during the election
campaign.

The General Election brought a complete victory to the
Labourites. The Labour Party polled 11,982,874 votes
against 6,660,560 for the Conservatives. It won 393 seats,
as compared to 166 in the previous Parliament, and the Conservatives won 189 seats as compared to 388. Both the
Conservative and the Labour leaders were surprised by the
election results, the Conservatives with the extent of their
defeat and the Labourites with the unexpected size of their
victory. The results of the elections were far-reaching
enough to be considered by one historian the type of "a
social revolution that contemporary Britain with its traditions of class differences and political continuity, was prepared to attempt." [2] The great majority of the British electorate expressed its conviction that it preferred to trust the
Labour Party with the complicated tasks of postwar reconstruction and with governing the country in time of
peace.

Many Britons cast their votes for the Socialists convinced
that they were serving their own interests, even if this conviction was mingled with a sense of guilt for turning out of

office a man who had their love and admiration and who had led them to a triumphant victory. British workers had no such compunctions. They believed that the Socialist planning and program would improve their lot, assure full employment, and give them the benefit of expanded social services. The Labour victory, however, would not have been possible had it not been for very large numbers of middle class voters, who supported the Socialist ticket motivated by fear that "a return to an unplanned private enterprise society would again mean economic inefficiency and social injustice." [3] Clement Attlee acknowledged the broader base of the Labour Party when he told the American Congress in 1945 that "our party is today drawn from all classes of society—professional men, businessmen and what we sometimes call the 'privileged' classes. It is really a pretty good cross section of the population." [4]

Attlee and Herbert Morrison, with the help of the Trades Union Congress, were determined to go slow on Socialist reforms in deference to their middle class supporters.[5] They were eager to reassure the British public that the Labour Party leaders were a far cry from the fiery radicals that some Tory speakers had pictured them to be during the election campaign. They went out of their way to show their respect for traditional British political mores and institutions, including the monarchy. After the opening of the Parliament by King George VI on August 15, 1945, Morrison stated that "pageantry lends color to democracy and helps it to work with smoothness and amid general respect." [6] Bevan and Sir Stafford Cripps, who had in the meantime returned to the Labour Party, were equally determined to press for a full and speedy realization of the Party platform, including the nationalization of basic industries.

The appointment of Aneurin Bevan as Minister of Health and Housing in Attlee's new Government is one of those rather beguiling puzzles of British politics. There was every logical reason why Bevan, the irreconcilable rebel who had been expelled from the Party in 1939 and who had then repeatedly, to the open glee of the Tories, attacked the policies of Morrison and Bevin representing his own Party in the Coalition Government, should have been refused a ministerial post. Attlee certainly did not forget his acute embarrassment when Bevan time and again attacked Churchill's conduct of the war. Churchill on those occasions was wont to state with mock innocence that all his policies had been approved by the War Cabinet, which included several Socialist ministers. On the other hand, Bevan's appointment made good practical political sense. There was a general agreement that Bevan, while exasperating, was an exceptionally able man with unusual leadership qualities. Attlee, the very much underestimated Prime Minister, gives in his memoirs a simple explanation of Bevan's appointment: "For Health Minister, I chose Aneurin Bevan, whose abilities have up to now been displayed only in opposition, but I felt he had it in him to do a good service." [7]

Ernest Bevin, who during the war years suffered from Bevan more than any other member of the coalition Government, related to Francis Williams, a wartime aide to Clement Attlee, that when consulted on the composition of the Government he told the Prime Minister, "You ought to give Nye housing. He may be awkward sometimes, but he's got his head screwed on right and he's got guts. He'll not let our people down." [8] He further explained to Williams how he first came to realize that Bevan "has his head screwed on right." During the war Nye Bevan came to see Bevin, who was then Minister of Labour, at the head of a workers delegation. The delegates presented their arguments and it was soon evident to Bevin that they were asking for the impossible. Suddenly Bevan threw his head back and let out a roar of laughter and said: "Chuck it, boys. He's too downy a bird for us to pull that particular wool over his eyes. I'll tell him what we really must have. And I'll show you how you can give it to us, Bevin, and why you ought to." "And he did," said Bevin. "And I [Bevin] said to myself 'There is some stuffin' in that fellow. He's got sense as well as blarney.' " [9] This story is fascinating not only because it gives an inkling of the intimacy and the spirit of familiarity and comradeship that characterized the personal relations among the Labour leaders. It is also undoubtedly true, as some have asserted, that Attlee gave Bevan the job because it was safer to have him inside the Government than to risk having him a free agent in the House of Commons and at Party conclaves. "Attlee," said an American writer, "dampened Bevan's power by making him Minister of Health." [10] By appointing Bevan, the Labour Party wanted also to make clear that it "meant business" as far as its Socialist program, especially in the field of housing and health, was concerned. Bevin knew quite well that, in effect, he was asked to put up or shut up. He put up and, it is generally conceded, did an outstanding job.

While he would have preferred the Foreign Office or the Exchequer, Bevan gladly accepted the challenge that the Ministry of Health presented to him. The memories of frequent illnesses, crippling diseases, and death that could have been prevented by prompt medical attention were deeply etched in his soul from his early days in the mines of South Wales. He never lost an opportunity to recall that a lung disease contracted in a colliery proved fatal to his father because the family could not afford the expensive medical treatment required, and that his mother and the children did not receive compensation for their tragic loss. Bevan's father was one of the founders of the Tredegar Workingmen's Medical Aid Society. Each member of the society contributed three pennies out of every pound he earned and the group hired doctors and dentists when the miners and their families became ill. The medical services were inadequate because the society's treasury was always nearly empty. After his father's death, Nye Bevan became active in the society and often castigated doctors for overcharging the miners. From the day he entered Parliament, at the age of thirty-two, Bevan fought for free medical services for British workers and their families.

The National Health Service Act was first introduced by Bevan in the House of Commons in March 1946. The bill did not become law until July 5, 1948. It took two years of patient and difficult negotiations, conducted by Bevan with exceptional skill, to bring about the final acceptance of the Health Service by the Parliament and the country. The initial and very strong opposition came from the doctors organized in the British Medical Association. To the astonishment of his friends and the chagrin of his enemies, the fiery Minister of Health did not declare war on the British doctors. On the contrary, Bevan was determined to delay the implementation of the act until the doctors became convinced of its usefulness and realized that the interests of their profession would be safeguarded.

Bevan faced a hard task. In the first poll, conducted by the British Medical Association in December 1946, 23,111 doctors voted against the scheme and only 8,972 were for it. Bevan was not dismayed and kept his temper in check. Instead of denouncing the doctors, he decided to negotiate with them, ready to consider their point of view and to compromise. Even the Conservatives were impressed with the businesslike and mellow Health Minister. Bevan told the press that he would proceed to consult with the doctors' groups and expressed hope that before long the B.M.A.

would see its way to approve the plan. He expressly stated that the bill was not final and might be changed as a result of negotiations.[11]

Bevan was convinced that the great majority of the British people wanted a national health scheme, and he shrewdly and correctly foresaw that "In a conflict between the [medical] profession and the general public, the latter will always win if they are courageously led. The pretensions of the medical profession as a special social group are resented by the generality of citizens." [12] He concluded that while individuals might be attached to their own doctors and trust them, there is a great deal of distrust between the people in general and the doctors. Since medicine is still more of an art than a science, many people are only too apt to deride the effectiveness of medical treatments and accuse the doctors of charging excessive fees.

In his long fight with the doctors, Bevan counted on and received the support of the people, regardless of party affiliations. There can be no doubt that the establishment of a free health service for all Britons was to Bevan a matter of deep faith and conviction. His brilliant exposition of the plan, contained in his book *In Place of Fear*, deserves to be read even by the outspoken opponents of socialized medicine. Bevan argues that the field of health protection should be eliminated from general private enterprise commercialism. "Society," he says,

becomes more wholesome, more serene, and spiritually healthier, if it knows that its citizens have at the back of their consciousness the knowledge that not only themselves, but all their fellows have access, when ill, to the best that medical skill can provide. But private charity and endowment, although inescapably essential at one time, cannot meet the cost of all this. If the job is to be done, the state must accept financial responsibility.[13]

Bevan related that some of his American friends (it was his practice to refer to his "American friends") tried to persuade him to limit the free health service to certain income brackets, above which payments would have to be made. He rejected this advice on several grounds. First, this plan would have involved the obtaining of proof of income, which consequently would have led to "lying and cheating and all sorts of insidious nepotism." [14] But an even more important objection in his eyes was the introduction of a "two-standard health service, one below and one above salt." [15] With Labour equalitarianism he declared, "The essence of a satisfactory health service is that the rich and the poor are treated alike, that poverty is not a disability, and wealth is not advantaged." [16]

Bevan was vehemently opposed to solving the problems of essential health services by medical group insurance offered through private insurance companies. Group insurance is in reality, he argued, a sale of the insured group to the insurance company at a considerable profit for the company. Such a profit is, in Bevan's Socialist opinion, ". . . wholly gratuitous, because it does not derive from the creation of anything. Group insurance is the most expensive, the least scientific, and clumsiest way of mobilizing collective security for the individual group. . . . There never can be a clearer case of the private exploitation of a product publicly produced." [17]

Bevan actually enjoyed the protracted negotiations with the doctors. He had long been convinced that he was a skillful negotiator. He knew from his Labour Party and trade union experience that it is important to "distinguish between the atmosphere of the mass demonstration and the quite different mood of the negotiating table." [18] This observation is significant because it provides a clue to the proper evaluation of Bevan's own fiery brand of "campaign oratory." He, as he says, enjoyed the challenge of dealing with the doctors also for another reason. He gleefully, although immodestly, testified that he outwitted his opponents by allowing them to storm at open doors. He related that he never intended to have the doctors become civil servants or to interfere with the principle of free choice of doctor. It required, therefore, no special sacrifice on his part to give in on one of the points. In order to reassure the doctors, who had no objection to the basic provision in the law of free medical service to all Britons, Bevan announced in the House of Commons that he did not contemplate the introduction of a full-time, salaried, state medical service. In the course of the negotiations, Bevan also agreed to liberalize the provisions of the act to enable the doctors to increase their income.[19] After the second adverse poll among the members of the B.M.A., conducted in February 1948, Bevan gave a full report to Parliament on his negotiations with the medical profession. He related that the doctors had four basic objections to the health scheme:

1. The B.M.A. objected to the basic salary of £300 for the doctors, fearing that they would become state employees. Bevan gave the assurance that it is not intended to create a statewide medical salaried profession, but maintained that the salary is necessary to make sure that young doctors, whose incomes from fees paid per number of patients would be limited, be assured of a decent living. Typically, he added that any doctor who did not want a basic salary might return it to the state "and the Chancellor of the Exchequer would be delighted."[20]

2. The B.M.A. felt that the doctors' partnerships would suffer. The Health Minister expressed his willingness to seek legal counsel on this matter in order to avoid any hardship on doctors who practice in partnerships.

3. Bevan rejected the B.M.A.'s objection to the prohibition, contained in the act, against the purchase and sale of medical

practices. He declared that it is not consonant with the ethics of a civilized modern society to buy and sell patients.

4. The B.M.A. pointed out that a doctor has no legal protection against dismissal from the service. Bevan retorted that he has the right to appeal to courts unless the dismissal is caused by neglect of duty or incompetence.

Bevan finished his brilliant exposition with a plea to the doctors to "consider the long record of concessions we have made." [21] He conceded that the B.M.A. had every right to try to persuade the House of Commons to change its mind, but it had no right to sabotage an Act of Parliament by influencing doctors not to join the National Health Service.

In a remarkable, if genuine, display of personal humility, Bevan disposed of the often heard accusation that a great deal of opposition of the B.M.A. to the health scheme stemmed from a personal antagonism to the Minister of Health. He said:

It has been suggested that one of the reasons why the medical profession are so stirred up at the moment is because of personal deficiencies of my own. I am very conscious of these. They are very great. Absence of introspection was never regarded as part of a Celtic equipment, therefore I am very conscious of my limitations. But it can hardly be suggested that conflict between the British Medical Association and the Minister of the day is a consequence of any deficiencies I possess, because we have never been able to appoint a Minister of Health with whom the B.M.A. agreed.[22]

In April 1948, the B.M.A. conducted another poll. This time the vote was 8,639 for and 9,558 against. Bevan again took a conciliatory attitude and met the remaining objections of the doctors by agreeing to review, within two years, the provisions which gave the Medical Practices Committee power to restrict the right of doctors to criticize and to publish such criticisms of the act as they might deem desirable.[23] In view of these concessions, the B.M.A. advised the doctors to join the plan. One year later, *95 per cent of all British doctors* had voluntarily joined the plan.

Bevan had every reason to be proud and happy with accomplishment. The National Health Act provides free medical, dental, and nursing care for all who want to use it, even for foreigners who are visitors in Great Britain. Bevan proudly stressed that there is no compulsion in the entire plan. It provides that

Those wishing to make use of the Service are asked to choose a doctor. A doctor has the right to refuse to accept a patient. Patients may change doctors and doctors may have patients' names removed from their lists. Thus the essential personal and confidential relationship between doctor and patients is protected.[24]

Significantly, it was Aneurin Bevan who in spite of the objections of his colleagues insisted that the Central Health Services Council and the regional boards, which run the program, must remain completely nonpolitical. "We have taken money out of medicine," Bevan said, "I will not let politics take hold." [25] Under the National Health Act, Britons pay nothing directly to the health service. They make a weekly payment, deducted from salaries, which covers all social security, unemployment, health, old age pensions, and even funeral expenses. The British people, on the whole, approved the plan and many people who needed medical or dental treatment but had hesitated to obtain it because of high cost were now visiting the doctors of their choice. Objective historians were to note in a perspective of a few years that "to the large group of underprivileged, the Act brought long needed assistance. The Act . . . proved far more successful and popular than its most enthusiastic sponsors dared to hope." [26]

Even the *Economist,* which in February 1948 warned that the failure of the health plan would fall squarely on Bevan's shoulders, was forced to concede in December of the same year that ". . . the figures bear out the general impression of the working of the health service." [27] The *Economist* still deplored the high cost of the service but conceded that "the treatment of sickness has a popular appeal that is very difficult to resist." [28]

The Conservatives did not oppose the plan, although Winston Churchill found it hard to restrain himself from delivering a strong attack on Bevan during a debate in the House of Commons. He accused Bevan of prejudicing "this important reform" by his "clumsy and ill-natured handling." Bevan's bad manners, said Churchill, caused unnecessary antagonism, especially on the part of the medical profession. "The whole process," Churchill concluded,

has been rendered more painful by the spirit of spite and class hatred of which Aneurin Bevan has made himself the expression. . . . He has chosen this very moment to speak of at least half the British nation as lower than vermin. We speak of the Minister of Health, but ought we not rather speak of the Minister of Disease? Indeed I can think of no better step to signalize the inauguration of the National Health Scheme than that a person who so obviously needs psychiatrical attention should be among its first patients.[29]

In speaking as harshly as he did, Churchill was obviously reacting not to Bevan's health act, but to his ill-famed speech delivered earlier in 1948 in Manchester, in which he attacked the Tory Government, which, in his opinion, had withheld unemployment allowances from the people of South Wales during the Great Depression. Bevan then added: "No amount of cajolery, no amount of ethical or social seduction can eradicate from my heart a deep burning

hatred for the Tory Party. . . . They are lower than vermin." [30]

The speech enraged the Conservatives and dismayed
many Labourites. The *Economist,* which made no secret of
its abiding dislike for Bevan, stated that

Mr. Bevan has long stood high on the list of those whom the
ordinary citizen, whether his politics be Opposition, Nonparti-
san, or even (one suspects) Labour of the less militant brand,
would clearly like to see psychoanalyzed. What, one wonders,
makes him tick? And how did he get that way? [31]

Not waiting for a professional opinion, the *Economist* did
a bit of analyzing on its own and reasoned that Bevan got
this way because in his youth he had to live on the earnings
of an elder sister.[32] It is to the "vermin" insult that Churchill
reacted, because it is generally conceded that Bevan came
through the struggle for the national medical service with
a greatly enhanced stature and reputation. One writer said
that Bevan as a member of the Labour Government had
developed into a brilliant Socialist administrator and Parliamentarian. The *Manchester Guardian* stated that he was
the ablest orator in the House, Mr. Churchill not excluded.
His success with the national health plan startled his most
devoted admirers. A *New York Times* correspondent wrote
that since Bevan became Minister of Health "he has
emerged triumphant from the battle with the doctors which
all soothsayers said would cripple him for good." Carried
away a bit too far with his enthusiasm, the same correspondent predicted that Bevan might soon be the Prime
Minister, because "the inner circle of the Labour Party has
created its own legend around him, which places the final
crown easily within his reach. When he will wear it appears
to be the only point in dispute." [33] Even some American
publications which made no secret of their animosity to

Bevan paid him, although somewhat grudgingly, well-deserved tribute for an excellent job done as Minister of Health.[34]

A few weeks after the National Health Service Act went into force Bevan refused to condemn the doctors in spite of a number of complaints voiced against them in a parliamentary debate. On the contrary, the Minister of Health was in a tranquil and happy mood. He praised the majority of doctors for their cooperation and told the House of Commons that over 36 million people had enrolled on the lists of patients under the service. He expressed deep and pardonable pride at the smoothness and efficiency which marked the inauguration of the vast and complicated nationwide service on July 5, 1948.[35] Again Bevan, the proud Socialist, said:

I take this opportunity of saying, as I think Hon. Members in all parts of the House will agree, that the transition on 5th July has been carried out with remarkable smoothness . . . with very little friction and dislocation. I venture to say that so great an administrative feat could not have been carried out in any other nation in the world as was carried out in this country on 5th July.[36]

The Conservatives did not challenge this statement of their archenemy.

The realization of the National Health Service was indeed an undertaking of staggering proportions, and Bevan deserved full credit for the efficient was his Ministry handled this enormous task. In all, 95 per cent of eligible Britishers put their names on the lists of recipients of the service, which cost the Exchequer £399,000,000 and was administered by a staff of 34,000 workers.[37] Bevan admits that he and all those who supported the scheme spent a very anxious year after the service was established worrying whether the expected abuses would not lead to public clamor for the cancellation of the entire plan. But these fears proved to be unjustified, because the British people after the first flush of novelty and excitement began to use the Service with prudence and intelligence. Bevan points out that

It is not generally appreciated that after only one full year's experience of the Service, I was able to put in an estimate which was firm and accurate. This was remarkable. It meant that in so short a space of time we were able to predict the pattern of behavior of all the many millions of people who would be using the Service in a particular year.[38]

The free National Health Service clearly won the approval of the British people, and the Conservatives lost no time in giving it their full approval. When Churchill returned to power in 1951, there was no suggestion of abandoning it.

There is general agreement that Nye Bevan also did an excellent job as Minister of Housing. In this difficult task he showed unusual administrative capacity, ability to get things done, and good planning and vision along with adherence to Socialist principles. His responsibility was staggering. The destruction of homes and dwellings from enemy bombings was considerable, and the cessation of home-building activity during the war years brought about a most acute housing shortage. In addition, a great percentage of homes in Great Britain were old and in need of extensive remodeling or replacement. In 1935, a Conservative member of Parliament, a surveyor by profession, made a survey and estimated that 4,600,000 houses should be pulled down because of age.[39] Out of 12,400,000 homes in Britain, 3,400,000 were over eighty-five years old. In 1945, it was estimated that 530,000 new houses were needed to replace some of the worst slum areas.[40]

Upon taking over his office, Bevan decided that what the majority of the people needed was new homes to rent, not to buy. He correctly reasoned that private enterprise would not be interested in erecting moderately priced family dwellings and putting them up for rent.[41] To supplement the building of permanent homes, the Ministry of Housing arranged for a supply of prefabricated houses. The achievements of this program were impressive. In the period between 1945 and 1949, 558,261 new permanent houses were built; 124,970 temporary houses were remodeled; and 141,654 war-damaged homes were repaired.[42] This record compared with 27,863 new houses built by private builders and local authorities in the first two years after World War I. It should, of course, be added that the cost of this program to the Government and the country was considerable.

While the policies of the Ministry of Housing encountered vigorous opposition from the Conservatives, Bevan, to the surprise of many, received support and cooperation from the local authorities and councils, many of which had a Tory majority. He explained the reason for this support when he proudly told the forty-sixth Annual Labour Party Conference: "We provided for local authorities the best housing subsidies that had ever been provided." [43]

In the field of housing, as in the area of public health, Bevan knew how to unite the efforts of many "self-motivating agents," [44] as he called them, to get the houses built. He said, "We have to build houses through a vast number of free and independent citizens and through a vast number of self-motivating agents, people who talk to you and who have the right to talk back. We want them to talk back." [45]

To supplement this program of public housing, Bevan was instrumental in the adoption by Parliament of the Town and County Planning Act. This act requested all cities and county councils to survey the needs of their respective localities and then draw up a development plan. After the adoption of the plan, the local authority was requested to implement it by a combined action by private and public building enterprises. An objective British writer pays Bevan this tribute for his accomplishments in the field of housing: "Mr. Bevan pursued his way for five years with a consistency of purpose, if not of method, unique among his cabinet colleagues, and while doing so, was able to confound his critics in every housing debate in Parliament." [46] In five years the Ministry of Housing repaired the damage to British houses and filled the need for new and better homes for the masses of Britishers who required public help in obtaining decent living abodes.

Speaking during a debate on housing, Bevan with his usual dash of partisanship proudly told the House of Commons: "Of course what is now happening is a grievous disappointment to the Tory Party. They can see the houses going up all over the country. It is no longer possible to . . . deny the fructification of the housing plans. . . ." [47] Bevan went on to inform the House that 20,000 new permanent houses were being erected each month and that his Ministry expected 24,000 new homes to be erected each month in 1948. Most of these homes would be available for rent to lower-income families. He stressed that the housing program was realized in spite of the strenuous opposition of the Conservatives and a large majority of the newspapers in the country. Bevan, with rare eloquence and with typical British pride, rose above his usual narrow partisanship to state that

And now that we have the houses, it ought to be for everybody —whether he be Socialist or a Liberal, a source of national pride and pleasure to see our people going into decent homes all over great Britain. . . . I would like to claim that, here and now, as a contribution and an achievement of all the members of the community, no matter to what party they may belong, because this job is a vast job of social cooperation and could not have been accomplished except by all kinds of persons in all walks of life.[48]

The *Economist,* which had no special fondness for the Minister of Health and Housing, admitted grudgingly in 1950 that the housing program was "erratic, expensive, and in some respect unjust. But judged by the paramount test, that of a number of dwellings completed, it has succeeded." [49]

Bevan built most houses for rent, but he also encouraged the building of homes for private ownership. He did not believe that Socialist beliefs should prevent anyone from owning a home. "I have made it possible," he told Parliament, "for far larger numbers of people to buy their own homes. I have never felt that there was anything wrong or unsocialistic in a person owning a home. I never thought it was wrong to own your own home." [50]

At the 1950 Labour Party Annual Conference, Bevan was handsomely praised by his Party leaders and comrades for his accomplishments in the fields of health and housing. While he proudly proclaimed that in the course of five postwar years Great Britain had built proportionately more new houses than all European countries put together, he vigorously opposed a resolution to nationalize the building industry.[51] Significantly, Bevan, when faced with a governmental responsibility and a practical job that had to be done, was ready and willing to compromise on Socialist dogma in order not to hamper the practical task at hand. He told the delegates to face facts: "If you nationalize the building industry, you do not make Great Britain twice as big." [52] He again gave credit for the success of the housing program to the excellent cooperation his Ministry had received from local councils all over the country, many of which were controlled by the Conservatives. Those who feared Nye Bevan's radicalism and extremism, if he should ever have become Britain's Foreign Secretary, would have done well to study his record as Minister of Health and Housing. There is enough reason to decry his love of power and opportunism, but there are also good reasons to believe that his hardheaded practical realism and strong desire to get a job accomplished would have outweighed his extreme leftist inclinations.

～VIII～ Bevan's break with his Party's foreign policy and resignation

BEVAN had become a potential asset to his Party, and his popularity in the Party was rising accordingly. His accomplishments received favorable appraisals in the British and even in the American press. But this happy state of affairs did not long continue. The cleavage within the Cabinet between the left wing—led by Bevan, Cripps, and Strachey—and the moderate wing—of Morrison, Bevin, and Gaitskell—was becoming wider. Clement Attlee found it increasingly difficult, in spite of his own great prestige, to minimize the differences and preserve the essential unity of governmental policies. After putting into effect an intensive nationalization program, which included the nationalization of the Bank of England, the coal industry, civil aviation, transportation, telecommunications, railroads, and steel, the moderate group demanded a slowdown in order to concentrate, in the words of Herbert Morrison, on "improving the efficiency of socialized industries." [1]

Morrison and Gaitskell deplored the attitude of the workers in many industries, especially in the coal mines. They decried absenteeism and the slackening of productiv-

ity. The workers in the state-owned industries and enterprises persisted in their antagonistic attitude to the
management and the public. "It is natural," said Morrison,

that men and women in industry should feel instinctively that
they must be against the management and there has got to be
a row with the boss from time to time, if only for the sake of
one's soul. It is all understandable. *But with public ownership
there must be a greater social responsibility in industry.*[2]

Gaitskell stressed that a halt was needed in the schedule
of nationalization in order to make a thorough study of the
entire industrial picture and particularly of the industries
which might be nationalized. Such a study required, he
argued, a great deal of time. In the meantime, the moderate
Labour leaders demanded from the British workers a
greater productivity, elimination of excessive absenteeism,
and a large measure of restraint in asking for wage increases.

This theory of moderation and gradualness in Socialist
planning and realization was utterly unacceptable to Bevan
and his left-wing followers. He received important support
from Harold Laski, the highly regarded although not very
influential Labour theoretician. Laski castigated the Labour
leaders for their theory of the "inevitability of gradualness,"
for their reluctance to apply the fundamentals of Marxism
to the British political and economic situation, and for believing that "there was some miraculous dispensation by
which we should achieve our socialist transformation without fighting for it."[3] While Bevan had never accepted
Laski's orthodox Marxist philosophy, he was vigorously
opposed to the principle of gradualness, especially as it
applied to the plans for nationalization of vital industries.
He did, however, reject the proposal to nationalize the
building industry when such a move, in his judgment, would

have hampered his practical efforts to provide better housing for the British people. The only mistakes that the Labour Party had made, Bevan maintained, were, not too much and too fast Socialist planning, but too little determination to realize the Socialist program quickly and effectively. "In so far as there are mistakes made in nationalization," he told his Party comrades,

they are the result not of the defects of Socialist principles, but of concessions we have been compelled to make to the barons of private enterprise. . . . There is no immaculate conception of Socialism. . . . The more *property you transfer from the private sector to the public sector the less exploitation there is of the possibilities of inflation.*[4]

The discomfort of Bevan at the Labour Government's foreign policy was growing more acute. The degree of his discomfort is difficult to assess, because Bevan's membership in the Government made it impossible for him openly to oppose Bevin's foreign policy. His position, however, can be surmised quite accurately by the attacks on British foreign policy that appeared frequently in the *Tribune* and by the periodic rebellions of a group of M.P.'s known to have been under Bevan's influence if not direct leadership. Bevan and his followers thoroughly disagreed with the principle of continuity of British foreign policy, to which Foreign Secretary Ernest Bevin fully subscribed. "Labour foreign policy," one observer stated, "has for the most part, been a generous and rather Wilsonian variant of well established British policies."[5] It should be remembered that Attlee and Bevin were members of the Coalition Cabinet and fully shared the responsibility for the policies of Churchill and Eden. Anthony Eden testified in the House of Commons, without contradiction, that Bevin and he, while in Churchill's Government, never differed on any important

issue of foreign policy.[6] Winston Churchill told the House
of Commons in 1948 that "on the whole, the Government
have maintained a continuity in foreign policy with that
pursued under the National Coalition Government of which
I was the head, and of which my right hon. Friend the
Member for Warwick and Leamington (Mr. Eden) was
Foreign Secretary. . . . In Greece, the Government have
pursued exactly the same policy as that which my right
hon. Friend and I did."[7] When Attlee and Bevin took over
the leadership of the British delegation from Churchill and
Eden, the Russians had little reason to rejoice. The British
Socialist leaders were equally determined on the defense
of the vital interest of the free world and intent on preventing the expansion of world Communism. In dealing
with the Russians, Bevin was, if anything, less conciliatory
than Eden. He recognized that until a genuine system of
collective security were established and until the Soviet
Union gave up its aggressive designs, it would be unwise
to fail to protect fully British interests and possessions.[8]
Bevin soon became quite popular with the permanent
officials of the Foreign Office and with the Conservatives
"although their support sometimes embarrassed Mr. Bevin's
relations with his own Party."[9]

The failure of the London Conference of Foreign Ministers in November 1945 because of Moscow's intransigence
brought the wrath of the *Tribune* and of left-wing
Labourites on Bevin's head. The *New Statesman and Nation*
blamed Bevin in an editorial for continuing the Tory
policies and for joining the United States in an anti-Russian
coalition.[10]

Gradually and quite reluctantly Bevin was coming to the
conclusion that the Big Three could not continue their wartime unity and that Russia was interested primarily in the
expansion of Communist rule and influence. "The only

thing," he said, "that will block understanding is, if any of us develop exclusive power politics, and do not use our perfectly legitimate interests in a way that will, as I said at the beginning, ultimately merge into a world security scheme . . . we will try again. But . . . we cannot be forced to acquiesce in an indefinite stalemate." [12]

In November 1946 a group of forty-six Labour M.P.'s led by Richard Crossman, a close friend, supporter, and admirer of Aneurin Bevan, submitted an amendment to the King's Speech, criticizing in essence Bevin's foreign policy of hostility to the Soviets and close alliance with the United States. The amendment said: ". . . and express the urgent hope that His Majesty's Government will so review and recast its conduct of International Affairs as to afford the utmost encouragement to and collaboration with all Nations and Groups striving to secure full Socialist planning and control of world resources and to provide a democratic and constructive Socialist alternative to an otherwise inevitable conflict between American Capitalism and Soviet Communism in which all hope of World Government would be destroyed." [12] The petition was signed by Bevan's wife, Jennie Lee, and his close friends and followers, such as Silverman, Stokes, and others. Richard Crossman explained the position of his group and presented arguments which in the course of years were to become the principles of Bevanism. Crossman urged that Britain, especially the British Labour Government, preserve a neutral position between America and Russia and become the "third force" which would "mediate fairly between Russia and America" and extend a hand of genuine friendship to both hostile giants. While praising the Labour Government's domestic program and policies, Crossman attacked it for drifting into the American camp, and he specifically demanded that Attlee disavow Churchill's Fulton speech on the necessity of full cooperation of the Western nations against Communism. Jennie Lee supported the amendment and concentrated her attack on the Government's policies in the British sector in Germany. Expressing views which she and her husband were to voice as late as 1957, Miss Lee contended that the denazification program was not far-reaching enough and denounced the revival of German big business.

The Prime Minister refused to give an inch in the debate. He refuted the contentions of the signers of the amendment and refused to disavow Churchill's speech. He praised Bevin's conduct of foreign policy and denounced Soviet obstructionism. Attlee suggested that the resolution be withdrawn or be voted down overwhelmingly. Richard Crossman then rose to request permission to withdraw the amendment. But the majority of the House, eager to rebuke the rebels, refused to grant the permission, and in the division the amendment was defeated by a vote of 353 to 0. The rebels, seared by Attlee's stinging rebuke, abstained and did not vote for their own amendment. Aneurin Bevan dutifully joined his colleagues on the Front Bench in voting "nay."

Attlee and Bevin were deeply distressed by Russian obstructionism, which caused the failure of the Conference of Foreign Ministers held in Moscow in March, 1947. The meeting gave concrete proof that the Soviet Union did not intend to negotiate seriously a peace treaty with Germany on the basis of free elections as previously agreed upon.

Moscow's hostility caused Bevin to strengthen the bonds of cooperation with the United States. This policy of close ties with America was deeply disturbing to the left wingers in the Labour Party and to Bevan. On May 1, 1947, fifteen Labour M.P.'s, including three of Bevan's close collaborators (Richard Crossman, Michael Foot, and Ian Mikardo), published a pamphlet entitled *Keep Left*. The authors de-

manded the abondonment of the "Tory idea of bolstering up
the British Empire with American dollars and fighting
America's battle with British soldiers." [13] The pamphlet
bitterly condemned the British alliance with the United
States and urged that Great Britain become the "third
force" between the Russians and the American antago-
nists.[14]

It is difficult to ascertain how much Bevan had to do with
writing the pamphlet, but the *Tribune* and the *New Statesman and Nation,* which consistently supported him, gave
full endorsement to it. It can also be reasonably assumed
that the "Keep Left" group, which later organized on a
semiformal basis, and of which Jennie Lee was a member,
kept in close touch with the Minister of Health. Only this
liaison can explain the fact that after his resignation in 1951
Bevan was able to take over quickly and effectively the
leadership of this group, known henceforth as the Bevanite
faction, which operated within the Labour Party until 1953.

The Government replied to its critics with a pamphlet
entitled *Cards on the Table,* which was submitted to the
forty-seventh Annual Conference, held in Margate. The
Labour leaders maintained that the Anglo-American alliance was not directed against the Soviet Union, but per-
tained only to common actions in areas where there was a
community of interest between the two countries. The
Government was careful to point out that it accepted no
dictation from the United States.

When America offered the hard-pressed British economy
assistance under the Marshall Plan, Bevin promptly accepted the offer.[15] The realities of the European situation
and the growing fear of Soviet aggression caused Bevin to
propose on January 22, 1948, a "Western Union" to take the
form of a military alliance between Britain, France, Bel-
gium, the Netherlands, and Luxembourg. After recounting

his many efforts to reach an agreement with Russia, Bevin
told the House of Commons,

All these developments, which I have been describing, point to
the conclusion that the free nations of Western Europe must
now draw closely together. . . . The time has come to find ways
and means of developing our relations with the Benelux countries. . . . If we are to preserve peace and our own safety at
the same time, we can only do so by the mobilization of such a
moral and material force as will create confidence in the West
and inspire respect elsewhere.[16]

Answering his Party critics, Bevin told them that America,
"is a country not only of great wealth and great resources,
but one whose people are moved by a goodwill and generosity which many of us in the Old World are apt to take
for granted." [17]

Anthony Eden, speaking for the Opposition, gave his
full approval to Western Union and endorsed Mr. Bevin's
foreign policy. "We welcome," Eden said, "the broad lines of
the statement made by the Foreign Secretary this afternoon.
I have no doubt at all that in the circumstances which
prevail in Europe today the policy which he has outlined
offers the best hope of restoring European political stability,
and through that, of providing a basis for an enduring
peace." [18]

While a left-wing Bevanite, Konni Zilliacus, delivered a
strong attack on the Western Union idea, it must be
assumed from a statement made by Ernest Bevin to the
Forty-seventh Labour Conference that Bevan voted for the
alliance in the Cabinet. Bevin, in order to disarm his critics,
made a point of telling the conference that his January 22
speech delivered in the House of Commons and proposing
the Western Union, which resulted in the signing of the

Brussels Treaty in March 1948, had the prior approval of the Cabinet.[19] Richard Crossman, another Bevanite, gave strong support to the Western Union and told the House that he "profoundly disagreed" with the speech made by Zilliacus.[20] Bevan, however, must have been quite unhappy when he heard Winston Churchill state in the Parliamentary debate that those who, like the Minister of Health, had criticized him for the Fulton speech, must now realize and admit that they were wrong because, as he put it, "in almost every detail and certainly in the spirit and in its moderation, what I there urged has now become the accepted policy of the English-speaking world." [21] Not without a touch of irony, Churchill continued, "The language used by the Prime Minister and the Lord President of the Council about Soviet Russia, and about the dangers of a new war, far exceeds in gravity and menace anything which I said at that time, or indeed, have ever said on the subject since the war." [22]

As could have been expected, under normal conditions Bevan would have leaped into this debate and drawn a distinction between the "warmongering, Russia-hating" Conservatives and the "peace-loving and peace-pursuing" Labourites, but he did not participate in the debate. This was not the first nor the last time that Bevan exercised the restraint of a self-imposed silence whenever there was a possibility that a speech, especially on foreign policy, might endanger his position or his aspirations of the hour within the Labour Party. In 1948 Bevan was determined to exploit his popularity as one of the most effective Labour ministers to gain a seat on the National Executive Committee of the Party. In spite of many temptations, he did not participate in the foreign policy debate at the Forty-seventh Conference of the Labour Party. His remarkable restraint was fully rewarded and Bevan was elected to the Executive by the largest vote received by any member chosen by the Constituent Labour Parties.

The Soviet blockade of Berlin and the successful American air lift caused the British Government, in collaboration with the Brussels Pact countries, to invite the United States and Canada to join with the free countries of Western Europe in a North Atlantic Treaty Alliance. The United States responded favorably, and on April 4, 1949, the North Atlantic Treaty was signed in Washington. The debate on the ratification of NATO took place in the House of Commons on May 12, 1949. Since the Labour Party and the Conservatives supported the treaty, there was only negligible opposition from a handful of rebels in the Labour Party and the Communists. Winston Churchill again, with thinly disguised irony, referred to the fact that those who condemned him for his Fulton, Missouri, speech, delivered in March 1946, were now supporting the North Atlantic Alliance, based on the closest fraternal association of the English-speaking world, an idea which he had been the first to advocate. He recalled that immediately after his Fulton speech, 105 Members of Parliament (among them many future members of the Bevanite faction) moved a motion of censure against him. Churchill mockingly said,

I do not see them all here today, some of them are here, but of course, I feel that there has been a large-scale process of conversion and, naturally, I welcome converts and so does His Majesty's Government. . . . Here, we have got about a hundred [converts] in a bunch, so far as I can make out, and though some of them have emphasized the change of heart which they have gone through by a suitable act of penance by abstaining from attending this Debate.[23]

The major opposition speech was again delivered by Konni Zilliacus. It was an unrestrained and hard-hitting speech, for which Zilliacus was subsequently expelled from the Labour Party on May 8, 1949. Zilliacus accused the Government of pursuing the policy laid down by Churchill in his Fulton speech. It is difficult to ascertain whether Aneurin Bevan agreed with Zilliacus' arguments. He probably agreed with his general line, but not with his decision to vote against the NATO Alliance. But Zilliacus based his major arguments on the *Keep Left* pamphlet, from which he quoted extensively and which undoubtedly had Bevan's endorsement. He quoted, for instance, from the pamphlet the following passage: "The Fulton policy has now become the official policy of the U.S.A. The American strategists are interested therefore to secure a system of forward defenses against Russia, manned by non-American forces." [24] In other words, Zilliacus explained the "Keep Left" group's point of view, that the United States is ready to fight Russia to the last Englishman. In concluding his violent attack on the treaty and on America, Zilliacus asked: "Are the present rulers of the United States right in assuming that Labour Britain with Franco Spain and a capitalist and partly renazified Western Germany are the only reliable bases, bastions and purveyors of cannonfodder for the American Century power politics and a counterrevolutionary war of intervention masquerading as the defense of democracy?" [25]

The Atlantic Pact was approved by a vote of 333 to 6, with a considerable number of Labour Members absent or not voting. The record discloses that Bevan did not vote. During his visit to the United States in October 1957, Bevan stated that he always was a supporter of NATO.[26] The one, and rather clear, support for this statement can be found in Bevan's speech to the House of Commons, made in 1952, in which he said in part,

I have no doubt whatsoever—I never have had any doubt that Western Europe is perfectly entitled to form whatever alignments and coalitions and take whatever measures it wishes for its own defense. We are as much entitled to take these measures in Western Europe as the Soviet Union is to take them in Eastern Europe.[27]

But in the same speech Bevan decried the general hostility to the Soviet Union and stated, "The fact is that whenever we approach a problem connected with the Soviet Union, it is almost impossible for some hon. Members not to do so in an anti-Christ state of mind." [28]

Bevan gave his full support to the Government's endorsement of United Nations resistance to North Korean aggression, which began on June 27, 1950.[29] The Bevanite group, however, soon began a sustained pressure on the Government to make sure that the conflict in Korea was localized and limited and the war stopped once the aggressors were thrown back of the Thirty-eighth Parallel.[30]

On November 29, 1950, a group of Bevanite Members led by Michael Foot submitted a motion urging British initiative toward ending the fighting in Korea. Another group of forty Labour M.P.'s, mostly trade unionists, called upon the British Government to take the initiative to arrange a Big Four conference in order to prevent the spread of the Korean conflict into a world war. The reason for this anxiety was the intervention of Red China in Korea and the fear that Americans might bomb military Chinese installations and concentrations in the Chinese sanctuary.

When on November 29, 1950, President Truman indicated that the United States Government had under active consideration the use of all weapons in Korea, including the atomic bomb, one hundred Labour M.P.'s signed a letter to Attlee, urging the Government to "disassociate Britain from the use of the atom bomb, emphasize that this country cannot be committed to any action outside the decisions of the United Nations and to warn that any unilateral action would be followed by the withdrawal of British forces from Korea." [31] The debate which followed in the House of Commons was described by the United States embassy in London as "the most serious, anxious and responsible debate on foreign affairs conducted by the House of Commons since the Labour Party came to power in 1945." [32]

President Truman adds in his memoirs, on the basis of information received from the United States Embassy in London, that "not only the followers of Mr. Aneurin Bevan, but also Churchill, Eden, and Butler, talked about 'disquiet' and generally indicated that they wanted to be assured that events in Korea would not propel the world into a major war." [33] Faced with this pressure in Parliament and with Bevan's insistence inside the Cabinet, Attlee decided to fly to Washington for a personal conference with Truman. The Attlee–Truman conference, which Attlee in his memoirs almost overlooked, but which Truman describes in his book with great detail, provides interesting proof that Bevan was successful in exerting considerable influence on Attlee on two cardinal points of British policy. Attlee made every effort to convince Truman that the United States should recognize Red China and vote for its admission to the United Nations. He gave as a reason a point of view which almost verbatim corresponds to the position taken by Bevan, as explained in his book, *In Place of Fear*, published in 1952, that "the Chinese Communists were potentially ripe for Titoism . . . the aim ought to be to divide the Russians and the Chinese who are natural rivals in the Far East." [34]

Attlee also told Truman that Britain could not go on increasing its armament. "The British austerity program cannot be further tightened," said Attlee, "because we can't cut back much more; we don't have any fat left to sweat off." [35]

In spite of his representations to Truman, Attlee and the

Labour Government, faced by the realities of the international situation in which the aggressive intentions of the Soviet Union and Red China became increasingly evident, decided to follow the lead of the United States and substantially increase the British military potential. Britain joined with the other NATO nations in building up a system of mutual defense and security. The Labour Party gave overwhelming support to the Government's policy. After Foreign Secretary Ernest Bevin appealed to the Forty-ninth Annual Labour Conference in October 1950 that the Party must give the nation "the necessary power to back up the United Nations, the necessary backing with your defense arrangements, so that aggression can never succeed," the conference backed him by a vote of 4,861,000 to 881,000.[36]

There were growing indications, however, that the influence of the Labour Government was gradually waning after five years of being in power. In the General Election, held in February 1950, the Labour Party won 315 seats in Parliament, a substantial reduction from the 393 seats held in the previous House; the Conservative strength rose from 213 to 296 seats. Attlee's new Government could count only on a bare majority of a few votes, clearly an insufficient margin of safety for an effective government. Churchill and the Conservatives were convinced that they had the Labourites on the run and were determined to make things difficult for the Labour Party, hoping that Attlee would have to dissolve Parliament and ask for a new election, which they were sure to win. Their tactics were quite successful. The Labour whips had to work overtime to assure the constant attendance of the Labour M.P.'s and were forced on several occasions to bring sick Labourites from the London hospitals to support the Government in the many votes of confidence forced by the Conservatives.[37]

The days of the Labour rule were obviously drawing to

a close, especially since the long-simmering rebellion of the Bevanite group against the pro-American, anti-Soviet and pro-armament foreign policy of Attlee, Bevin, and Morrison was threatening to explode at any moment. The man who would touch off the explosion was Aneurin Bevan. He was only waiting for an appropriate *casus belli*. He was soon to find it. During March and April, Bevan was feuding with the new Chancellor of the Exchequer, Hugh Gaitskell, who proposed to establish charges under the National Health Service for dentures and glasses. The feud was growing more bitter, especially since Attlee, who usually mediated in such interministerial squabbles, was in a hospital, having his ulcers healed. As Attlee relates, "the disagreement spread to the effect on the economy of the level of armaments on which we had embarked." [38] Bevan found Gaitskell a much tougher man to deal with than Cripps and Dalton who preceded him in the Treasury. Gaitskell refused to yield to Bevan's cajolings and threats, and won the approval of the Cabinet on the inclusion of the health charges in the Budget. Bevan decided to use his quarrel with Gaitskell as the occasion for his resignation from the Government. On April 22, 1951, he and Harold Wilson, President of the Board of Trade, and John Freeman, Minister of Supply, who subsequently resigned from the Government with Bevan, demanded that the National Executive Committee call a special conference of the Labour Party to debate the subject of rearmament. When the Executive refused and reaffirmed its wholehearted support for the Government's policies, the three ministers charged that the Executive was subservient to and taking orders from the Government.[39]

On Monday, April 25, Aneurin Bevan rose in the House of Commons to explain the reasons for his resignation. The London *Times* reported that he "started quietly and a little hesitantly . . . then his voice gathered resonance, his gestures became more expansive and as he developed his case, he repeatedly leaned to admonish his own Front Bench with vivid phrase and pointing finger." [40] Bevan told Parliament that he was resigning primarily because of his conviction that the United States' and Britain's armament program would undermine the British civilian economy, lower the standard of living, and eventually cause large-scale unemployment. "The fact is," he stated, "that the Western World has embarked on a campaign of arms production, and upon a scale of arms production, so quickly and to such an extent, that the foundations of political liberty and Parliamentary democracy will not be able to sustain the shock." [41] Such a policy of accelerated armaments and the resulting lowered standard of living in the Western countries, Bevan continued, would aid Russia, which was not interested in a military test, but in social-economic competition. [42] The Government's armaments policy, Bevan charged, would furnish for Soviet Communism "a whole series of Trojan horses in every nation of the Western community." [43] The resigning Minister of Health had also decided to square his accounts with Mr. Gaitskell by launching a bitter, unrestrained, and thoroughly unfair personal attack on the Chancellor of the Exchequer. He accused him of mutilating the health program, of allowing himself to be dragged behind the wheels of American diplomacy, and finally of taking money out of the national insurance funds to "finance the rearmament of Great Britain out of the contributions of the workers." This last demagogic and patently untrue charge was clearly designed for internal consumption in the Labour Party. Bevan hoped to damage Gaitskell's standing and prestige in the Party and improve his own stature as the fearless defender of the hard-won rights of the working class. Bevan concluded his speech with a hope that "the dramatic nature of a resignation might cause even some of our American friends to think before it is too late." [44]

The speech was received in a generally hostile silence[45] and, as Bevan left the House, only his wife, Jennie Lee, "hurried after him to pat his back and whisper something." [46] Bevan's vindictive onslaught on Gaitskell received the general condemnation it deserved. The sober *Times* stated editorially, "Mr. Gaitskell's bitterest political enemy could scarcely have been less fair." [47] The *Spectator*, with its hearty dislike of Bevan, hopefully predicted that the fear that his resignation will win him support in the country "may be largely discounted." [48]

Before examining the false hopes of Bevan's foes, it might be in order to consider, in some detail, the reasons for Bevan's resignation. There is evidence to substantiate the conclusion that neither the health charges nor the armament question were the real reasons for Bevan's resignation. Bevan must have known that the charges for glasses and dentures were put into effect not to save money, because the amount involved was comparatively small, but to prevent abuses discovered in the administration of the National Health Service.[49] Some Conservative newspapers charged that in the initial flush of excitement and enthusiasm over the general provisions of the act, many Britishers were prone to order unnecessary dental work and extravagant glasses.

The armament issue was also a blown-up argument without much merit. The London *Times,* commenting on Bevan's resignation, recalled that only ten weeks earlier Bevan had *supported* the rearmament program when he told the House of Commons, "We shall carry out the rearmament program. We shall fulfill our obligations to our friends and allies." [50] In a pamphlet which Bevan and Wil-

son published two and a half months after their resignation
and entitled *One Way Only*, the authors conceded some rearmament to be necessary, but argued that the degree of
the armament program must not be allowed to affect adversely the British economy. As we have seen, Attlee fully
agreed with this point of view and made every effort to
explain the British dilemma to President Truman in their
Washington conference in 1950. Indeed, one cannot quarrel
with Attlee's view that Bevan's big ado about armaments
was blown out of all proportion and unjustified.

Attlee points out that he had stated publicly that the degree of rearmament would be conditioned by "the availability of raw materials and machine tools and the level of
prices. *There was, therefore, in my view, no real difference
of principle.*" [51] A year later, Bevan claimed (he was not
contradicted) that Attlee made the rearmament program
conditional upon the availability of raw materials and machine tools at his suggestion. He admitted, however, that
he did not suggest to Attlee that "it [rearmament] was also
dependent upon the viability of the British economy." [52]
Furthermore, at the 1950 Annual Labour Conference, Bevan
supported the rearmament policy, enunciated by Bevin and
Attlee and endorsed by the National Executive Committee.

At the conference held in October 1951, only seven
months before his resignation, Bevan was on his best behavior. He praised the attainments of the Labour Government and ascribed them to the "greater degree of unity
than I have ever have known before in my experience in
the Labour Party." [53] He spoke in support of the policy
statement submitted to the conference by the National Executive and gave handsome praise to Attlee and Morrison.

Was the resignation, then, a rash emotional decision made
at the spur of the moment without much prior consideration? There is every reason to assume that the contrary was

true and that the resignation was the result of a carefully
thought-out plan. Aneurin Bevan, throughout his political
career, reacted emotionally and impulsively on relatively
unimportant situations, but was deliberate and coldly practical when matters of great importance were at stake. He
devoted several weeks to careful negotiations with Wilson
and Freeman and to consultations with other friends and
followers, and, one must assume, to serious private delibera-
tions and introspection. It is therefore reasonable to assume
that there were other considerably more important and
compelling reasons for the resignation. Bevan was thoroughly dissatisfied with the post of Minister of Labour and
National Service, which Attlee gave him in the new Government formed after the 1950 election. Having done an
excellent job in the Ministry of Health and Housing, he had
reason to assume that he would be given the post of Chancellor of the Exchequer. Attlee, however, assigned that post
to Hugh Gaitskell. Bevan knew that in his capacity of Minister of Labour his main task would be to keep the unions
in line and to discourage them from asking for substantial
wage increases. This assignment Bevan, the radical foe of
the employers and the uncompromising Socialist, did not
cherish. Ernest Bevin had succeeded in preventing the British workers from asking for higher wages and shorter hours,
but that was during war years when the Government could
and did appeal to the patriotism of the entire population.
Bevan knew that his enemies inside and outside the Labour
Party waited with glee and anticipation for the inevitable
conflicts to arise between the trade unions and the Minister
of Labour. He considered Attlee's offer for two weeks before accepting it. When he did accept it, his left-wing
friends on the Labour backbenches, who had looked to him
to lead them in a rebellion against Attlee and Morrison,
were bitterly disappointed. They complained that Bevan

was outmaneuvered by the right wingers who had appealed to Bevan's love of important office.[54]

After a short time in his new post, Bevan realized the mistake he had made and looked for a way of freeing himself from the new responsibility. He also knew that the days of the Labour Government were numbered, because it was becoming increasingly impossible to rule with a majority of a few votes in the House of Commons. Bevan anticipated that Attlee would have soon to recommend the dissolution of Parliament and declare new elections. Such a possibility was undoubtedly discussed by the Cabinet. He wanted to make sure that he would leave the Government as the acknowledged leader of the left wing of the Labour Party which, while increasingly vocal, was amorphous and heterogeneous and badly in need of a strong leader. The dramatic resignation, with its attendant publicity, would serve, he correctly surmised, to rally and energize all dissatisfied elements in the Party, especially in view of the anticipated defeat in the next elections, which was widely predicted by the opinion polls and the press. He would be pictured as the martyr for the interests of the British workers.

Bevan was aware that his quest for power within the Labour Party was progressing too slowly. To be sure, his prestige was growing and he was easily elected to the National Executive Committee, but he still was kept out of the inner circle of the top leadership by the coalition of trade union leaders and the moderate or right-wing intellectuals of the Party. The resignation and the assumption of the leadership of the Bevanite group (of which Harold Wilson, Michael Foot, Richard H. Crossman, and Barbara Castle were the leading members) were to serve notice to the entrenched leadership of Arthur Deakin, Morrison, and Bevin that the best interests of the Party demanded that Bevan be taken, on terms of full equality, into the inner ruling group. Bevan knew that the Party leadership had duly noted that in the 1950 elections to the National Executive he got 849,000 votes to 671,000 votes cast for Herbert Morrison. The issue on which Bevan decided to challenge the Party leadership and gain his power objective was not the rearmament question and certainly not the additional health service charges, but the *entire* area of Britain's foreign policy. Bevan decided to single out for special attention the alleged abdication by Britain of its decisions in international politics in favor of blind obedience to and abject following of American leadership. He also knew the fear of the British people of another war and decided to exploit it.

In spite of the fact that the resignation was deliberate and well thought out, it was nevertheless a gamble. Bevan staked his entire political future on it, since there was considerable resentment within the Labour Party against him for kicking the Government in the teeth when it was struggling for its life. But those who hopefully predicted, primarily on the basis of the hostile reception of his tactless resignation speech in Parliament, that Bevan would go into political eclipse were greatly mistaken. Bevan was not headed into the wilderness of political oblivion, but on the contrary "the minority supporting him was growing" [55] and more and more unions came to his support. The Gallup Poll reported that 60 per cent of those interviewed supported Bevan's opposition to the health changes and the majority endorsed his reasons for resignation.[56] In a short time, a large group of Labour M.P.'s overcame its fear of Party discipline and sanctions and declared its support for the Welsh rebel.

Bevan's followers were happy that their leader's resignation gave them the freedom to launch a vigorous attack on the Labour Party's leadership and policies. The *Tribune,* whose co-editors were Jennie Lee and Michael Foot, joyously announced:

Now that the first shock of the resignation is passed, the Labour Movement is lustily enjoying its new freedom. It is no longer tongue-tied . . . the dynamism of the free discussion is already carrying us forward to new positions of Socialist strength and Socialist unity.[57]

Bevan and Wilson made an effort to expound their views more fully and comprehensively and in July 1951 published a pamphlet entitled *One Way Only.* They declared that the most important task of the free countries was to raise the living standards of their populations, an aim which could not be reconciled with a rearmament program. Bevan and Wilson correctly assessed the importance of winning the underdeveloped and uncommitted nations of Asia for democracy, and urged large-scale economic aid for these areas. The whole argument, however, which contained a number of truths and half-truths, was based on an entirely fallacious premise that the Soviet Union had no aggressive intentions against the West and would not exploit Western military weakness. The authors "proved" this contention by pointing out that Russia did not attack Yugoslavia when Tito declared independence of the Kremlin. They conveniently forgot to mention the Greek civil war, the Korean conflict, and the Berlin blockade, where only the armed power of the West halted the Russians. Had Bevan's and Wilson's views not been rejected by the great majority of their countrymen, Labourites and Conservatives alike, the free world would have been in mortal danger.

Bevan's fortunes improved after the dissolution of Parliament by Attlee, which came only six months after his resignation in September 1951. True to its traditional custom, which Bevan once aptly defined as "putting the differences in the cupboard in order to face the main enemy," [58] the Labour Party suppressed all intention of disciplining Bevan and closed ranks in a show of party unity and solidarity to assure success in the forthcoming elections. Speaking at the traditional preconference *Tribune* meeting, Bevan affirmed the right and even the desirability of members of the Labour Party to have honest differences of opinion but ". . . what I object to, and always have objected to, is the assumption that every new and vital growth in the party should be smothered in a demand for unity." But fighting the Tories, Bevan continued, takes precedence over everything else. "I made up my mind," he said, "that our argument is over. . . . I have been fighting Tories all my life, ever since I was a nipper." [59]

The *Times* reported on October 3, 1951, from Scarborough, the scene of the Fiftieth Labour Party Conference: "The Fiftieth annual conference which opened at Scarborough on Monday, found Mr. Bevan and his supporters working in close unity—for the time being—with the Government leaders, with the majority of the Executive and with the trade union leaders." [60] Mr. Bevan was one of the small group which agreed on the terms of the election manifesto before it was presented to the National Executive on Sunday. Mr. Bevan sealed the truce in a good-humored but quite unrepentant speech, which entertained a packed audience.

Aneurin Bevan once again demonstrated his political acumen and agility. He was a rebel, but a very cautious one. In spite of his dramatic resignation on basic policy principles, he held his peace at the Party conference and apparently convinced his Party leaders that he was a man who could be negotiated with. He, the outspoken radical and uncompromising Socialist, voted for a vague and watered-

down platform which called for the "taking over of industrial concerns that fail the nation" and readily accepted a
foreign policy plank which piously stated that peace is the
first objective of the party. The Labourites lost the 1951
election. They got only 296 seats to 321 won by the Conservatives. It might be that Sir Norman Angel gave at least
a partial explanation for the Labour defeat when he wrote,

It is no secret at all that a great many in the Labour Party, especially on the trade union side, regard Mr. Aneurin Bevan a
far greater menace than Mr. Churchill to the world of the British workers' desires.[61]

~IX~ Bevan on Russia, Socialism, America, and Red China

HAVING BROKEN with the Labour Party leadership, Bevan felt the need for a full exposition of his views in a form of a guide book for his followers. He devoted several months to collecting and editing his speeches and scattered newspaper and magazine articles. Several new chapters were written to summarize his life's story and political philosophy. The book appeared in April 1952, published under the title *In Place of Fear*. If the book was intended to be the "Bible" of Bevanism, it fell short of its goal. It hardly did justice to its author, a generally acclaimed orator, or equal second to Winston Churchill. *In Place of Fear* fared badly in the hands of the reviewers. There was general agreement that Bevan, "a man of speech and action is not a theorist or a writer." [1] The book is poorly written, it rambles and lacks the conviction, the verve, and the infectious enthusiasm of many of Bevan's speeches. In spots it is downright dull. One reviewer correctly observed that the book is "a curious piece of work, which over large stretches gives the impression of having been dictated in a hurry, then laid aside and forgotten." [2] Even Kingsley Martin, a close friend and collaborator of Bevan, while agreeing with the main thesis of the book, had no words of praise for its style and persuasiveness.[3] What was disappointing to many reviewers was the conviction that the book did not reflect, even in a small measure, the attractive and magnetic personality of its author. This magnetism and attractiveness is admitted even by his enemies. A reviewer who virtually demolished Bevan's political arguments began his review by stating that "Mr. Aneurin Bevan is the most exciting political figure in Britain today. His qualities would be outstanding anywhere; a vigorous, original mind, vivid imagination, a great personal force. He has passion and political courage."[4] A veteran correspondent of *The New York Times,* who heartily disapproved of Bevanism, had no hesitancy in admitting that "one hour with Bevan made me a convert . . . the man is as persuasive as an insurance salesman, has lots of charm, real simple charm . . . with a golden Welsh gift of gab."[5] While the book does in spots reflect Bevan's original mind, it mirrors none of his vivid personal force and magnetism. It is a pedestrian book, which while occasionally persuasive can hardly be classed with the fighting revolutionary books which stirred men's souls. And what is even more surprising, Bevan emerges from the book not the shining knight of Socialism, the rebellious proletarian bent on changing the prevailing social order, but as a practical, hardheaded and rather moderate Socialist whose one truly strong emotion is his pronounced anti-Americanism. One reviewer aptly said, "The ogre turned out to be surprisingly mild-mannered, introspective and somewhat old-fashioned."[6]

This mild and moderate Aneurin Bevan was really no surprise to those who knew him best. An old Socialist comrade says, "he is of the left in politics but not so far left as he sometimes seems to his enemies—or to his friends. But never so far left, I think, as to get out of touch with practical politics or the realities of political life."[7]

Likewise, the Anglican vicar of the London Church of St. Matthew, in which both Cripps and Attlee were active members, related that after meeting Bevan he hesitated whether to invite him to his home because he had heard that Bevan was not fond of parsons. He finally did extend the invitation. Bevan came, saw, and conquered the parson and his family by his kindliness, generosity, and humor. The vicar found him a most stimulating companion and became convinced that Bevan was not a dangerous radical as he was often pictured to be. "Many look upon him," he wrote, "as an ogre who with the help of Russia is determined to ride roughshod to Downing Street and foist a dictatorial regime upon the country. Nothing could be further from the truth. Nye is a passionate democrat and an arch-individualist." [8] A distinguished British journalist and political writer for the *Observer* also felt pleasantly reassured when he visited Bevan in his comfortable home in Chelsea, the artistic center of London, where he lived with his wife, Jennie Lee, and her parents. He too found that "Bevan may be an ogre to his enemies but in private life no one has greater charm." [9] There seems to be an overwhelming weight of evidence to support these dispassionate and objective appraisals of Nye Bevan. How, then, can one explain some of his extreme and often demagogic utterances? Francis Boyd has an explanation which merits attention and consideration. He argues that the key to the many puzzling aspects of Bevan's career is his incessant and determined search for the "source power." [10] The poor, deeply hurt miners' helper determined early in his life to become a somebody, settling later on attaining the leadership of the British Labour Party. Having a keen and sharp mind, he quickly understood and analyzed the power structure of the Labour Party and decided to force the existing leadership, based on an alliance of the big trade unions and the moderate intellectuals, to make him a member of the ruling group. Since they refused to take him in willingly, he became the rebel leader of a heterogeneous group of dissidents and malcontents, which he led and molded by the sheer power of his personality. It had been said, correctly, that the Bevanite group constituted a miniature Popular Front. Its cohesion and effectiveness depended in a very large measure upon the personality of the leader. In his constant pursuit of power Bevan often mixed extreme radicalism and emotionalism with down-to-earth practical politics and almost conservative moderation. He was the able, moderate, and practical politician as Minister of Health and Housing, but became the turbulent political extremist when he saw an advantage in leaving a "decaying Government before it finally disintegrated" [11] and thus became the leader of a powerful opposition group. The resignation was a gamble, but Bevan confounded many who foresaw his political demise by winning, in 1952, seats for himself and for six of his followers on the Executive Committee of the Labour Party and by becoming shortly thereafter a member of the Shadow Cabinet.

Bevan deliberately did not let his enemies—or his friends —forget that even in his amiable and compromising moods he still had a hand grenade behind the door. It would be wrong, however, to assert, as some did, that Nye Bevan lacked principles or that he was always ready to sacrifice his principles to satisfy his political ambitions.[12]

Being a veteran and wise politician with a rich experience in the inner politics of the British Parliament and his own Party, Bevan was willing and ready to bend with the wind and enjoyed a down-to-earth political give-and-take; but he had a political philosophy and political ideals to which he remained true all his life. There can be no doubt of Bevan's wholehearted dedication to Socialism and of his devotion to the improvement of the lot of the British workers. While he had a cohesive political philosophy, he occasionally compromised and moderated his views whenever in his opinion conditions required such compromises. Bevan was convinced that he could make an important contribution to the peace of the world once he achieved a position of international importance. He correctly considered himself a skillful negotiator and thought that, had he gotten Russian and American representatives around a negotiating table, he could have brought about a settlement of the major outstanding issues between the two strongest countries of the world. He apparently did not consider this task much more difficult than the long and complicated negotiations which led to the adoption of the National Health Service, or the patient negotiations he conducted so often and so skillfully within the National Executive Committee of the Labour Party to bring about unanimously endorsed foreign and domestic policy statements for submission to the Annual Conferences.

The central theme of Bevan's book is his profound conviction that Britain must conduct its own independent foreign policy, because its continued alliance with and reliance upon America will bring either the bankruptcy of the British economy or World War III or both. Bevan maintained that the British people have more to fear from the fear of Communism than from Communism itself, because this constant and morbid fear jeopardizes the gains of the welfare state, lowers the standard of living, and diverts the nation's wealth toward expenditures on armaments instead of expanded social services. Such a fear, said Bevan, is without foundation because the Soviet Union does not want war, fears war as much as the West does, and wants to compete with the West, economically, ideologically, and socially, but not militarily. "There is no evidence to show," writes Bevan, "that the Soviet Union wants a trial of strength." [13] If there is a danger of the spread of Communism, it comes not from armed intervention of the Soviets, or even from their subversive underground activity, but from the failure of the Western countries and society to redress and alleviate social wrongs and injustices.[14] "An effective answer to Russian aggression [*sic*]," says Bevan, "involves a re-examination of our attitude to the social problems in our own country!" [15]

These basic ideas, which he states and restates in his book, may suffice to explain the universal condemnation of Bevan's views which followed the publication of *In Place of Fear*. There are, however, several relatively more important questions for which answers should be sought on the pages of the only volume ever written by Nye Bevan. What did Bevan think of the Soviet Union, of Red China, of Communism? Was he a Communist or a fellow-traveler? Was he anti-American? What was the nature of his Socialism? These questions need serious and objective study, first because of Bevan's one-time potentially crucial role in world politics, and even more because of the great diversity of answers given to these questions by writers, diplomats, and common citizens on both sides of the Atlantic.

That such a careful and objective examination of Bevan's views and world outlook is needed is further highlighted by a thoughtful and typically British observation made in the House of Commons by Julian Amery, one of the most empire-minded and right-wing Tories. Following Bevan in a debate, Amery once said,

First, I should like to consider one aspect of the right hon. Gentleman's [Bevan's] argument. *I think he has often been misrepresented.* [Italics mine.] People have said he is pro-Russian. As I understand it—and I have followed his speeches and the speeches of his supporters with care—he does not deny that there is a certain danger from the Russians and does not deny the need for a measure of re-armament. What he does say is that by re-arming as much as we are at present doing, we run the risk of overstraining our economy.[16]

Amery went on to say that he disagreed with Bevan but sympathized with his point of view and certainly did not consider him a Communist or a fellow-traveler.

What did Bevan think of Russia and Communism? There is overwhelming proof that Bevan detested Communism, and had no illusions about the despotic nature of the Soviet Union. He wrote:

We all know that there are features of the Soviet system which are repulsive. The existence of huge forced labour camps, the ruthless punishment meted out to political offenders, the disappearance without trace of people who offend against the ruling clique, the appalling doctrine of 'associative crime,' all these are deeply offensive.[17]

This indictment of Russia is powerful and conclusive. Typically, however, Bevan's blind hatred of the Conservatives caused him, without a shred of logic or justification, to blame the Tories for the worst features of Soviet tyranny. According to him, Churchill contributed more to the aggravation of this tyranny than Stalin. "Let us remember," he said,

that the Soviet revolution would not have been so distorted, would not have ended in tyranny, would not have resulted in a dictatorship, would not now be threatening the peace of mankind, had it not been for the behavior of Churchill and the Tories at that time [of the Russian Revolution]. Do not forget that in the early days when the great mass of backward people were trying to find their way to the light, were trying to lift themselves from age-long penury and oppression, they were diverted from their objectives and thrown back into darkness, not by the malignancy of Stalin [*sic!*] at first, but by the action and the malignancy of Churchill, the City of London, New York and all the rest of the capitalist world.[18]

Bevan had not forgotten that at the time of the closest Anglo-Soviet collaboration during World War II, Winston Churchill had expressed his regret that the British Archangel expedition did not succeed in strangling the Bolshevik Revolution in its early days.

Bevan, in spite of his insistence on the advisability of continued negotiations with the Russians, had no illusions as to the sincerity of the Soviet recurrent peace propaganda. "Russian peace propaganda," he stated, "is a sham and a cynical sham at that as Vishinsky's behavior in the United Nations Assembly in Paris revealed to all not blinded by fanaticism." [19] During World War II Bevan, together with the anti-Communist English writer George Orwell, in his *Tribune* repeatedly exposed and denounced Soviet tyranny. They bitterly opposed the Yalta Pact as an appeasment of Russia. After a visit to Russia in 1930, Bevan stated that while the British people are slaves of the past, Russians are slaves to the future,[20] because their basic needs for food and housing are sacrificed for the requirements of the "Plan." He wrote, "The economic function of the police state is to hold down the consumption of the people, especially of the peasant population, while their surplus production is drained off for the purpose of fixed capital investment. . . . Herein lies the tragedy of the Soviet Union." [21] Bevan cheered when the Yugoslavs "threw down the gauntlet to the Soviet Union, [and] . . . challenged the most sacred thesis which has held all the Communist parties of the world in subjection to Russia. . . . Yugoslavia is the first instance of a Communist country rebelling against this dogma. China will be next." [22] He visited Yugoslavia several times after its break with the Soviets, and encouraged and befriended Tito and his closest collaborators. He had also, often, on behalf of the British Labour Party, worked with the Italian Socialist parties to influence them to disassociate themselves from Communist domination.

Bevan devoutly hoped and expected that the higher standards of education, the growing industrialization would gradually cause the Soviet students and intelligentsia to press for more and more political freedom and thus slowly eliminate the most obnoxious features of the Soviet dictatorship. "The economic enfranchisement of the Soviet workers," Bevan believed, "is proceeding and their political enfranchisement must follow." The Soviet Government, Bevan felt, is aware of this and that is why it makes "desperate attempts . . . to insulate themselves from the rest of the world. . . ." [23] There have been increasing reports coming out from the Soviet Union to provide substantiation to these predictions made by Bevan in 1952. The Soviet masses, Bevan predicted, will some day express their dissatisfaction with the dictatorship and the lack of freedom. "What form that protest will take," Bevan wrote, "when it comes, is difficult to conjecture." [24] Remarkably, Aneurin Bevan foresaw two basic developments in the Soviet Union. As early as 1952, he prophesied that the Soviet Union would have to decentralize its industrial set-up, because of the enormous growth of a vast bureaucracy.[25] This decentralization was ordered by Khrushchev in 1955, for the exact reason cited by Bevan. Bevan also showed remarkable foresight when he foretold that the expansion and improvement of the Soviet educational system would result in political ferment and unrest among the Russian scientists, engineers, and students. He said:

The totalitarian states are bound to fail because you cannot educate a man to be intelligent inside the workshop and a fool outside the workshop. That is what the Soviet Union will discover. . . . Once you start educating the working class to use all the complicated machinery of a modern civilization and it learns to read blueprints, it reads other things as well.[26]

While Bevan admitted that "insofar as I can be said to have had a political training at all, it has been in Marxism," [27] he maintained that the Marxist school of political thought was arid and outdated. He particularly condemned the fact that Marxism consistently understated the value and the importance of a political democracy with its inherent right of universal franchise. He detested Communism because he was a dedicated admirer of Parliamentary British democracy. Kingsley Martin was correct when he said that Bevan "has never in thirty-five years of rebellious activity advocated anti-Parliamentary or unconstitutional behavior. He sincerely believes in Parliamentary democracy." [28] Bevan once paid this tribute to the rule by Parliament, where he spent most of his adult life: "It has always been held to be one of the glories of the British Constitution, and especially of the Parliamentary system, that we can at one time bend it, adjust it, arrange it, reform it and adopt it to national needs." [29] In 1953 Bevan again affirmed the supremacy of Parliament in British political life. "Once Parliament has debated and decided on a legislative act by a majority vote," he argued, "it is entirely improper for any action to be taken outside the House of Commons in order to coerce the will of Parliament. That is my view." [30] He explicitly decried the right of any political group or party or trade union to disobey or sabotage the expressed will of Parliament. The only way, according to Bevan, to seek redress and change the law under the British political system is for the opponents of the law to obtain a majority in the House of Commons and repeal it or change it.

Bevan stated his political credo in simple and clear

words: "I look upon free institutions as not only the most desirable of political systems, not only as the one most congenial to the flowering of human genius, but as indispensable in a modern industrial community." [31] On another occasion, Bevan very aptly observed, "I believe that modern civilization can solve its problems better by counting heads than by breaking them." [32] It takes very little political clairvoyance to state that Aneurin Bevan, the individualist and the rebel with bohemian tastes, would have fared badly under a Communist regime.

In spite of his abhorrence of the Soviet system, Bevan consistently advocated negotiations with Russia for a *modus vivendi* based on peaceful coexistence. He felt that there was a chance for such negotiations to succeed because there are in the Soviet Union elements that desire peaceful accommodation with the West. "Do not let us believe," he said, "that behind the monolithic face of the Soviet Union, there are no differences of opinion. Dictatorship has schisms, as well as democracy." [33] Bevan surmised that there are in Russia two schools of thought. One wants adventure and war and the other believes that it is possible to obtain the goals of world conquest by peaceful competition. Bevan believed that the latter school is in the ascendancy. He was firmly convinced that the Soviet Union made a tragic mistake in annexing the Baltic states and in subjugating a number of eastern European countries. These aggressions, he felt, contradict Russia's "own" stated creed. "But they move restlessly," he told Parliament, "in the hug of the bear and *nothing is more certain than that they will never be reconciled to their oppressors* [italics mine]. . . . She conquered but she cannot digest, and never will be able to digest, because people nowadays will not accept a decree at the hands of a foreign dictatorship." The liberation of the Soviet satellite states will come, Bevan foresaw, gradually and in a peaceful manner. The process can be termed gradual self-liberation.[34]

Bevan was a full-blooded, dedicated Socialist who heartily disliked the capitalist, free enterprise system, especially as it functions under a Tory Government. He testified that when he was a young miner in South Wales, he had asked himself this one central and practical question: What is the source of power in Great Britain and how can it be attained by the workers? [35] His analysis led him to see this source of power in the British Parliament, which Bevan considered ideally suited to become the instrument, in the hands of the workers and the Labour Party, to obtain a social-democracy in Great Britain. Parliament can and should be used "to expose wealth and privilege to the attack of the people." [36] Because it determines its own rules and its own scope of authority, Parliament, says Bevan, can and should become "a weapon and the most formidable weapon of all in the struggle of poverty over property and privilege." [37] There are, according to Bevan, three main forces in modern society—private property, poverty, and democracy.[38] There is and will be a constant struggle between poverty and property, and both make every effort to use democracy and its instruments in this constant competition. The arena of this titanic struggle in Britain is Parliament. The House of Commons, Bevan alleged, was subservient to the British propertied class until 1928, when the law of universal franchise for all Britons over twenty-one was enacted. From that year on (which incidentally is the year Bevan entered Parliament), it became possible for the British underpriviliged classes to bring about the rule of democratic Socialism. Bevan genuinely admired and loved Parliament. He took pride in the fact that, unlike the American Congress,

No courts can construe the power of the British Parliament. It interprets its own authority, and from it there is no appeal. This gives it a revolutionary quality, and enables us to entertain the hope of bringing about social transformations, without the agony and prolonged crises experienced by less fortunate nations.[39]

This remarkable statement deserves careful study. Bevan is convinced that because of the unique institution of the British Parliament, there is no need for a social revolution to obtain for the workers control of the means of production. This can be done by the Labour Party obtaining a majority in Parliament and nationalizing British industries. The allusion to the "less fortunate nations" obviously applies to Russia and Red China. In those countries with a primitive economy and a lack of long tradition of political democracy, a social upheaval was inevitable, although Bevan regretted the cost in human lives and human freedoms. Bevan correctly maintained that the General Strike of 1926 demonstrated that British workers would not wish to seize power and control of the Government even if the opportunity presented itself. In 1926 Bevan wrote, "The workers and their leaders paused even when their coercive power was greater than that of the State." [40] He saw the explanation for this typical reaction of the British workers in the "subjective attitude" of a people which is not ready to sacrifice the right of free vote and other freedoms even for the opportunity to seize power. Bevan, the proud Britisher, said with rare fluency of expression: "The opportunity for power is not enough if the will to seize it is absent, and that will is attendant upon the traditional attitude of the British people toward the political institutions that form part of their historical heritage." [41]

In his oversimplified social analysis, Bevan exaggerated the opportunities of the British workers and the Labour Party to use Parliament as a revolutionary weapon to obtain basic changes in the British economic system. Fortunately, these opportunities are rigidly circumscribed by the periodic General Elections which can and do shift the control of Parliament from one party to another and thus provide an opportunity for a re-evaluation and changes of acts of the previous Parliament.

This is exactly what the Conservatives did when, after returning to power in 1951, they made a study of the effects of the nationalization policies of the Labour Government and decided to denationalize those industries where, in their opinion, nationalization was contrary to national interest. They retained the state ownership of the coal industry, where nationalization was found to be necessary and useful, but they partly denationalized the transport and steel industries. Bevan apparently realized the danger of carrying his conception of the power of Parliament too far. On one occasion, when he became annoyed by an alleged slight to the dignity and the prerogatives of the House, allegedly committed by Churchill's Government, Bevan restated his view that the flexibility of the British Parliament system is one of the glories of British Constitution. However, he recognized that this flexibility had its dangers, because the British people "cannot be protected by a written Constitution, so that any time a majority in the House of Commons can, if it wishes, not merely adjust the Constitution to the needs of the circumstances, but can distort the Constitution according to its own wishes." [42] Obviously, according to Bevan, when the "distorting" is done by the Labour Party it is harmless or even beneficial, but this discretionary parliamentary power becomes a calamity when exercised by the hated Tories.

Socialist democracy, in Bevan's conception, does not lead to the abolition of private property or the capitalist system of free enterprise. It does imply the abolition of poverty, want, unemployment, and disease. "The victory of socialism need not be universal to be decisive. . . . *It is neither pru-*

dent, nor does it accord with our conception of the future [italics mine], that all forms of private property should live under perpetual threat." [43] This moderate and calm view of the place of private property would hardly be acceptable to many American Socialists. Bevan even foresees that once a proper balance is achieved between public and private property and the welfare state which would eliminate unemployment and disease, it is quite possible to achieve a great measure of social tranquility and abolish class war and class hatred. "The philosophy of democratic socialism," he says,

is essentially cool in temper. It sees society in its context with nature and is conscious of the limitations imposed by physical conditions. It sees the individual in his context with society and is, therefore, compassionate and tolerant . . . it eschews all absolute proscriptions and final decisions. . . . It struggles against the evils that flow from private property, yet realizes that all forms of private property were not necessarily evil. . . . Consequently, it is not able to offer the thrill of the complete abandonment of private judgment, which is the allure of modern Soviet Communism and of Fascism, its running mate [*sic*].[44]

No wonder that these mellow, thoughtful, and idealistic statements, which could undoubtedly have been subscribed to by Attlee and Gaitskell, and yet were written by the fiery Welsh rebel, had puzzled the reviewers and the public after the publication of *In Place of Fear*.

Bevan advocated a far-reaching degree of public ownership of industry, and vigorous Socialist planning and control of the State's social services. In the society of the future, he maintained, public ownership must dominate.[45] Poverty, inequality, and injustice must be eliminated in all democratic countries by action of the government along Socialist principles. The British Free Health Service is, in Bevan's opinion, "a triumphant example of the superiority of collective

action and public initiative applied to a segment of society
where commercial principles are seen at their worst." [46] The
Labour Party must never hesitate to put into effect its complete program of nationalization of basic British industries.
If the Party had made mistakes during its terms in power, it
was not that it pursued "its principles too roughly or too far,
but by making too many concessions to conventional opinion." [47] Socialist principles must be adhered to in a clear and
direct fashion and the Labour Party must be prepared to
fight, if necessary, for its nationalization policy. "Are we
seriously," Bevan asked, "going to be told that in 1952 we
have discovered some royal road, some ingenious way of
trying to achieve our socialist purposes which would not
lead us through the old hard agony of public ownership?" [48]
Fear of unemployment, which haunted Bevan from his
childhood days, caused him to emphasize time and again his
conviction that unemployment can be prevented in Great
Britain only by Socialist planning.[49] Bevan summarized and
characterized his own brand of Socialism when he answered
a question put to him by a British journalist, "Would you
deny that you are a left winger?" Bevan answered, "Certainly not, if by that you mean an ardent Socialist." [50] When
asked to define his conception of Socialism, he said, "Nationalization is the transfer of property from the individual
to the state. Socialism is the full participation of the people
in the administration and operation of that property." [51]

There is no way of glossing over the fact that Aneurin
Bevan was bitterly anti-American. There is a conclusive
body of evidence to prove that he had a strong dislike of
America, its policies, and way of life. In Bevan's generally
consistent political philosophy, his anti-American bias was
the most stable factor. And yet Bevan went to unusual
length to deny this bias. Opening his bitter attack on the
United States in his book, he bemoaned the fact that it had

become impossible to express critical views about a policy
of a nation to which you do not belong without exposing
yourself to the charge of being "anti" that nation.[52] In answer to a journalist's question, he stated categorically, "Of
course, I am not [anti-American]. . . . I have far more
friends among Americans than I have among the British
Tories. To be against a particular American policy is not to
be anti-American. Such phrases are the coinage of illiterate
minds." [53] But these denials notwithstanding, one can search
in vain through the pages of *In Place of Fear* and his many
speeches delivered to the House of Commons and at Labour
Party conferences for a single favorable reference to the
United States. Franklin Roosevelt's New Deal left him, unlike Harold Laski, cold and unappreciative. He has often
expressed his fears, especially during the Coughlin and Mc-
Carthy episodes, that America might become a Fascist state.

On the other hand, Bevan had spoken on many occasions
critically and even contemptuously about Britain's closest
ally. He was unhappy about the powerful capitalist country
which has given its workers a very high standard of living,
provided full employment and extensive welfare state services without a Socialist government, without Socialist planning, and even without the existence of a politically influential Socialist Party. It is easy to understand that American
political and economic realities negate everything that
Bevan believed in and fought for during his long career in
British politics and in British Socialism. He never forgot the
image of America and American business he received from
reading Jack London's *Iron Heel*.[54] He believed that American big business faced with a serious economic depression
might seize power in a Fascist coup. He pointed out that in
America during national emergencies big business men take
over the control of governmental machinery. "In time of
war," he said, "the British business man is mobilized in the

government machine. But the difference is just there. In Britain the business man is mobilized. In the States he mobilizes." [55]

The leadership and guidance given to the Western world and particularly to Great Britain by America, is, in Bevan's view, wrong and dangerous.[56] "The scale of armament urged upon the democracies by the United States," he wrote, "is a source not of strength but of weakness." It is the misguided American economic and military policy, he firmly believed, that has more than any other factor upset the British economy and threatens the standard of living of British workers. A British historian reviewing *In Place of Fear* summed up Bevan's views on America in these words: "The United States, obsessed with a fear of imminent Russian aggression, has imposed on Europe an economic burden that may wreck it and certainly cannot save it in the unlikely event of a military move by Russia." [57] In view of subsequent events in Europe, and especially the Soviet rape of Hungary, Bevan's optimism on the unlikelihood of Russian use of its military power was completely misplaced. Bevan's distorted view of American leadership for providing, through NATO, a deterrent to Soviet aggression, was at variance not only with the views of Churchill and Eden, but also of Attlee, Morrison, and Gaitskell. Nevertheless, as Brogan points out, Bevan's making the United States the scapegoat for British economic ills was popular in the Labour Party and in Europe "not because it was true, but because they want it to be true." [58] The United States, in Bevan's opinion, did not have "the experience, sagacity and self-restraint for world leadership." [59] Britain, in his view, had all three characteristics of a world leader, but unfortunately lacked the wealth of America.

The basic cause for the tragically wrong and misguided American foreign policy, Bevan saw in the fear that per-

vaded the United States. This conviction remained un-
changed after Bevan's two visits to the United States, one
made with Jennie Lee in 1954, and the other a brief lecture
tour in 1957.

The following three quotations are ample evidence on
how consistently Bevan held to his conception of the United
States as a giant ruled by a central emotion of fear:

1. In his book he wrote,

Fear is a very bad adviser. Its companion is hate, and hate is the
father and mother of cruelty and intolerance. Fear of Soviet
Communism has led the United States, and those who follow
her lead, to take a distorted view of the world situation and of
forces which are at work at modern society.[60]

2. Addressing the Fifty-first Annual Conference of the
Labour Party, in 1952, Bevan said,

The United States of America is a very peaceful and very rich
country, and if great wealth, if great productive capacity can
rid a country of fear, then America ought to be the most self-
satisfied and the most tranquil country in the world. But on the
contrary, America is hag-ridden by two fears, fear of war and
fear of unemployment, which is fear of peace.[61]

3. Summing up his impressions from the 1957 tour of
America, Bevan wrote that he received a very hospitable
reception and was impressed by the friendliness of the people of the United States, but

in a curious way they do not add up to a total social climate
that I found in the least attractive. The frame is more magnifi-
cent and glittering than ever, but the picture inside is shallow,
unrewarding, and in places even tawdry.[62]

And again, Bevan reaffirmed his earlier conclusion that
fear is at the bottom of all American troubles. American
advertising, he asserted, created a climate of American

opinion in which the dominant note was fear. "Fear that you will fall behind in display of ostentatious personal expenditure," he writes, "fear that dandruff or body odor might lose you your sweetheart, fear of this, fear of that, fear of everything." [63]

In the distorted picture of America to which Bevan clung so tenaciously, the American bankers and industrialists feared peace because any let-up in the armament production would bring unemployment and economic depression. This sad state of affairs could, of course, be changed, Bevan asserts, if Americans would accept Socialist rule and Socialist planning.[64] It is of importance to stress that the pronounced anti-American views of Aneurin Bevan were not shared by the leaders of the British Labour Party. Ernest Bevin spoke of the United States not as a fear-ridden giant but as a "young and vigorous democratic people." [65] Unlike Bevan, he readily acknowledged the generous help and assistance, both economic and military, given by America to Great Britain and to Western Europe. "It is a country," Bevin said, "not only of great wealth and great resources, but one whose people are moved by a good will and a generosity which many of us in the Old World are apt to take for granted." [66] Herbert Morrison repeatedly stated that England must cooperate closely with America to maintain her economic health and to prevent Soviet aggression.[67]

Attlee had been a staunch friend of the United States during his entire active political career. He specifically denied that the United States did not fully cooperate with Great Britain when Socialists were in power. Attlee told his Party comrades, "I have never found on the side of America that they would not work with us because we were a Socialist Government." [68] Attlee rejected Bevan's attacks on America and British rearmament, and declared that he had little respect for those who always clamor for reduction of armaments by the "defenders of freedom, but entirely ignore the fact that this armed, dangerous State [the Soviet Union] has not shown her readiness to discuss disarmament." [69] Winston Churchill told the House of Commons in 1952 that members of a delegation of the United States Senate which visited him at his country home bitterly complained about the anti-American feelings they thought existed in Parliament. Churchill then assured them that their fears were without foundation because,

The anti-American elements in Parliament are only a quarter of the Labour Party and the Labour Party is only half of the House. Therefore, you might say that one-eighth, at the outside, gives vent to anti-American sentiments. The Labour Party as a whole and the Government of the day supported by the Conservative Party are wholeheartedly friendly to the United States and recognize and are grateful for the part they are playing in the world and for the help they have given us.[70]

Bevan's views on the lack of aggressive intentions of Russia were generally rejected and condemned by the reviewers of his book and by the overwhelming majority of the British press. One of the most effective answers to Bevan was given in an open letter to him, written by the distinguished Spanish exiled diplomat and statesman, Salvador de Madariaga. The latter quoted Bevan as saying that "the danger from communism, if dangers there are, come not from military plans but from the failure to redress wrongs that exist in Western society. . . . The only answer to Soviet communism is an alteration of social practices and social principles." [71]

Madariaga asked Bevan if he knew one single country of Europe which went Communist because of bad social practices and principles. He further asked him whether it was not true that the only reason eastern European countries became Soviet satellites was the naked power of the Red

Army, which ruthlessly suppressed all freedoms and exter-
minated all political opposition. Madariaga quoted a speech
made by Bevan in Jarrow, in which he said, "I say to my
American friends that their economic and fiscal policies are
doing more harm to Western Europe than Stalin can ever
do." [72] Answering this demagogic and intemperate statement, the Spanish diplomat—more in sadness than in anger
—comments: "Often your utterances and those of your
friends sound as if you were ready to hand over, for good
and all, the peoples of half of Europe to Moscow, provided
the standard of living of the British working classes remained unimpaired." [73] Bevan's statements gained for him,
however, some rank and file support because of his stress
on combating Communism by raising economic standards
and by directing British productivity for the economic and
industrial help and assistance to the underdeveloped countries of Asia and Europe. These were attractive slogans for
the British workers, whose employment and prosperity depended upon increased exports and a free and unhampered
foreign trade.

Aneurin Bevan had been an outspoken and consistent
advocate of a policy of granting full diplomatic recognition
to Red China, and its admission to the United Nations. He
had repeatedly expressed his dislike and contempt for
Chiang Kai-shek and his regime. Bevan wanted Great Britain to break fully and openly with the American policy,
which opposed the supplanting of Nationalist China by Red
China in the Security Council and the United Nations Assembly, and which encouraged and supported the Nationalist Chinese regime on Formosa. He urged the handing
over of Formosa to Red China.

Bevan condemned the American policy of nonrecognition
of the Red regime as unrealistic and unwise because it had

driven Red China into a close alliance and dependence upon the Soviet Union. This alliance, he maintained, need not have happened, because "China is not the natural ally of Russia." [74] As a matter of fact, Bevan said, China and Russia are natural historical enemies. China needs industrial products and the industrial know-how, which only the West can supply her. The policy of nonrecognition has forced China to turn to Russia. Bevan was convinced that Red China was not happy with this total dependence upon the Soviets. "From the beginning," he wrote, "we believed that China was not anxious to sever all connections with the Western world. We felt that she would not want to be wholly dependent on the Soviet Union." [75] Bevan was not unaware of the grave shortcomings of the Red Chinese regime and he fully exposed its evil features after a visit to China in 1954 with a Labour Party delegation, headed by Clement Attlee. As a matter of record, Bevan, with characteristic courage and bluntness, was more critically outspoken in his conversations with the Red Chinese leaders than some of his more moderate and right-wing colleagues. He insisted on a visit to a prison to interview political prisoners. But he considered the American policy vis-à-vis China completely indefensible and injurious to the best interests of Great Britain. This policy, he believed, stifled the possibilities of expanding British trade in the Far East, and deprived England of the very important Chinese market. ". . . The refusal to admit the new China," he wrote,

to the United Nations and the continued recognition of Chiang Kai-Shek regime is peevish and unrealistic. . . . The time will come for the reconsideration of the status of Formosa. It is impossible to justify a refusal to cede it to China. Its eventual assimilation in the Chinese People's Republic is an essential condition for the pacification of the Far East.[76]

Bevan stood at that time alone in the Labour Party in his readiness to hand over Formosa to Red China. It is difficult to understand how he reconciled his position on Formosa with his strong adherence to and respect for the right of free franchise. Why should the Formosans be denied at least the right to self-determination? The British Labour Party at the time advocated a free plebiscite on Formosa which would have given the Formosans a chance to decide whether they wished to remain independent, accept a United Nations trusteeship, or join Red China. The Labour Party declared in 1953

. . . that the problem of Formosa should be referred to the people of Formosa. Formosa should be neutralized for a period and Britain should be prepared to contribute to an international naval force for this purpose. Thereafter, the people of Formosa should be enabled freely to determine their own destiny.[77]

While Bevan's stand on Formosa had in 1952 little or no support in England in general, and in the Labour Party in particular, his position on the recognition of Red China and its admission to the United Nations was fully shared by the Labour Party and by the Conservatives. The British recognition of Red China by the Labour Government, in spite of the strong disapproval of the United States, received the full support of Winston Churchill and Anthony Eden. The British people and their leaders were and are convinced that a *de facto* recognition of Mao's regime and a resumption of trade with the Chinese mainland is in the national British interest. An objective observer put it this way: "America regards Bevan as the architect of Britain's China policy, whereas it springs from the inevitable marriage of convenience between British geography and British security." [78] The reference to British security applies to the conviction of the British leaders that refusal to recognize Red China would have endangered the status of Hong Kong and possibly brought an open Chinese assistance to the Communist guerillas in Malaya. H. C. Allen added that Great Britain "was certainly not unaware of her great commercial investments in China, and of the hostage-like character of the island colony of Hong Kong. . . ." [79] The Labour Party is on record as demanding the seating of Red China in the United Nations. The National Executive Committee of the Labour Party stated in a formal policy statement:

The Labour Government recognized the Peking Government as the legal government of China and pressed frequently in the United Nations that the representative of the *de facto* government should occupy China's seat. It is clearly a travesty that the delegate from the rump regime of Chiang Kai-shek should speak in the name of the Chinese people who have rejected him, and the Labour Party believes that there can be no lasting political settlement in the Far East which is not based on the recognition that the Peking Government is the effective government of China and, as such, should represent that country in the United Nations. [80]

Clement Attlee did everything in his power to convince President Truman in 1950 of the advisability of recognizing Red China and abandoning Chiang. In 1953, in an address to the Fifty-second Annual Conference of the Labour Party, he abandoned his usual mildness and moderation when he declared his forthright disagreement with the American China policy. He said,

It is absolutely ridiculous not to recognize what is the effective government of China. That is not the government of Chiang Kai-shek. As soon as aggression has been halted and support for aggression has been withdrawn, then is the time when the Peoples's Government of China should be brought into full consultation and should take its rightful place with the United Nations. [81]

While Attlee and Bevan were in full agreement on the necessity to limit the Korean conflict, on the avoidance of a war with Red China, and on the seating of Mao's Government in the United Nations, they were nevertheless far apart on the timing and the methods to be used in the implementation of these basic policies. It is this difference that was of great significance to the American people. Attlee, sensitive to American views and emotional involvement in the question of recognition of Red China, was cautious and avoided the exacerbation of the Anglo-American differences. Bevan, on the other hand, used every occasion for a bitter and unrestrained attack on the United States for its China policy. During the Korean conflict he accused America of "conducting" an anti-Communist crusade and of attempting to involve Great Britain in a war against Red China.[82] He demanded, in effect, a complete surrender of the United States on all issues concerning China. In a speech in the House of Commons Bevan stated that in exchange for an armistice in Korea the United States should give "effective assurances to the Chinese Peoples' Government that they accept the Chinese revolution as an accomplished fact; that they are prepared to disband Chiang Kai-shek's forces on Formosa, and not to connive—as the Chinese people think they are—in a counter-revolutionary movement at some time or other." [83]

Bevan apparently considered the conquest of China by the Communist armies as an inevitable result of the oppression and corruption of the Kuomintang regime. To him, the "Chinese Revolution" should have been accepted and welcomed, just as the Russian Revolution was hailed and applauded by the South Wales miners. He once recalled that when the news of the overthrow of the Czarist regime reached his home town, the miners, with tears streaming down their cheeks, shook hands and exclaimed: "At last it happened." [84]

Bevan was at odds not only with Churchill and Eden on the appraisal of the nature of the Red Chinese regime, but also with the official leadership of his own Party. They agreed with him that the safety of Hong Kong and the needs of British trade necessitated the recognition of the Red regime, or, as Attlee was in the habit of calling it, the Peking Government, but they had no illusions about the oppressive and tyrannical aspects of the Mao Tze-tung regime. One can easily surmise that Attlee and the Labour leaders shuddered when Bevan told the House:

Everybody here knows—at least every miner, railwayman and agricultural worker knows very well that if he were in China he would be a Communist peasant. He would not be a Chiang Kai-shek, he would be a Communist. Anyone who had lived under the regime of Chiang Kai-shek would become a Communist. He would not be forced to be a Communist, because everybody knows that when the Peoples' armies marched, they occupied a country where people received them willingly.[85]

It is difficult to believe that Bevan, whose basic abhorrence of Communist tyranny is unquestioned, really believed in this statement.

After his visit to Red China in 1954 with a Labour Party delegation, Bevan acknowledged the accomplishments of the Peking Government in the fields of education, industrialization, and sanitation, but was critical of the ruthless control of political life by the Chinese Communist Party. He particularly criticized the suppression of the opposition parties.

Bevan's position on recognition and admission of Red China to the United Nations and the advisability of expanding trade with the Peking Government has gradually become the position of the British people and the British Governments, whether Labour or Conservative. The *Manchester Guardian,* commenting on the return of a delegation of British businessmen to Red China, added: ". . . Sooner or later, we hope, political relations will improve and political restrictions on trade with China will be lifted." [86] In December 1957, F. J. Erroll, the Conservative Parliamentary Secretary to the Board of Trade, told Parliament that Britain is eager to expand trade with Communist China and has, therefore, enlarged her diplomatic representation in Peking. "There is," he said, "a great scope for trade with China despite the present embargo list. . . ." [87]

In Place of Fear, in spite of its general moderation, increased the fear of many Britishers that the unwary Labour leaders might allow Bevan to climb the ladder to the Labour Party's leadership.

~ X ~   Next objective: the Shadow Cabinet

THE SHOW of unity at the Fiftieth Labour Party Conference, held in Scarborough in 1951, to which Bevan so generously contributed, did not save the Labourites from a defeat in the General Election. The Conservatives obtained a majority of twenty-six seats in Parliament and Churchill continued in office. Aneurin Bevan returned to the House by a substantial majority received from his faithful constituency. He made strenuous efforts to organize a strong and well-functioning Bevanite faction within the Parliamentary Labour Party. The objective was not to cause a schism in the Party but to gain a position of strength vis-à-vis the hostile coalition of trade union leaders and the entrenched Party leaders, including Attlee and Morrison. Bevan was strongly opposed to schisms and splits in Socialist parties. He told the Fifty-first Conference ". . . no matter what our differences, we must never allow the British Labour Movement to become schismatic. We must avoid at all costs a repetition here of what has happened to continental Socialist movements. That is why we must never carry our doctrinaire differences to a point of schism." [1] This was not an easy task because Bevan's supporters were a heterogeneous group of malcontents and rebels that included idealistic traditional Socialist pacifists, disgruntled union officials, fellow travelers, and genuine supporters and admirers of Bevan. The Bevanite faction had in its ranks a large number of intellectuals and professionals. Out of approximately fifty members, fourteen were journalists and eleven lawyers. The extreme leftist views of some of his followers were often embarrassing to Bevan, but he needed all the support he could get, and by the beginning of 1952 the Bevanite group became a faction with its own separate caucuses and whips. It met before important debates and votes were scheduled in the House to determine its position and instruct its members. "The Bevan group," wrote Francis Williams a few months later, "has now caught up within it—not always perhaps with its leader's entire wish, for he finds himself attracting to his cause some curious bedfellows—what may be accurately described as many of the congenital dissidents in the Labour Party." [2]

The Bevanites were united in their opposition to a vigorous rearmament program, they held pronounced anti-American views, and advocated the old-fashioned class war approach to Britain's economic problems. They were agreed on the proposition that the official Labour Party leadership was timid, too eager to compromise on Socialist principles, and ineffective. Bevanism meant a repudiation of the middle class support so eagerly sought and solicited by Attlee and Morrison. A bright young intellectual Bevanite, Michael Foot, summarized the quarrel between the left and right wings of the Labour Party in these words:

The aim of the right wing was to make British socialism mildly reformist in its domestic aspirations and bipartisan in foreign policy accepting the Churchillian thesis of agreement with the United States at all costs. Bevanism marked a revolt of the rank and file of the Labour Party against these tendencies. [3]

Foot exaggerated the extent of Bevan's support among the rank and file, because millions of trade union members continued to support their leaders, Arthur Deakin and Sir William Lawther, both strong foes of Bevan. However, the support that Bevan gained in the local Constituent Labour Parties was considerable and was growing stronger.

In January 1952 Bevan's stock rose considerably when Churchill told the House of Commons that Britain could not afford to rearm on the scale demanded by the United States. That had been Bevan's contention all along. A writer in the *Spectator* asked, "Is Churchill a Bevanite?" His answer was, of course, negative, but he pointed out that "both Mr. Churchill and Mr. Bevan were up against the same set of unpleasant facts." [4] Bevanites acted with an increasing self-assurance and virtually ignored the official Party leadership. There were persistent rumors that Bevan was out to challenge Attlee's leadership. The Welshman vigorously denied the accusation, and he was undoubtedly sincere. He knew only too well that any attempt to oust Attlee would end in a dismal failure because the Labour Party traditionally preferred moderate leaders like Lansbury and Attlee. Its experience with the strong and independent leader Ramsay MacDonald ended in a disaster for the Party. Bevan, shrewd and astute in his Party's history and traditions, knew that even his friends would not back him for the post of Party Leader. He had long decided to make his ascent to the Party's leadership gradually through the traditional channels of membership in the Party's Executive and then through increasingly important posts in the Shadow Cabinet. For the time being, the goal was a seat in the latter body. Bevan and his supporters used every opportunity to prove their contention that the Labour Party leaders lack the courage and determination to stick to Party principles and decisions. They made full use of Churchill's disclosure during a debate on a motion of censure, introduced by the Labour Party, that Herbert Morrison when he was Foreign Secretary promised the United States Government that Britain would join actively with America outside of Korea if the United States forces should be attacked from bases in Red China. Morrison, who moved the motion of censure criticizing Churchill's submission to American leadership in Korea, was painfully embarrassed by the disclosure, but did not deny its veracity. Bevan, who considered Morrison to be his most powerful rival in the Party, made the most of this incident and accused Morrison of disregarding the Party's wishes. Morrison's stature suffered serious damage, the extent of which became evident at the October Labour Party Conference. On the other hand, Bevan's stock rose, especially among backbenchers and the regional Labour parties.

The relations between the Bevanite group and the official leadership grew progressively worse. A serious clash came in March when Churchill presented a defense program at a cost of 13.1 billion dollars. Attlee in a private letter instructed the Labour M.P.'s to abstain in the vote on the bill. But when the vote came, fifty-seven Bevanites voted *No.* Flushed and angry, Attlee left the House immediately after the vote to consider disciplinary action against this clear defiance of his authortiy and position. Next day he called an emergency meeting of the Parliamentary Labour Party. Bevan, aware that the day of reckoning had come, hastened to find out whether in this fight for his political life he would have the backing of his home constituency. He need not have worried. His South Wales voters were not in a mood to let their "Nyrin" down. He was received by prolonged ovations in crowded and enthusiastic meetings. The constituents were rather proud that their favorite son was giving battle to the Party bosses. Emboldened by this support, Bevan vowed a fight to the finish. He said that he wanted unity but, "if we cannot go on together, we shall go on alone. . . . If they ask me to recant I say, 'No, we can't.'" [5]

Clement Attlee came to the meeting of the Parliamentary Labour Party with a resolution demanding that Bevan recant, give a firm pledge to follow the Party's directives, or face expulsion. He had the backing of the other leaders who felt that the time had come to stamp out the rebellion. But the majority of the Labour M.P.'s thought otherwise— they did not want to see a split in the Party and feared that Bevan had, especially on the issue of rearmament, considerable support. Tom O'Brien, a respected trade union leader, changed the temper of the discussion when he suggested that the meeting transfer to Westminster Hall where a plaque might be inserted with the inscription: "On this spot, the Labour Party committed suicide aided and abetted by Clement Attlee and Aneurin Bevan." [6] The search for a face-saving compromise was on. George Strauss and John Strachey, old friends of Bevan, although not Bevanites, introduced a compromise resolution in the form of an amendment to Attlee's motion which provided that henceforth all Labourite Members of Parliament must vote with the Party except on matters of conscience, like pacifism. Both Attlee and Bevan accepted the compromise and the amendment carried by a vote of 162 to 73. Attlee's motion lapsed and was not put to a vote. It is difficult to disagree with the view taken by the *Spectator* that the vote represented a victory for Aneurin Bevan, because it merely gently slapped his wrists and, "instead of Attlee's authority over the party being reaffirmed, it was seriously compromised." [7] Bevan's gamble paid off. He was neither expelled nor censured. He compromised, but the bosses of the Transport House were put on notice that an attempt to expel him would mean a split in the party. A Gallup poll revealed that nearly half of British organized workers supported the rebel leader, and Bevan could usually count on the active support of over fifty members of Parliament and on the sympathetic neutrality of many others. What was the secret of his strength? A British writer saw the secret in Bevan's "romantic vision of a land governed by the best elements of its working class . . . this continues to be the vision worth dying for, when the programs of the realists are scarcely worth living for." [8] Bevan was also aided by the Conservatives' inability to provide even partial employment to the half million idle British workers.

The strength of the Bevanite faction infuriated those among the Labour members of Parliament—like George Brown, Woodrow Wyatt, and Richard Stokes—who were firmly convinced that Bevan was a menace to the Party and should be expelled, with his followers if necessary. The *New Statesman and Nation*, sympathetic but not committed to Bevan, demanded that a *modus vivendi* be achieved between the official leadership and Bevan. The editors stated that Bevan was strong enough to demand concessions but must not ask too much. Such a compromise, middle-road position would include the Party's position on rearmament and Anglo-American relations.[9] The Liberal and Conservative newspapers did their best to deepen the rifts and advised Attlee to reject any further compromises and insist on Bevan's submission or expulsion. The showdown was to come at the forthcoming Labour Party conference. Several foreign policy issues contributed to the intensification of the dispute. After the United States Air Force bombed the enemy installations on the other side of the Yalu River, without prior consultation with the United Kingdom, Bevan pulled all stops in attacking the United States for allegedly dragging Britain into a war with Red

China. He demanded that the Labourites introduce a strong motion of censure against Churchill's Government. When Attlee demurred, Bevan in a caucus of the Parliamentary Labour Party accused him of appeasing Churchill and got the group to agree on a strong censure motion. In the debate Churchill lost no opportunity to chide Attlee for submitting to the extreme anti-Americanism of his "rival." In the continuous debate on British rearmament, Bevan could not resist the temptation and revealed in a speech in Parliament that it was at his insistence that Attlee inserted several qualifying clauses when as Prime Minister he introduced the armaments bill. This breach of a Parliamentary code that prohibits the disclosure of inner Cabinet discussions and conflicts drew the ire of many Labourites.[10] When a Labour M.P. angrily interrupted Bevan's disclosures, he was told,

If my right hon. Friend is interrupting, all I can rejoin is that there is no personal rancour on my part about what I am saying. After all, I can assure my hon. Friends, that if they disagree with me I shall not try to get them expelled from the party. I shall just hammer the point out properly.[11]

The issue of the rearmament of West Germany provided another point of dispute with the Bevanite faction. Bevan and his wife, Jennie Lee, were long distrustful of the revival of Germany as an economic and military power in Europe. They doubted the sincerity of the denazification program and feared that the growing strength of German cartels and big business would bring about the rebirth of reactionary and aggressive German militarism. The Labour Party was on record in a resolution adopted by the National Executive of April 30, 1952, that before any German rearmament began, two prior steps must be taken. First, another attempt should be made in a four-power conference to reach an agreement with Russia on free elections in all of Germany; and second, in case of continued Russian refusal, new elections should be held in Western Germany to ascertain whether the people of Germany supported the rearmament policies of Chancellor Adenauer or the policy of neutrality of the German Socialist Party. The second condition was designed to give the German population an opportunity to reject the entire rearmament plan by giving the German Socialist Party a majority in the Bundestag. The Soviet's reneging on its pledge for German free elections and American pressure brought about a renewed consideration of the problem. Herbert Morrison came out in favor of the Government's support of the agreement reached between the United States and Chancellor Adenauer for German armed contribution to the defense of Europe, but Aneurin Bevan with the unexpected support of Hugh Dalton got a four to one majority of the Parliamentary Labour Party to vote against German rearmament. Bevan's victory was primarily the result of the position taken by Dalton, an implacable foe of Bevan and of the natural inclination of many Labour M.P.'s to support the German Socialists who were battling Adenauer on the same issue. Bevan's foes immediately began to howl for his scalp. The *News Chronicle* in an editorial accused Bevan of a conspiracy within the Labour Party to form a Party-within-a-Party, and George Brown, M.P., wrote in the Labour paper, the *Daily Herald,* that the Bevanites did not believe in the democratic processes and Party loyalty. Attlee was urged to move decisively to smash the revolution.

The *New Statesman and Nation* warned that "there are still quite a number of Anti-Bevanite fanatics in the Transport House, in the T.U.C., and the Parliamentary Committee, who regard the Left as a 'foreign body' to be smashed and expelled." [12] The *Statesman* went on to assert, correctly, that Bevan's enemies were out to isolate him, deny him any position of power and influence, and if possible expel him from the Party. They considered Bevan's ascendancy a real menace, first because of his hostility to the entrenched trade union hierarchy, and second because Bevan was antagonizing the middle class without whose support the Labourites could not win an election.

It was probably the thought of elections and Party unity that caused Attlee to reject the advice of a showdown and to make another attempt to compromise his and Morrison's differences with Bevan. He was the man to effect a compromise because he was personally liked and respected by Bevan. After short but intense negotiations, the National Executive Committee issued two statements of policy. Both statements, adopted unanimously, were to be submitted to the Annual Conference. One short statement expressed its opposition to *immediate* rearmament of Western Germany; the second endorsed the British arms program, with Bevan's limiting and qualifying conditions, and concluded with a general statement restating Labour's positions on state ownership of key industries. It was a moderate compromise statement which represented important mutual concessions made both by Morrison and Bevan. Bevan agreed to underwrite an endorsement of NATO in these words: "The Labour Party believes that close cooperation with the United States of America is vital to Britain and to the Commonwealth as a whole. It supports the North Atlantic Treaty Organization." [13] In consideration of Bevan's position, the statement urged NATO to pay more heed to social and economic problems of its members. Bevan asked for and got a strong endorsement of his views on China. The statement said, "The Labour Government recognizes the Peking Government [not the Chinese People's Republic, as Bevan was wont to say] as the legal government of China and pressed frequently in the United Nations that the representative of the *de facto* government should occupy China's seat." [14] Chiang Kai-shek's Government was denounced as a "Rump regime" which deserved no support.

The *New Statesman and Nation* was pleased to note that "the National Executive, by its unanimous endorsement of these documents, is recognizing that for the Labour Party to achieve power it must have a Left and Right wing and that party policy must be born of a coalition of ideas." [15] The anti-Bevanites were not reconciled by this show of unity. Sir Arthur Deakin, the head of the Trades Union Congress, Sir William Lawther, president of the National Union of Mineworkers, Herbert Morrison, and Hugh Gaitskell were hoping that the delegates to the conference would cut Bevan down to size and hand him a stinging rebuke for his frequent breaches of Party regularity.

Bevan and his lieutenants were concentrating on gaining the support of the Constituent Labour Parties, which long resented the domination of the Labour Party by the large trade unions. The showdown came in the election to the National Executive Committee, and Bevan's victory exceeded his fondest hopes. The Constituency and Central Labour Parties elected Bevan and five of his supporters, including Tom Driberg, Harold Wilson, and Richard Crossman. The seventh seat went to James Griffith, who was acceptable and popular both with the left and right wings. Bevan received the highest vote among all the candidates elected by the Constituent Parties. He got 965,000 votes, almost the maximum possible. The sensations of the election were the defeat of Herbert Morrison by Richard Crossman, who had a majority of 40,000 votes, and the elimination from the Executive of Hugh Dalton and Emanuel Shinwell. Morrison's defeat stunned the conference and enraged Bevan's foes. Bevan regretted Morrison's defeat because he feared that the reaction of his opponents would be violent. And so it was. George Brown, M.P. and former member of the Labour Government, told the delegates: "It seems to me this conference is rapidly going mad." [16] The election, however sensational, did not give Bevan the control of the Executive Committee. He could only count on six votes out of twenty-seven; the majority was still controlled by the Trades Union Congress.

Arthur Deakin, infuriated by the Bevanite strength and by a Bevan-supported resolution introduced by the Salford West Labour Party, which called upon the Trades Union Congress to call strikes if necessary to cause the downfall of the Conservative Government, bluntly warned the conference that the trade unions provide most of the money for the Labour Party machinery and election expenditures. [17] Deakin's crude reminder that he held the Party's purse strings aroused widespread protests. Deakin reaffirmed the traditional policy of the trade unions, which was opposed to committing the "Trade Union Movement to industrial action for political purposes." [18] It was a reflection of the temper of the Morecambe conference and of Bevan's growing strength that this extreme resolution, while defeated, drew 1,728,000 votes against 3,986,000.

The major exposition of the Bevanite point of view was given to the conference by Richard Crossman, who urged faithful adherence to Socialist principles. Crossman argued the advisability of Britain becoming the "third force" between Russia and America. In complete contradiction to the NATO resolution for which Bevan voted, Crossman expressed no preference between two great rival powers. The danger of war he diagnosed as "the hysterical fear in Washington and the Kremlin. . . . If war should come, we cannot, as Socialists, want a victory for either side. The victory we want is the prevention of either side winning.

Each must learn to co-exist with the other. . . ." [19] One can imagine how distasteful such views must have been to Attlee and Morrison, and there is ground to doubt whether Bevan himself would have subscribed to this upside-down logic. It was not for the first time that Crossman, Mikardo, and Zilliacus expressed fellow-traveler views which Bevan, the sophisticated individualist, found hard to swallow. These leftist intellectuals thought that they were using Bevan to propagate their convictions, but as it later became apparent, it was Bevan who used their considerable talents to attain his own objectives. Bevan, however, undoubtedly subscribed to the position taken by his wife, Jennie Lee, on the German question. She warned against the re-establishment of the Krupp industrial empire and urged support for the German Socialists.[20]

The major fight of the conference developed on a resolution introduced by Walter Padley, M.P., on behalf of the Union of Shop Distributive and Allied Workers. In line with Bevan's position, the resolution for a "re-examination and reduction of the rearmament program which threatens to render it impossible for Britain to achieve economic stability and solvency through increasing exports and ensuring satisfactory minimum standards of life and adequate social services. Financial aid from the U.S.A. for this re-armament program provides no solution and involves the risk of further sacrificing Britain's right to put forward an independent policy." [2] At last the two major issues—the relation between the arms program and the British economy and British independence in foreign policy from the United States, which Bevan cited were his reasons for resigning from the Labour Cabinet in 1951—were to be fought out by the delegates to the Labour Party convention. The battle was furious and both camps made every effort to marshal all of their respective forces. It was the first time that a major trade union, representing a conference voting strength of 317,000 votes, gave its support to the Bevanite position. Up to now such support was limited to the Constituent Labour Parties and small and relatively weak unions. Harold Wilson pleaded that the resolution should be voted upon not as a test between Bevan and Deakin, but on its contents and merits. He stressed that the correctness of his and Bevan's positions on rearmament had been proven by Churchill's cutback in the arms expenditures because of growing economic difficulties.[22] Hugh Gaitskell argued that the adoption of the resolution would give Europe the impression that British Socialists are opposed to the shoring up of Britain's defenses, and would also endanger the Anglo-American alliance.[23]

The closing speech in the debate was given by Clement Attlee. A careful reading of his address proves again that it was only Attlee's lack of oratorical talents and his slight stature that caused so many people on both sides of the Atlantic to underestimate his personality and influence. It was a strong and well-reasoned speech. Attlee began with recounting all the attempts made by the West to reach a fair accommodation with Russia. The attempts had ended in failure and the West had no choice but to build, for its survival, adequate defenses through the Brussels Treaty and NATO. "It is curious," said Attlee, "that in so many of the resolutions on the Agenda there is a total ignoring of even the existence of a great armed State like the U.S.S.R." In an obvious reference to Bevan, Attlee delivered this powerful indictment of the Bevanite position: "I have not much respect for other people who clamor for reduction of armaments by the defenders of freedom, but entirely ignore the fact of this armed, dangerous State which has not shown her readiness to discuss disarmament." [24] In an atmosphere of great tension, the conference voted against the U.S.D.A.W. resolution by 3,644,000 to 2,288,000.

The size of the opposition mustered by the Bevanites was astonishing. It proved that Bevan had strength and support not only in the Constituent Labour Parties but also among the rank and file of several of the big trade unions. The resolution drew the support, in addition to the U.S.D.A.W., of the powerful Amalgamated Engineering Union (voting strength, 595,000) and the National Union of Railwaymen (voting strength, 366,000). His bitterest foes had to acknowledge that Aneurin Bevan had become a power to be reckoned with in the Labour Party. They were impressed but not awed. A prominent Labour M.P., Denis Healey, delivered a slashing attack on Bevan's anti-Americanism. Noting that Bevan denied that he was anti-American and claimed he was as pro-American as Herbert Morrison, Healy went on to say: "The only difference in fact between Nye Bevan and Herbert Morrison is that Nye thinks that the best way to win friends and influence people is to kick them in the teeth. . . . I am quite prepared to accept Nye Bevan's word that he is not anti-American, though as a master of the English language it is remarkable how much and how often he gets himself misunderstood." [25]

The behavior of Aneurin Bevan, the hero of this dramatic conference, deserves serious contemplation. During the most exciting days of the conference, during the furious debates involving his entire political philosophy, he, the spokesman and the leader, was silent. He spoke once, on behalf of the Executive, in closing the debate on a relatively unimportant resolution on unemployment. While he called on the Party not to compromise on its stand toward nationalization and denounced America as a bewildered and fearful giant, it was, for Bevan, a mild speech. He jokingly remarked, in the course of his address, that he had promised not to stir up a controversy. "I know," he said, "I must be careful lest I make a controversial speech." [26] This was the only time that Aneurin Bevan took the floor of the conference. He did not speak on the Salford West resolution, he did not react to Deakin's threat, and he did not use his oratorical powers to push through the U.S.D.A.W. resolution, which aimed to make his views on British rearmament and relations with America the official policy of the Labour Party. How could he, who in the opinion of some was governed by his passions and emotions, keep silent during the exciting and tense hours of the crucial debates? There seem to be several answers to this puzzle. First, Aneurin Bevan did not allow his emotions to rule him in truly important junctions of his life. He could be and was cool and deliberate as the hour demanded. The Morecambe Conference was a decisive one for Bevan and he was too astute to throw away his victory by an ill-tempered and provocative speech. Bevan was also bound by two important restrictions. He was bound by the compromise policy statements for which he voted in the Executive Committee, and he could hardly speak for resolutions which were at variance with the agreed policies. Bevan also knew that the defeat of Morrison and Dalton by his supporters deeply angered many of his Party comrades and he did not wish to add to their irritations by breaking the traditional principle of collective responsibility, which is usually binding on all members of the Executive. On the contrary, it served Bevan's purpose and objectives to appear as a modest victor and a fellow leader, who although heading a rebellious faction is ready to compromise and be reasonable. He was out to convince the leaders of the Party and of Transport House that if they decided to share their power with him, he would be a responsible and reasonable colleague.

The objective was no secret to anyone. Bevan wanted and was entitled to, on the strength of his showing in the elections to the Executive, a seat on the Shadow Cabinet. As the conference progressed, it became clear that Bevan's opponents had decided to put up a strong fight to thwart his ambitions. The gauntlet was thrown down by the powerful Arthur Deakin. He was bitter and uncompromising. He correctly told the conference that the rearmament issue was an artificial one because it involved no real difference of opinion, the real issue was "that there is a great struggle for Leadership going on." [27] He denounced the defeat of Hugh Dalton in the elections to the Executive as an act of ingratitude on the part of the Bevan faction, for Dalton had made repeated efforts to make peace between Bevan and the Party leadership. Deakin saw only one solution to the internal struggle in the Labour Party, namely,

The complete abandonment on the part of this dissident element within our midst of the tactics they have so recently been employing. Let them get rid of their whips; dismiss their business managers and conform to the party constitution. Let them cease the vicious attacks they have launched upon these with whom they disagree, abandon their vituperation and the carping criticism which appears regularly in the *Tribune*.[28]

Deakin and the trade union leaders served notice that they did not intend to tolerate Bevan's intransigence any longer, and that they would press for the unconditional dissolution of the Bevanite faction within the Parliamentary Labour Party and an end to the *Tribune*'s attacks. The disquiet, if not the alarm, exhibited by Deakin and the Parliamentary leaders of the Labour Party can be ascribed to their fear that Bevan's ascendancy and the growing strength of the Constituent Labour Parties would upset the traditional and controlling alliance between the Parliamentary leaders and the conservative and moderate leadership of the majority of the big unions.

The reaction to Bevan's victory at Morecambe in the American and British press was one of hysterical indignation. Only eighteen months elapsed from the time that Aneurin Bevan was the generally respected, although not generally liked, member of the British Government. What caused the uproar which followed his election to the Labour Party's Executive, a post which would be quite easily within reach to a former important Cabinet member? The answer lies in the fact that in the span of eighteen months Aneurin Bevan succeeded, by the organization of his own faction in Parliament, by vituperative attacks on meeting platforms, in the *Tribune,* by his anti-Americanism and by his "lower than vermin" speech, in frightening British public opinion and many of the Conservative and Labour Party leaders. It became obvious that Bevan aimed to become Britain's Prime Minister and the "stop Bevan" slogan became the universal cry.

The *Manchester Guardian* wrote that "Morrison has gone down to the wild men of Labour's backwoods, the tea-time Socialists of the suburbs and the revolutionaries of the tiny local parties in rural areas." [29] The *Guardian* described Bevanism as a xenophobic movement, which if it should seize power would introduce a statist economy, but it concluded that "there is a facade of rebel victory, but there is also a weight of sensible opinion to keep rebellion in its place." [30] The *Spectator* with unconcealed glee noted, "The split [in the Labour Party] now stands glaringly revealed" and hoped that Bevan would be made to pay for Morrison's defeat. The editorial urged Attlee to act to stamp out the rebellion.[31]

On the other side of the aisle, the *New Statesman and Nation* was happy with the results of the conference. The showdown at Morecambe, the *Statesman* wrote, proved to the right wing that it could not hope to defeat or eliminate the left faction, but must learn to coexist with it. The editors recognized the fact that Bevan's victory divided the Party "into two armies arrayed for battle" [32] but ascribed Bevan's growing support to the following factors: (1) The desire for a militant leadership; (2) Protest against the drift to the right; (3) Rebellion of the younger generation against the old guard. The *Statesman* called upon Morrison and Bevan to reconcile their differences and, with the help of Attlee, to restore Party unity.

Hugh Gaitskell, commenting on the conference, said in a speech at Stalybridge that the Labour Party leadership suffered a defeat at Morecambe because it treated Bevan like a respected opponent instead of fighting him as rebels should be fought. He strongly intimated that the Constituent Labour Parties were infiltrated by Communists who were instrumental in throwing their support to the Bevanites. He urged that Bevan be fought with no holds barred.[33] In a subsequent article in the *Spectator*, Gaitskell wrote that the real root of the feud with the Bevanites was in foreign policy. "The most worrying feature of Morecambe to me," Gaitskell stated, "was the fact that so many local party delegates seemed to favor a foreign policy which was not just slightly different from the official view, but totally opposed to it. The views they [Bevanites] express are very much what the Communists would like them to express." [34] These local parties, he maintained, are run by Communists and the Party leaders ought to take steps to explain their point of view to them. The Party must, he concluded, counteract the vicious and misleading propaganda of the Bevanite organ, the *Tribune*.

Lord Pakenham, a Labour member of the House of Lords, expressed alarm at the growing strength of the Bevan faction and called upon Bevan to disband his "separate organization." He added, "I agree wholeheartedly with Mr. Gaitskell and Mr. Deakin that if they continue their present tactics, they must be tackled much more bluntly and vigorously than hitherto." [35] Like Gaitskell, Pakenham also ascribed Bevan's successes to the latent anti-Americanism which is pronounced among the rank and file members of the Party. He quoted a comrade, who told him, "Mr. Bevan was the man who would stand up to the Americans and prevent them dragging us into war." [36] Concluding, Lord Pakenham urged the Party leaders to adopt a clear and constructive policy which could provide a counterweight to the Bevanite program. Both Gaitskell and Pakenham indirectly admitted that the official Party leadership was weak, confused, and ineffective, a weakness which Bevan very cleverly exploited. The Bevanites and their supporters, on the other hand, rejoiced over the victory and demanded a position of power for their leader. Jennie Lee, with an engaging wifely devotion, told a correspondent that the peace of the world depended upon three people—Nehru, Tito, and her husband.[37] Bevan's friends claimed that they were as strong as their opponents, which, while an exaggeration, had some plausibility if the vote on the rearmament issue was considered. The *New Statesman* claimed that the principles of Bevanism had now become the official Party line, and Richard Crossman openly demanded that Bevan be given a place on the Shadow Cabinet. Gaitskell's accusation of Communist infiltration of Bevanite ranks was rejected in the *Tribune* and the *New Statesman* with anger and derision. An editorial in the *Statesman* said that "such charges are below the level of serious debate and they do public harm to Labour's cause at the time which demands great restraint." [38] The *Manchester Guardian* bluntly called on Attlee and Morrison to crush the "Bevanite Cabal." [39]

Aneurin Bevan watched the storm which was raging all around him and kept his peace. He felt misunderstood because he did not desire to *control* the Party—he only wanted a *share of the control*, because of a sincere conviction that such a position of power and leadership would make it possible for him to make a contribution to peace and Socialism. He was not prepared, as some of his hotheaded and pink-eyed supporters advised him, to exploit his victory and engage in a knockdown fight with the Party leaders and with the Transport House. He knew that his differences with the leadership were not irreconcilable and that a time wouuld come when he would join forces and collaborate with them. Bevan was not ready to burn any bridges. Once again he was calmly ready to make a cautious retreat and demonstrate his ability and readiness to compromise. He realized that the time for compromise had arrived when Attlee in a speech accused the Bevanites of sectionalism and endorsed in part Gaitskell's anti-Bevan position. Four days later on Wednesday, October 15, 1952, the Bevanite group in Parliament announced that henceforth its meetings and caucuses would be open to all Labour M.P.'s. The move was designed to kill the accusation that the faction was a Party-within-a-Party. Bevan's compromise proved to be too little and too late. Attlee and Morrison became deeply concerned by the genuine alarm expressed by British and American public opinion at Bevan's victory. They were determined to restore the respectability of the Labour Party in the eyes of the British electorate, especially the middle class, whose support they always considered essential to a Labour victory in any General Election.

On October 29, Attlee demanded that the Parliamentary Labour Party order the disbanding of all unofficial groups and factions. This time, the Parliamentary group accepted Attlee's recommendation by a vote of 188 to 51, and the Bevanite faction was ordered to disband or face expulsion. Bevanites were also instructed to cease all attacks on adopted Party policies and Party leaders from meeting platforms and in the *Tribune*. The order was a prompt response to Bevan's article in the *Tribune* in which he offered himself, Harold Wilson, and John Freeman for election to the Shadow Cabinet. The article was written carefully, skillfully mixing veiled threats and sweet reasonableness. He warned that "we will not abandon our right to carry our Socialist education in Great Britain, in order to provide an enlightened Socialist movement behind a Socialist majority in the next Parliament." [40] But he also suggested as a gesture of conciliation to open the meetings of his group to all Party members.

Bevan convened a caucus of his group to consider the ultimatum and urged the unconditional submission to the Party. He was not ready to jeopardize his chances in the forthcoming elections to the Shadow Cabinet, even if some of his more radical friends were ready to continue the fight. They were unhappy over their leader's decision to seek a seat on the Parliamentary Executive Committee which if attained, would make it impossible for him to continue his opposition to the Party's policies and leadership. Bevan had no such scruples. To him the Bevanite movement and faction were not an end in themselves but means to shift the Party's platform toward greater consonance with his views and toward attaining for himself a position of power in the Labour Party, and through it in the British Government. For the time being he wanted to become a spokesman of the Party on Labour's Front Bench in Parliament, and the abandonment of his faction was the price he was willing and ready to pay. The Bevanite group went out of existence with a rather mild letter of protest published in the *New Statesman and Nation* under the signature of Harold Wilson. Wilson wrote that the group decided to accept "the majority decision of our colleagues and, for our part, we will abide loyally by it." [41] But the faction denounced the decision "as illiberal . . . and based on allegations that are not true . . . [and] prejudicial to Party unity." [42]

Bevan decided not only to seek a seat on the Shadow Cabinet but also to challenge Herbert Morrison for the post of Deputy Leader of the Parliamentary Labour Party. He knew that he had no chance to defeat Morrison but wanted a test of strength. He lost but got a surprising 82 votes out of 290. The Party leadership got scared, and Attlee proposed a change in the voting procedure for the Shadow Cabinet designed to make it harder for Bevan and Wilson to win. Instead of a straight ballot for twelve men to be voted upon by the 290 Labour M.P.'s, he proposed an exhaustive ballot. After the first ballot, six old-timers were elected and neither Bevan or Wilson made it on the first try. Bevan finally squeaked through on the subsequent ballots and became the twelfth man on the Shadow Cabinet.

His initial goal was attained. After many years of hard work and astute if unorthodox tactics, he gained admittance to the small inner group that controlled the destinies and the policies of the British Labour Party. In case of a Labour victory, he would automatically get an important post in the Cabinet. Bevan had his eye on either the Exchequer or the office of the Foreign Secretary. He moved to the Front Bench and promptly joined Attlee in speaking for the motion of censure that the Labourites introduced against the Churchill Government for alleged incompetence and failure to consult the House on important decisions. In fact, the motion was in retaliation to the Government's action on denationalization of the iron and steel industry. True to form, Bevan, in contrast to Attlee, delivered a brilliant and slashing attack on the Government. Winston Churchill, who took the Labourite motion in stride and good humor, gave every indication that he was enjoying the opportunity to cross swords once again with his old adversary. He congratulated Attlee on the mild tone of his address and added that he hoped that "he [Attlee] will not be left at the post, as it were, when the right hon. Gentleman the Member of Ebbw Vale resumes his role of virtuous indignation reinforced with the abuse for which he is celebrated." [43] Churchill chided Attlee for changing the method of electing the Shadow Cabinet "in order to isolate the right hon. Member for Ebbw Vale." [44] Interrupted by Bevan during his address, Churchill gracefully yielded the floor, remarking, that he did so, "as the right hon. Gentleman is so lonely, I will treat him with chivalry." [45] The *New Statesman and Nation* paid deserved tribute to Bevan's triumph and his return to Parliament's Front Bench, which came as a shock to foes and as a surprise to his friends. The editorial said,

A month ago anyone would have been laughed to scorn for predicting that Mr. Attlee and Mr. Bevan would this week be jointly leading the attack on the Government in the first Censure Motion of the Session. Yet this is just what has happened . . . the leading contestants can congratulate themselves on having averted a split. . . . It became clear after Morecambe that neither could win because neither could capture the other's stronghold.[46]

Attlee could not overcome Bevan's control of the Constituent Labour Parties and Bevan did not even attempt to seize decisive power over the trade unions.

His foes were mournful and his friends were pleased, but Bevan was quite unperturbed. He took his place as the spokesman of the Labour Party with grace and ease, as if the honor would have naturally belonged to him. He did not gloat over his victory. His eyes were already focused on his next objective.

~XI~ The growing strength of Bevanism

BEVAN was obviously not content to remain for long the twelfth man in the Shadow Cabinet. His heart was set on getting an important post in the Cabinet—to become the Party's official spokesman on financial or foreign affairs. His chances for attaining a higher post were good, because although the Bevanite faction was inactive, Bevanism was alive and growing in strength. The sources of its strength were in the latent anti-Americanism of a large segment of the British people and the genuine fear of another war. There was also a strong sentiment against any further involvement in the Korean conflict and especially against the possibility of a United Nations war with Red China. Bevan exploited these fears to the utmost of his considerable abilities. He relentlessly attacked "American imperialists" and "militarists" who were, in his opinion, advocating an all-out war against Red China, even at the risk of World War III.

Bevan demanded that Nationalist China be ousted from the United Nations as a gesture of good will toward Red China, which then might agree to negotiate an armistice. "Is it not a fact," he asked, "that it might be possible to create a better atmosphere for successful negotiations in

Korea if the Chinese were not continually threatened by a recrudescence of counter-revolutionary action by Chiang Kai-shek and would it not be better to move on this matter rather than encourage this perpetual stalemate?" [1] He conceded that Red China should not be allowed to take a seat in the United Nations while the Korean war was on, but urged that the Chinese seat be declared vacant. While Bevan pressed the issue with special vigor and virulence and with a strong dose of anti-American animus, he did represent the views of his party on the Chinese question.

After the Prime Minister, Sir Anthony Eden, returned from a visit to the United States, Clement Attlee, the leader of the Opposition, asked him "whether in the course of those discussions, they debated with our American friends at all the question of Formosa, and in particular the very anomalous position by which the seat on the Security Council is still held by the representatives of Chiang Kai-shek instead of the real and effective government of China?" [2] In spite of some illusions entertained by many Americans, Attlee's and Bevan's views on Red China and Chiang Kai-shek were getting ever closer. Eden patiently but with little conviction answered Attlee that the majority of the United Nations continued to recognize Nationalist China, and Great Britain was not in a position to recommend the admission of Red China to the United Nations while the Korean war was on. In a later debate, Attlee again endorsed Bevan's conviction that Red China was not a natural ally of Russia and that isolating her was a tragically wrong policy. He said, "I do not believe that China is a mere puppet in the hands of Russia. I think that she will wear her Communism with a difference. . . ." [3]

The Conservatives offered little resistance to this pressure except to plead that the Government's hands were tied because of its determination not to give offense to its great

American ally. Winding up a debate in the House on the Korean situation, Selwyn Lloyd, Minister of State, surprisingly gave Churchill credit for being the first to suggest Britain's recognition of Red China. He unequivocally declared that the Conservatives "supported the recognition of the Central People's Government of China [*sic*]; I think in fact, my right hon. Friend [Churchill] was the first to suggest it. We did that not because we particularly liked that Government but because it was the effective Government of China." [4] British public opinion was in general agreement with this bipartisan China policy and even right-wing Conservative M.P.'s urged the expansion of trade with the Red Chinese. "Trade with China," wrote a Conservative M.P., ". . . on the large assumption of an early and successful armistice at Panmunjom, is in the minds of all those manufacturing and commercial communities whose munition output may soon be greatly reduced." He urged a simple, nonpolitical approach to the question of trade with Red China, concluding, "When the 'drummer,' whether the big shot on the board, the technician, or the salesman, sets out for China, let him leave behind prejudice, the habit of comparing unfavorably something which is merely different, and take with him in his sample case the right goods at the right price." [5]

While Bevan's position on China was in consonance with the Labour Party's policy and to some extent even with the Conservative Government's position, his anti-American attacks had a unique quality. The leader of the Bevanite movement was constantly drumming into the ears of his enthralled listeners that Britain should not follow the American colossus, but conduct its own independent policy. To the consternation of the Government, the Conservative right-wing rebels found themselves on some occasions in complete agreement with the left-wing rebel when the latter, sounding like a dyed-in-the-wool Tory, proclaimed that Great Britain was strong enough and wise enough to lead the world without American tutelage and supervision. The Conservative right wingers, who felt that American pressure and meddling had forced Britain to give up its dominant position in the Middle East, were not distressed by Bevan's biting attacks on America. They too, like Aneurin Bevan, were deeply convinced that Britain, with its rich tradition of freedom and political democracy, need not and should not accept the lead of the United States. Anti-Americanism had become the one most distinguishable feature of the movement which became known as Bevanism. "The foundation of Bevanism," wrote a British political writer, "appears to be the conviction that British policy must be separated from American policy on the ground that American policy might otherwise drag Britain unwillingly into either bankruptcy or war or both." [6]

Bevanist views were expressed in the House with increasing frequency. Bevan's wife and political ally, Jennie Lee, made on May 12, 1953, a remarkable speech in the House of Commons which brought her many compliments from both sides of the aisle. Since Miss Lee did not address Parliament often, and since she and her husband had for many years worked in closest political association and harmony and by all accounts led a happy married life, her speech provided important clues to the political philosophy of this remarkable couple in British politics. Miss Lee stressed that Great Britain must lead and not follow in international politics. "It is absolutely essential," she said, "that Great Britain speaks as Great Britain and that we no longer either hedge or apologize if in the contribution we are to make to international affairs we disagree with the United States of America. . . ." [7] She further denounced British reliance on American economic help and proudly recalled that she voted against the acceptance of the first American loan in 1945. She then paid tribute to "a few independent Tories . . . who felt that Great Britain was throwing aside its real powers of influence in the world at the time when she accepted *that rather disgraceful loan.* . . . I am grieved and shamed when I hear that the contribution which our country can make to international affairs is lost because of the clatter of the dollars falling into the begging bowl." [8] She went on to deliver, almost in passing, a biting attack on incidents of discrimination against the Negroes in America, and recalled that her first experience during a visit to America was to meet a Negro who was neither entirely black nor white and who made pathetic attempts to "pass" as a white American.

Gracefully and graciously Miss Lee paid tribute to her husband's great adversary. Winston Churchill is, she said,

a Prime Minister for whom all of us have a certain respect and a certain affection. Every soldier in the line of battle respects the soldier in the opposite trenches if he feels he believes in what he is fighting for and is a brave man for his side. It is in that sense that I pay my respects to the Prime Minister. [9]

She concluded her speech by reaffirming another basic principle of Bevanism, namely the "third force" idea. Great Britain had little to choose between America and Russia and must chart its own way and destiny between these two opposing powers. "I do not believe," Miss Lee declared, "that the 20th Century world wants to live under the domination of either the American dollar, of American values or under the domination of Soviet Russia." [10]

While his wife, Crossman, Mikardo, and others propagated his views—sometimes perhaps going a bit too far for his own taste—Bevan himself was under wraps and on his best behavior. He was concentrating on improving his position in the Shadow Cabinet by trying to convince the leaders, many of whom openly distrusted him, that he believed in Party regularity and loyalty. He faithfully carried out the assignments given to him on Labour's Front Bench and tried to appear as the official and restrained spokesman of the Labour Party. He was not very successful. After his rather lusterless speech on the National Health Service, the Conservative Minister of Health, Ian Norman Macleod, described Bevan as behaving like a sucking dove. The *Manchester Guardian* commented that "Certainly he seems like a reformed character. . . . The cyclonic Bevan we have not seen for a long time." [11]

Bevan was not happy with his own moderation and restraint, nor with the Labour Party's weak and ineffective opposition to the Government's determination to denationalize the transport and steel industries. Both the transport and the iron and steel bills, which the Conservative Government submitted to Parliament early in 1953, were bitter pills for Bevan to swallow. If he had his way, the Labour's Party's opposition to the turning over of the key industries which the Labour Government nationalized when in power would not have been weak and ineffective, as it was generally conceded to be. "Something like a fatalistic acceptance of both measures," wrote the *Guardian*, "has developed in the Labour Party, made bearable by the promise it keeps making that it will re-nationalize both industries when it is returned to power." [12] In fact, while the leaders of the Labour Party and the powerful Transport Union were genuinely interested in nationalizing the coal industry in the first place, the nationalization of steel was originally a reluctant concession to the Bevanite extremists. Whenever the opportunity presented itself, and Aneurin Bevan was assigned to speak on behalf of the Party with some latitude, he showed flashes of temper and anger.

Speaking on the transport bill, Bevan delivered a slashing attack on the Conservative Party, charging that it was "fundamentally authoritarian and had never been a democratic party at all." [13]

In March 1953, Bevan made a tour of the Far East, during which he visited India, Pakistan, and Burma. He was warmly received by Government officials and leaders of political parties who were long impressed with his neutralist-third force idea. Bevan made a thorough study of the attempts made by the Indian Government to raise the standard of living in the Indian villages and to put into effect a long-needed land reform. He liked what he saw and contrasted favorably the Indian local village-community projects with the centralized agricultural policies of the Soviets. "The theory [in India]," he wrote, "is the reverse of the centralism which has distinguished the Soviet approach to rural life. It is an attempt to make democracy work, where it can be expected to be most vigorous and self-reliant, at the bottom of the social scale." [14] He told his Asian audiences that he was proud of having been a member of the British Government that had granted independence to many of its former dependencies. With a typical Welshman's longing for the mountains, he went to seek respite in the Himalayas: "The mountains worked their old magic on me. They smoothed the fretfulness from my spirit like wrinkles from a worn garment." [15]

Upon his return home, Bevan wrote a series of articles for an American magazine to warn his "American friends" once again that the United States policy on China was unpopular in Asia and was fraught with dire dangers to the free world. In Red China, he argued, just as in Russia, there are two groups, the extremists, who are pushing for aggression and war, and the moderates, who are in the majority and favor a policy of peaceful coexistence. "Any American

sabre-rattling," he warned, "encourages the extremists." [16]
America and Britain must work for a settlement with Red
China and the formula for such a settlement, as Bevan
saw it, was simple. The first step would be "the immediate
disbanding of Chiang Kai-shek's army on Formosa"; the
second, "return [Formosa] to the Chinese Government to
whom it belongs." [17] He became convinced on his tour that
while the people of India, Pakistan, and Burma understood
and supported the United States and United States policy
on resisting the North Korean aggression, they were at a loss
to understand why the foremost member of the United
Nations coalition was itself ready to commit or to help
Chiang commit an act of aggression against Red China.
As was sometimes his custom, Bevan added a threat to the
warning: "Let me ask my American friends—and despite
what is said to the contrary, I have many American friends
—whether they seriously imagine that we here in Britain
are going to involve ourselves in a third world war in order
to put Chiang Kai-shek back in China?" [18]

Summarizing the series, Bevan used his sense of historical
analysis, of which he was proud and which he considered
unique, to teach his "American friends" a lesson in history.
He warned the American people not to make the same
mistake in regard to the "Chinese Revolution" as the British
committed in regard to the Russian Revolution. The British,
he wrote, led by Winston Churchill rejected his advice and
that of many Labourites to accept the Russian Revolution as
a *fait accompli* and help the Bolsheviks to industrialize
Russia. Churchill instead decided to make an attempt to
overthrow the Soviet Government. "We did stop Winston
Churchill," wrote Bevan, "from murdering the Russian
Revolution," [19] but the Labour Party could not stop the
Conservative effort to starve the Soviets to submission.
The Russians then were forced, according to Bevan, to

use the methods of a police state to force industrialization. Bevan then gave his own interpretation of Soviet brutality, ruthlessness, and excesses. "Most of the fault of the Communists in Russia," he wrote, "stems directly from the fact that the Russians had to industrialize with their own resources and with no assistance from the industrialized West." [20] Following Bevan's arguments to their logical conclusion, one would have to assume that if Britain, America, and France had provided Lenin and Stalin with credits, loans, and machinery, the Soviet Communists would have created in Russia a political democracy and lived ever after in harmony and friendship with the rest of the world.

Aneurin Bevan solemnly warned the Americans not to make the same blunder as did the British after the 1917 Bolshevik Revolution. "That is why," he continued,

I say to my friends in America: don't make the mistake about the Chinese revolution that we British made about the Russian revolution! Even if you give up the idea of destroying it militarily, don't try to starve it to death, because all you will accomplish is to drive the Chinese administration into the same monolithic excesses that you witness in the Soviet Union. [21]

Bevan did not acknowledge that international Communism has an irresistible compulsion to dominate the world by infiltration and naked aggression. He repeatedly and with obvious seriousness blamed Churchill for all the brutality and degradation inflicted by the Soviet rulers on its subjects.

Back in Parliament, Bevan was busily mending his fences in the Labour Party, managing even to improve his relations with Hugh Gaitskell. They united in opposing the Budget Estimates. The main speech against the budget was made by Harold Wilson, who followed Hugh Gaitskell, the Party's official spokesman of financial matters. The Parliamentary correspondent of the *Manchester Guardian* observed that both Gaitskell and Bevan were on the front bench after Wilson delivered his speech:

The lively communion between the three might have suggested that they were bound to each other by "hoops of steel" and that no breath of discord had ever sullied their relations. . . . This speech of Wilson's for the front Opposition bench, following that of Gaitskell demonstrated, and was no doubt designed to do so, that the official party and the Bevanites are united for attacking the Budget.[22]

To show the complete unity of the Party, Bevan was given the task of closing the debate on the Budget. While otherwise mild and subdued and ineffective, he concentrated on a favorite topic—the expansion of British trade. He emphasized his conviction that Britain cannot hope to expand its trade with the United States because "the markets in Great Britain and America are not mutually complementary, whereas markets in other parts of the world are." [23] The allusion to the desirability of British trade with Russia and Red China was obvious.

Bevan's patience and volatile temper must have been sorely tried by the obvious inertia and placidity that seemed to have gripped the Labour Party. Its official leaders were in no mood to fight anybody, especially not Winston Churchill. The general debate on foreign policy conducted in May 1953 was replete with mutually expressed assurances of respect and affection between the Prime Minister and the Leader of Her Majesty's Opposition. Attlee and the Labour Party cheered Churchill for getting the Order of the Garter and the Conservative spokesman expressed his profound gratification at Attlee's return to the House after an operation. Clement Attlee, replying to a brilliant review of world affairs made by the Prime Minister, accepted Churchill's general tone and approach to world

affairs, endorsed Churchill's proposal for a Big Four conference, and praised him for the moderation of his address.
The Conservatives joined in the spirit of mutual admiration,
and Selwyn Lloyd, Minister of State, graciously said, "The
right hon. Gentleman began by paying a compliment to the
tone and the tenor of the speech of the Prime Minister. I
hope he will not regard it an impertinence in a junior
Minister to say that we on this side thought the tone and
tenor of his speech also was admirable." [24] Bevan, mindful
of his objectives, the short- and the long-range ones, said
nothing to disturb the tranquility of the occasion. But not
all elements and groups in the Labour Party were satisfied
with the ineffectiveness of the opposition, and the *New
Statesman and Nation* openly claimed that the banning of
the Bevanite faction was responsible for the lack of vitality
and dynamism in the Labour Party's fight against the
Churchill Government.

While the Parliamentary Labour Party was in the
doldrums and Bevan seldom spoke in Parliament, Bevanism
was making great strides in capturing the minds of British
workers and large segments of the British people. The
restrictions that Bevan imposed on himself did not pertain
to the *Tribune,* the *New Statesman and Nation,* and to his
fiery and able lieutenants like Wilson, Crossman, Mikardo,
Silverman, and Castle, who exerted every effort to propagate the basic Bevanite philosophy. The results of this
campaign were soon evident. The National Executive Committee, determined to preserve the Party's unity, devoted
several months to the preparation of a programmatic statement to be presented at the annual conference, scheduled
for October 1953. The statement, entitled *Challenge to Britain,* was published in June 1953, and was adopted unanimously by the entire Executive, including Aneurin Bevan.
In the tradition of the Labour Party it was a compromise

statement which faithfully attempted to reconcile the views
of the Bevanites, the right wing, and the center group. It
was a "compromise program designed for party debate and
public propaganda." [25] The Conservative and the Liberal
papers found the statement weak and uninspiring. The
Spectator in a lead article wrote that "the Labour Party's
policy statement *Challenge to Britain* never at any time
justified its title.[26] The Liberal *Manchester Guardian* expressed its disappointment by stating that "the Labour
Party Executive's policy statement *Challenge to Britain* was
not an imposing document. . . ." [27] The organ of the
Bevanites, the *Tribune,* denounced the statement as weak
and lacking the courage of its Socialist convictions. The
critics were only partly correct. *Challenge to Britain* was
cautiously and carefully written, but its content, especially
in the field of foreign affairs, was bold and far-reaching
and reflected the extent to which Bevanism has influenced
the official policy of the Labour Party.

The Party outlined a program for improving Britain's
economic position in order to achieve "independence of
American aid, which was one of the Labour Party's major
objectives." [28] The statement went on to advocate, in line
with an often expounded Bevanite principle, a greatly increased trade program with Communist countries, but
pointed out that the cold war put certain limitations on such
a trade. It said, "Labour will endeavor to maintain and
expand East-West trade within the limits imposed by the
Cold War. We shall constantly seek a relaxation of international tension to widen those limits and make possible a
reduction of the arms burden." [29]

Challenge to Britain accepted Bevan's thesis that the
danger of Communist infiltration in the underdeveloped
countries of the world came from internal causes and not
from Soviet subversion. "We believe," the statement de-

clared, "we have a duty to help countries in Asia and Africa to combat hunger, poverty, ignorance and disease. We further believe that the biggest contribution to the forces of freedom and peace must come from an organized attack on the causes of misery which breed unrest." [30] That part of the document which dealt with the issue of nationalization was wary and restrained. This restraint was the result of a long process of re-evaluation and re-assessing of the principle of public ownership of basic in-dustries. While in power, the Labour Party leaders had an ample opportunity to see that the nationalization of an im-portant industry was a complicated task, which even when successfully accomplished did not automatically make the management of a particular industry easy, efficient, and profitable. They also became convinced, especially Gaitskell and Morrison, that any further extension of public owner-ship must be preceded by a considerable period of study and preparation. Finally, the Labour Party came to the conclusion, which contradicted the doctrinaire Socialist philosophy, that there are limits to nationalization and that some industries cannot and should not be taken over by the state. Even Aneurin Bevan, when Minister of Health and Housing, opposed suggestions for the nationalization of the building industry, because in his opinion such a step would have hampered rather than aided his housing program. *Challenge to Britain* promised that the Labour Party, when returned to power, would renationalize trans-port and steel, but it added: ". . . though the general case for nationalization is compelling, we advocate nationaliza-tion here only for these industries where the immediate national need makes the case overwhelming." [31] The sober and cautious Labour leaders decided that national interest and not Socialist dogma would determine the limits of public ownership. They were well aware of the fact that this approach would sit well with the floating middle class voters who were essential for a Labour victory at the polls.

Bevan voted for the watered-down version of nationalization, which obviously contradicted his famous dictum of the "agony of public ownership," but he had to compromise in order to improve his position in the Shadow Cabinet, and he was as eager as his colleagues to see the Labour Party return to power. The *Spectator* shrewdly appraised the situation when it wrote, ". . . the power which Mr. Bevan has avowedly been seeking all his life is not merely for his party, but also for himself. Anyone who thinks he has abandoned that particular struggle is either in possession of a most remarkable piece of inside information or is ignoring the evidence of his senses. Mr. Bevan is not like that. Political life is not like that." [32]

Consistent with his habit of compromising with an engaging smile, Bevan remembered to keep a grenade behind his back. His enemies and friends had always to be reminded that he compromised because he wanted to, not because he had to. These reminders began to pour into the offices of the Transport House in the form of scores of resolutions to be submitted to the conference by the Constituent Labour Parties, whose political thinking was generally dominated by Bevan and his supporters. The resolutions, almost all on foreign policy, demanded the end of the cold war, unconditional trade with Russia and Red China, denounced "American imperialists and militarists," and urged the cessation of "American dictation" in British foreign policy. The official Labour Party leadership was again put on notice that it needed Aneurin Bevan to help keep those wild-eyed radicals in check. The Constituent Parties also gave expression to their disappointment with the Executive's stand on the nationalization issue. As usual the big trade unions were quick to come to the aid of the

Executive. Their leaders were still smarting from the blow their entrenched prestige suffered at the Morecambe conference. The trade union leaders long looked upon local Labour Parties with unconcealed disdain. In their eyes they were in the main a conglomeration of uninformed radicals manipulated by scheming left-wing intellectuals and Bevanites. The big unions resented the sudden emergence of the Constituent Parties as a factor of strength in the Labour Party. They were not used to encountering any serious opposition in directing the Party's policies. Ernest Bevin once said that it was not Keir Hardie who founded the Labour Party—the Labour Party grew out of the bowels of the T.U.C. The defeat Herbert Morrison suffered at the hands of the Constituencies at the Morecambe conference was considered by the big union leaders as a challenge and provocation which could not go unanswered.

The Trades Union Congress, which met in September 1953, on the Isle of Man, gave full support to the Executive Committee's moderate position on nationalization. The congress approved the "Interim Report on Public Ownership," issued by the T.U.C. General Council, which stated: "It would not be true to say today that public opinion is strongly prepared for the transfer of further industries to public ownership." [33] The *New Statesman and Nation* complained that the T.U.C. Congress put "public ownership into cold storage." [34] The "big four" of the congress, Sir Arthur Deakin, Sir William Lawther, Tom Williamson, and Sir William Tewson, proceeded to redress the wrong that they thought was committed at the last conference, and agreed to support Herbert Morrison for treasurer of the Party to replace the incumbent Arthur Greenwood. Greenwood had become unpopular with them because he had attempted to reconcile the differences between Bevan and the official Party leadership. Morrison could return to the Executive only through the treasurership, for he lost the support of the Constituent Parties mostly through his harsh and uncompromising opposition to Bevan and Bevanism.

Tom O'Brien, the president of the Trades Union Congress, praised the trade unions for providing an effective check, within the Labour Party, to the ambitions of eccentric individuals in pursuit of personal power. The reference to Bevan was clear. He warned that the General Council of the T.U.C. would not tolerate much longer the Bevanite intrigues and machinations and the attempts to create a chasm between the leaders and the rank and file trade union members. "The unions," concluded O'Brien, "will support leaders whom they trust, but will not have leaders foisted upon them." [35] The Labour Party was put on notice that it might have to choose between Bevan and the support of the big trade unions.

This open challenge of the trade unions to Bevan alerted the country to the probability that the forthcoming Margate Conference would be an exciting rambunctious meeting where the issue of Bevan and Bevanism would be finally fought out. The British press readied itself for exciting news. When the conference finally assembled at Margate on September 28, everybody soon realized that the fireworks and the fight were cancelled. Bevan, the master political strategist, refused to come out and fight. As far as he was concerned, this was the wrong place and the wrong time for a contest. The wrong place because Bevan knew the limited power of the Annual Conference; the wrong time because he still lacked enough strength and support. He realized that in spite of the Labour Party Constitution, the Annual Conference as a rule made no real decisions and gave no directions to the Party. It was a good propaganda show, a fine place to let off steam, but the binding decisions and the real power rested in the leaders of the Parliamentary Labour Party and in the Executive. The Parliamentary Labour group was completely autonomous and Bevan himself on several occasions warned the conference delegates not to issue directives to the Labour representatives in Parliament. Both Ramsay MacDonald, when he was Labour Prime Minister, and Clement Attlee, as the head of the Labour Government, openly declared that they were not bound by any decisions or instructions from the annual conferences with the exception of general Socialist principles. Attlee did not feel that it was necessary for him to consult the Labour Party Executive or even its leaders, except a few personal friends, when he formed the Labour Government in 1945. The bloc voting at the conference ensures that the National Executive usually controls the decisions of the conference. The final speaker in each debate is selected by the Executive and it is his task to advise the conference, on behalf of the Executive, how to vote on a particular resolution. Since nineteen out of twenty-six members of the Executive are virtually selected by the leaders of the trade unions, the powerful union as a rule is thrown for the resolution supported by the Executive and is more than enough to crush any opposition. At the 1950 Conference, trade unions controlled 5,014,000 votes as compared with the 985,000 votes of the Constituent Labour Parties. The voting strength of the five largest right-wing unions was as follows:[36]

Transport and General Workers (T.&G.W.)	830,000
National Union of Mine Workers (N.U.M.)	651,000
Amalgamated Engineering Union (A.E.U.)	595,000
General and Municipal Workers (G.&M.W.)	400,000
National Union of Railwaymen (N.U.R.)	366,000
74 other smaller unions had the remaining	1,855,000

The Executive Committee could generally count on the complete loyalty and support of the great majority of these unions. R. T. McKenzie summarized the status of the annual conference in a succinct statement: ". . . history shows that the leaders of the P.L.P. (through the N.E.C.) advise the Party Conference as to what the Conference should advise the P.L.P. to do." [37]

Aneurin Bevan, who had attended Party conferences from 1929, was well aware of the real structure of power in the Labour Party, and considered it futile and wasteful to give battle to his enemies on the floor of the conference without adequate preparation and without an assured substantial following. He again decided to resort to his great Welsh charm and persuasiveness to compromise and conciliate. The Party leaders were notified that Bevan was ready to do business in the preconference caucuses. Since unity was always a magic word in Labour Party councils, Bevan's overtures were not rebuffed. First, an ingenious compromise was worked out which averted a fight between Morrison and Greenwood for the post of Treasurer. Herbert Morrison got a seat on the Executive through a resolution, passed later at the conference with Bevanite support, by which the Deputy Leader of the Parliamentary Labour Party became an ex-officio member of the Executive. Greenwood was then unopposed in the election for Party Treasurer. In exchange for considerable concessions in the foreign policy resolutions to be submitted to the conference by the Executive, Aneurin Bevan agreed to go down the line in support of the entire *Challenge to Britain* statement. He faithfully kept to the bargain. He told reporters before the opening of the conference that "it may be now and again somebody will say rather rough things . . . [but] don't let anyone make any mistake. . . . When we have had our row and made up our minds, this movement is going to be a solid, united movement." [38]

Clement Attlee contributed to the spirit of unity by accepting many Bevanite ideas in the foreign policy resolutions he submitted to the conference. In doing so, he undoubtedly considered not only the importance of preserving Party harmony, but also the necessity of adopting some of the popular slogans of Bevanism and thus stealing Bevan's thunder. The modest and unassuming but wily British Party leader was well aware that Bevan's demands for negotiating with Russia, his anti-Americanism, and his advocacy of the recognition of Red China had widespread support among the rank and file members of Labour and the British people. Thus many of the Bevanite principles have become the official Labour Party policy. Attlee proposed: "Conference . . . deplores the failure of the Western Powers to maintain the initiative in efforts to break the East-West deadlock. . . . Conference urges renewed efforts to convene at the earliest date, a Four Power Conference at the highest level in order to seek out any possibility of agreement on outstanding issues." [39] While affirming support for the NATO, the conference cast a dart at Senator McCarthy for "the harm done to Anglo-American relations by political witchhunting in the U.S.A." [40] On the controversial issue of the extent of the British rearmament program, the Executive accepted Bevan's warning that the program "must be reviewed periodically in the light of the international situation and our *economic position*" [italics mine].[41] Attlee and Morrison agreed with Bevan's opposition to German rearmament, although this opposition was made conditional upon Soviet acceptance of a peaceful reunification of Germany.

The official Party leadership also appeased Bevan by adopting a clearly anti-American set of resolutions concern-

ing the Far East. "Conference . . . reaffirms," Attlee's motion read, "that a settlement must be reached with the
Peking Government as the effective government of China
and that the Peking representatives should be admitted to
the U.N." [42] On the matter of the future of Formosa, the
Executive did not accept Bevan's suggestion that the island
be turned over to Red China, but demanded that Formosa
be neutralized by an international naval force, and "thereafter, the people of Formosa should be enabled freely to
determine their own destiny." [43] Since, as one writer observed, the Trade Union "lambs" did lie down with the
Bevanite wolves, [44] the Executive had no trouble in beating
down any and all objections that were raised against *Challenge to Britain* and against Attlee's foreign policy motions.
When J. F. Fagan, representing the Barrow-in-Furness Constituent Labour Party, proposed an amendment urging "an
immediate reduction of armaments to a level commensurate
with our economic strength," [45] neither Bevan nor his lieutenants rose to support it, in spite of the fact that the proposal represented one of the basic principles of Bevanism.
It was this issue which ostensibly caused Bevan's resignation from Labour Government. During the entire conference
Aneurin Bevan spoke only once, when he addressed the delegates on behalf of the Executive on an inconsequential resolution on health. Arthur Deakin, the stormy petrel of the
Morecambe Conference, gave full support to the truce. The
Manchester Guardian ironically observed that "Mr. Bevan
and Mr. Deakin have gone out of their respective ways to
be courteous to each other and to exchange pleasantries in
public." [46]

All in all, the Margate Conference was peaceful, harmo-
nious, and—dull. The peace was really not peace but a
truce. The trade union bosses did not choose, or could not

risk, expelling the rebels from the Party; Bevan, always with an eye cocked on the top Party leadership, had not the slightest desire to secede. He happily noted that he received the highest vote from the Constituencies (1,142,000) in the election to the Executive, but he also realized that a decisive battle with Morrison and the trade union leaders would eventually be unavoidable if his goal was to be attained. He needed more strength and more support. The real contest was to come in the Parliamentary Labour Party with his old adversary and rival for Attlee's post, Herbert Morrison.

In November 1953, Bevan announced again his candidacy for the post of Deputy Leader, then held by Morrison. He knew that he had no chance to unseat Morrison, but the showdown was intended to put the Party and the nation on notice that the Margate show of unity had not changed Bevan's determination to wrest the Party leadership from the trade union–Attlee–Morrison coalition. Bevan lost by a vote of 181 to 76. As compared with the same vote in 1952, Bevan lost six votes, but Morrison lost thirteen. The leadership remained more firmly than ever in the hands of Clement Attlee who alone among his colleagues considered himself best fitted for the job.

The relative peace and tranquility of the post-Margate period was completely shattered in December 1953 when Aneurin Bevan became again the object of a storm of protest and abuse in the British press and in Parliament. This time the uproar, which Bevan must have deeply regretted, resulted from an article by Bevan which appeared in the Egyptian newspaper *Al Goumhouria*, the official organ of the Egyptian revolutionary Government headed by General Naguib and Colonel Nasser. While Great Britain was in the midst of delicate negotiations with the intransigent Egyptians, who pressed for the complete withdrawal of British troops from the Suez Canal Zone, Bevan wrote that British troops had no right to be on Egypt's soil.

The presence of troops of another nation on one's own soil is a circumstance to be borne only when it is voluntarily conceded. . . . The presence of American airmen is tolerated in Britain but not accepted. If their presence comes to be actively resented, then they will have to withdraw; and for the same reason we shall have to withdraw from Egypt, because a military base is useless if it is surrounded by a hostile population.[47]

Again ignoring the long record of Soviet aggressions, Bevan asserted that British withdrawal from Egypt would not be an invitation for Russian troops or Russian influence to move in. "When the British walk out of Egypt," Bevan continued, "the Egyptians and only the Egyptians will walk in."[48] British newspapers of all shades of political opinion, the Conservatives, and the great majority of the Labourites heaped scorn on Bevan for giving aid and comfort to the Egyptians, who were intent, with some American encouragement, on forcing the British out of the Canal Zone and on the unilateral control of the Suez Canal. Many argued that Bevan, as a Privy Councillor, had no right to publish articles abroad damaging the nation's interest.

In an earnest, long, but thoroughly unconvincing speech in Parliament, Bevan cited excerpts from articles published by Winston Churchill in European and American newspapers, attacking the policies of Neville Chamberlain's Government in the years immediately preceding World War II.[49] This argument and Bevan's explanation that the article which appeared in the Cairo newspapers was previously published, without any adverse reaction, in the Indian newspapers, fell generally on deaf ears. Bevan's article was in the opinion of a great majority of the members of Parliament reckless and irresponsible. Some even considered it outright treason. Martin Lindsay, Conservative M.P., accused Bevan of inflaming anti-British passions in Egypt, and concluded his address by stating, "In giving his sponsorship and encouragement to the revolutionary movement in Egypt, I think the right hon. Gentleman has done a dastardly thing and forfeited the respect of this House and his fellow citizens." [50] Bevan's position was repudiated by his own Party when half the members of the Parlimentary Labour Group, in an unprecedented step, signed a motion supporting the Conservative Government in its negotiations with Egypt. Clement Attlee withheld comment on Bevan's article, but he made it unmistakably clear that the British Labour Party did not share Bevan's view on the Egyptian question. He denounced the Egyptian extremists and assured Prime Minister Eden that the Labour Party stood behind him in protecting British interests in the Suez Canal. It was a bitter and disappointing day for Bevan. The mildness and moderation he exhibited in 1956, when he spoke on behalf of his Party against the British military action against Egypt, might well be traced to the effects of that incident. Bevan could have conceivably blamed himself for contributing in some measure to the disastrous chain of events which culminated with Nasser's seizure of the Suez Canal.

Bevanism was gaining ground, but Bevan's climb to power was getting to be quite a tortuous and demanding chore. He was clearly wasting his time and talents sitting in the furthest corner of the Opposition's Front Bench.

∾XII∾   Bevan resigns from the Shadow Cabinet

A FEW WEEKS after the unfortunate uproar in the House of Commons that followed the publication of his article in an Egyptian newspaper, Aneurin Bevan left with Jennie Lee for a visit to Egypt and Israel. In view of Bevan's advocacy of a British withdrawal from the Suez Canal Zone, it was generally assumed that the Egyptian nationalists would welcome him with open arms. But his reception was restrained and almost cool; the Egyptian leaders were well aware of Bevan's long-standing sympathy for Zionism and his close friendship with many leaders of the State of Israel. Naguib and Nasser remembered Bevan's attacks on Bevin, when the latter as Britain's Foreign Secretary fought Jewish immigration into Palestine and opposed the establishment of a Jewish State.

It soon became clear that Bevan decided to make up for the painful impression created by his pro-Egyptian position in the midst of delicate Anglo-Egyptian negotiations. He saw General Naguib, Egypt's Prime Minister, and Colonel Nasser, the head of the revolutionary junta, but refrained from endorsing the Egyptian demands for the withdrawal of British troops. He told reporters that he merely listened to Nasser's arguments, and when asked what he thought of

Egypt's revolution, he threw caution to the winds and aptly answered, "There is no revolution, what happened was a *coup d'etat* with a revolutionary facade. The revolution has still to come." [1] He specifically refused to endorse Egypt's claims to the Suez Canal, and while agreeing that America sometimes was close to being imperialistic, he also stated that he had no admiration for Russia because the Soviet system had failed to produce a happy society. Bevan got a poor press in Egypt, but the British papers praised him for using his generally admitted ability to discover the heart of a political issue. He exposed the sham of the Egyptian military upheaval, which had overthrown the corrupt King Farouk only to substitute for his regime a thinly disguised military dictatorship.

Upon his return to Britain, Bevan became increasingly disturbed by the ineffectiveness of Labor's opposition to the Churchill Government. While he respected Clement Attlee and, unlike many of his colleagues, considered him a shrewd and wily politician, Bevan was irked and irritated by Attlee's moderate and conciliatory attitude on issues of foreign policy, by his pronounced pro-Americanism, and his tendency to exchange compliments with Winston Churchill. He felt frustrated by his limited influence in the councils of the Shadow Cabinet, where he was the "twelfth man" and, on most issues, a minority of one. His membership on the Executive Committee was also of little avail because the majority which was selected by the trade unions consistently supported the policies and positions taken by Attlee and Morrison. On the contrary, his membership in the Shadow Cabinet and on the Executive were proving to be a distinct handicap, for he was bound by the rigid discipline of the standing orders and subject to the principle of collective responsibility. Nor was he free to express his views, which were generally in complete disagreement with official Labour policies. This was particularly irksome because Bevan thought that he finally had several issues which, if properly fought out, could conceivably catapult him to the leadership of the Labour Party through a revolt of the rank and file members. The most important of these issues were the question of the rearmament of West Germany, the manufacture by Britain of the H-bomb, and the South-East Asia defense organization. Bevan sensed that his position against arming West Germany and against the manufacture of the hydrogen bomb had widespread intellectual and emotional appeal, and he felt well equipped to carry the fight to the mass of the British people. But to be able to do this he had to free himself from the restraints that his membership in the Shadow Cabinet and the Executive placed upon him.

The opportunity came on April 13, 1954, when Foreign Secretary Anthony Eden reported to Parliament on his conversation with the American Secretary of State Dulles, who had visited London. Eden reported to the House that the British and American governments had decided to take part, with other concerned governments, in a South-East Asia defense alliance, patterned after NATO. The purpose of the new set-up was to "assure the peace and security and freedom of South-East Asia and the Western Pacific." [2] Attlee, leader of the Opposition, followed Eden to the floor of the House and suggested that the new organization include Asiatic nations in order that it "should not in any way be represented, as it may be misrepresented, as a defense of obsolete colonialism." [3] Attlee approved of SEATO, but asked that steps be taken to assure India's participation in it.

Eden, obviously gratified, warmly thanked Attlee for his support, but Aneurin Bevan, flushed and angry, barged into the polite exchange with a statement that electrified the House. "Is the right hon. Gentleman aware," he asked, "that the statement which he made today will be resented by the majority of the people in Great Britain? Is he further aware that it will be universally regarded as a surrender to American pressure?" [4] He concluded by stating that the South-East Asia defense organization would be interpreted by the people of Asia as aimed to perpetuate the European colonial rule in that part of the world. Bevan's open defiance of his Party leader and of the elementary rules of Party discipline stunned the Labour M.P.'s and made sensational headlines in the British press. On the whole, the newspapers were delighted that Bevan finally threw down the gauntlet, and called for his expulsion from the Labour Party. On April 14, Bevan announced his resignation from the Shadow Cabinet in order to be free to head a national campaign against the Party's leadership on the whole field of foreign policy. The resignation was received with open glee and satisfaction in most quarters.

The mass circulation pro-Labour *Daily Mirror* again chose to misinterpret Bevan's action as the impulsive and rash act of an irresponsible hothead. It wrote ". . . again he has shown that the greatest blunder the party could make would be to elect him leader. . . . For who can follow a whirlwind? How can a man who does not give loyalty expect to command loyalty from others?" [5]

The *Spectator* called Bevan "a very special disaster for Labour" [6] because he had no positive intellectual contribution to make to the Labour Party, which was in great need of a cohesive and positive leadership. The influential weekly pleaded with the official Labour Party leadership to stop temporizing and expel the rebel, who "has his eyes on the Labour Party Conference in Scarborough in October and on the next General Election—not on Indo-China and Germany." [7] Attlee was urged to stop Bevan without fear of consequences. Dennis Healy, a Labour M.P. and a sworn foe of Bevan, declared that Bevan by his latest action had shown that he was "impossible as a colleague and would be intolerable as a leader." [8] He expressed his hope that this time Attlee was committed to fight Bevan openly to the bitter end.

The *Economist* in a front-page editorial asked whether Attlee, Morrison, and Gaitskell were finally this time determined to fight not only Bevan but also Bevanism.[9] The editorial correctly pointed out that in the past Attlee and other Labour leaders felt compelled, even when resisting Bevan personally, to adopt his ideas and policies and to appease his followers. The *Economist* bluntly warned Attlee not to appease Bevan on the central theme of Bevanism—his virulent anti-Americanism—in spite of its wide popular appeal. It urged him not to yield or compromise or buy Party peace by ditching Bevan and then go on to a ". . . sly acceptance of Mr. Bevan's policies." [10]

The *New Statesman and Nation,* whose editors were close to Bevan, did not share the gloomy predictions on his political future. It stated that those who foresaw the isolation of Bevan were misreading public opinion and greatly underestimated the public appeal of Bevan's views. The *Statesman* disputed the views of the anti-Bevanites who accused him of splitting the Party for the sake of personal ambitions. On the contrary, it commended him for placing his convictions above any personal considerations.[11]

Attlee, who had his ear attuned to the temper and views of the rank and file of the Party and had an instinctive disinclination to take drastic actions, ignored the goading of Labour's right wing and of the Conservative press. He was not ready for a showdown with Bevan, and Harold Wilson was allowed to take Bevan's place on the Shadow Cabinet after expressing his complete agreement with his comrade's views. The Executive Committee of the Labour Party went through the motion of reaffirming the doctrine of collective responsibility of its members and threatened severe punishment against any minority which would only defy the Party's discipline or adopted policies. Significantly, however, recognizing the powerful influence of Bevan's views on German rearmament, the National Executive specifically exempted the issue of German arms from collective responsibility and allowed its members full freedom of expression. This was an important concession, which Bevan lost no time in exploiting. He and Wilson and other prominent Bevanites opened an active campaign among the members of the big trade unions to influence them to oppose arms for West Germany. "No Guns for the Huns" became a popular slogan which received an ever greater measure of support among the rank and file trade unionists in spite of the anti-Bevanite views of their leaders.

Herbert Morrison did not share Attlee's forbearance toward Bevan, and in an article in an obscure magazine, the *Socialist Commentary*, blasted Bevan's resignation, stating that this impetuous act would cost the Labour Party thirty seats in the next election. He also estimated that Bevan's "vermin" speech lost the Labour Party from thirty to fifty seats in 1950. Morrison argued, as he had done often in the past, that Labour could win a majority in Parliament only by gaining the support of the middle class, and this was impossible as long as the Party did not disavow once and for all the revolutionary slogans and the radical nationalization promises of the Bevanites.

Morrison's personal attack on Bevan was a flagrant breach of the rules laid down at the meeting of the Parliamentary Labour Party of October 23, 1952, which called on all Labour members to refrain from making personal attacks on one another, either in Parliament or in the press. While the article was gleefully quoted in British newspapers, it backfired on its author because it stamped Morrison as a violator of the standing orders of the Party and evoked widespread sympathy for Bevan as the victim of a harsh and vindictive personal attack. Attlee shrewdly exploited Morrison's mistake by delivering, at the meeting of the Parliamentary Labour Party on May 19, 1954, a gentle but firm rebuke to Morrison and Bevan for mutual personal attacks, thus strengthening his own position as the middle-ground and generally accepted leader.

In spite of the hopes of his enemies and the fears of his friends, Bevan's position grew stronger even as he returned to his obscure seat as a Labourite backbencher in the House. The Cooperative Party and two large trade unions went on record as supporting his oposition to German rearmament, and sixty-five Labour M.P.'s put their names to Bevan's motion that Parliamentary approval be secured before Britain start to manufacture the hydrogen bomb. Three Labour whips who were among the group were subsequently forced to recant or resign. The *New Statesman and Nation* answered Morrison's accusation that Bevan was responsible for Labour's election defeats by stating that Labour wants the floating vote, "but not if the price of that marginal gain is the sacrifice of the faith and the enthusiasm on which the Party depends on its existence." [12]

In June 1954 Bevan took the final step toward obtaining complete freedom of action. He announced his candidacy for the post of the Labour Party Treasurer, which was held by Hugh Gaitskell. He knew that he had no chance to unseat Gaitskell, who had the full support of the big trade unions and of Attlee and of Morrison, but the announcement of the candidacy automatically forced him to give up his sure seat on the National Executive. Bevan put the official leadership on notice that he intended to continue the fight for his views and for a position of power in the Party, and to attain freedom from the oppressive discipline and restraint which had hampered him in speaking out on issues which in his opinion had great popular appeal. He intended to carry the fight for his views on SEATO, the H-bomb, negotiations with the Soviet, and German rearmament to the floor of the Annual Conference. The *New Statesman and Nation* gave two reasons for Bevan's decision to enter the contest for Gaitskell's post: first, to free himself of the gag rule of the Executive, ". . . a position as intolerable to him temperamentally as it was unprofitable politically; secondly, because he was anxious to dramatize the contest for an office virtually in the gift of the trade union leaders. . . ." [13]

Michael Foot, a close collaborator of Bevan, frankly explained that Bevan had reached a saturation point in the support he received because of the firm opposition to him of the big trade unions. "His decisions to fight for the treasurership," Foot wrote, "therefore was part of an attempt to carry the argument into the trade unions." [14] The next step in Bevan's uphill and turbulent quest for power within the Labour Party was to obtain the support of the big trade unions in spite of their leaders' bitter hostility, or at least to obtain enough of a trade union following to force the big union bosses to give him their support for a top Party post.

In the early summer of 1954, Bevan, to the surprise of many, bought a country home, the Asheridge in Buckinghamshire, and the Tory newspapers began to refer to him sarcastically as the Squire of Asheridge. When asked by a reporter how he reconciled his Socialism with becoming a member of the landed gentry, Bevan replied that it was the typical land hunger of the farmer. This remark contained more than a kernel of truth, for Bevan's father had been a dispossessed farmer who had to earn a meager livelihood as a miner at Tredegar. Aneurin Bevan had not as yet, how-

ever, mellowed with age and with the attainment of moderate financial security and social success. Pictures of the
hard years of his childhood and young adulthood, spent in
the poverty-stricken depressed area of Ebbw Vale, were
deeply seared in his mind and gave him no rest. He remembered the degrading poverty of the miners living in the
grimy valleys, and the large country homes on the hills
above where the Tory mine owners lived. The Conservatives remained identified in his mind with the hated and
haughty owners of the mines, and he was determined more
than ever to fight them. He wanted power for himself because of his conviction that he was destined to assure for
the British workers a better deal, and for Britain a position
of leadership in the world based on independence from
"American dictation" and a negotiated peace and accommodation with the Soviet Union. He was a gentleman
farmer devoted to scientific raising of pigs on his Buckinghamshire farm, but to his constituents in Ebbw Vale he remained the poor miner's son who made good in London
and who was fighting with the Tory blighters for a better
deal for the Welsh workers and miners.

Shorn of Party rank, Bevan played the role of the perse-
cuted obscure backbencher to the hilt. A gullible American
reporter saw Bevan as a tragic and rejected figure of a man.
"Nye Bevan," he wrote, "was a changed and embittered
man. . . . Night after night he sat brooding in the 'Bevanite' corner of Commons Smoke Room. . . . The tragic figure of a saviour to whom nobody was grateful." [15] The hostile British press unintentionally created more sympathy for
Bevan when it made a sensation of a minor traffic accident
in which he was involved. Driving his flashy sport car,
Bevan sideswiped a bus at Gerrard's Cross in Beaconsfield,
recovered control, and went on without stopping. The bus
suffered no damage, but Bevan was identified and called

before a magistrate on a charge of hit-and-run driving. He told the judge that he did not stop because he wanted to avoid publicity, was fined the equivalent of $166.10, and his driver's license was suspended for three months. The newspapers made a *cause célèbre* of the prominent traffic offender, and Nye Bevan obligingly played the role of long-suffering martyr on whom misfortunes seemed to pile up almost daily. It is doubtful that he lost much sleep during these "tragic" months. He knew full well that the publicity did him no harm and helped to keep his name in the papers during a relative lull in his political activity.

In the summer of 1954, Aneurin Bevan, as confident, energetic, and affable as ever, agreed to lead with Attlee an official Labour Party delegation to Russia and Red China. This good-will visit, under the direct sponsorship of the Labour Party's National Executive, was evidence in itself of the strength of Bevan in spite of his minority status. The official Party leaders realized that it was easier to fight Bevan than to cope with the popular issues of Bevanism. They decided to steal Bevan's thunder and minimize the appeal of his popular position on Red China by sending an official delegation headed by Clement Attlee. Before leaving for the trip, Bevan went to his faithful constituents in Ebbw Vale to tell them exactly where he stood and to get a refreshing fill of their cheers and applause. He told them:

If you South Wales miners were in China, you would be communists, of course you would, I know you would. The Labour Party delegation is going to China, because they have been bottom dogs for a long time. We are going because we believe that the only people who can talk the language of the peasants and workers of China are the representatives of the peasants and workers of Great Britain.[16]

The audience cheered and hundreds patted good old Nyrin's broad shoulders.

Typically, after delivering himself of this revolutionary peroration and scaring the London *Times* and *The New York Times,* Bevan became a meek, agreeable, and well-disciplined member of the Labour delegation. He gave full deference to Attlee and steadfastly referred reporters to the leader of the delegation for statements. Bevan quickly impressed even the right-wing members of the group by his sharp questioning of the Red Chinese leaders and guides about political freedom, the right of free franchise, and the protection of rights of workers. He made no secret of the fact that while he held to his views on Red China's admission to the U.N., he was not impressed by Mao's "people's democracy." These tactics paid off handsomely. Bevan had no need to sound off and speak his mind on China. As was happening more and more frequently, his views were expressed by others who carried much more political weight. In this case, Bevan's job was done by none other than Clement Attlee, when he reported on the trip to the Annual Labour Party Conference at Scarborough. Bevan sat back smugly when Attlee, after expressing some grave doubts about the monolithic character of Red China, adopted Bevan's China policy, lock, stock, and barrel. There was absolutely nothing with which Bevan could disagree or which, as a matter of fact, he had not said many times before. Attlee reaffirmed Bevan's view that Red China was not "a mere satellite of Russia," [17] and that the Communist rulers were in effective control of the mainland of China and "have managed to unite the mass of the Chinese people behind them." [18] While he deplored the lack of political democracy, he praised the Red Chinese regime for abolishing corruption and crime and for raising health and sanitation standards. Mao's government, said Attlee, could also claim tremendous advance in the field of education and public housing.

In a remarkable change from his previously held position, Attlee for the first time endorsed Bevan's view that "Chiang Kai-shek and his immediate adherents, who are utterly discredited, should be retired, away to some safe place to end their lives in peace. . . . And I believe that after a period Formosa should be united back to China." [19] He also strongly supported Red China's claim to membership in the United Nations Assembly and to China's permanent seat on the Security Council.

Aneurin Bevan must have grinned with satisfaction when he heard Attlee's exposition of his stand on the SEATO defense organization. On April 13, 1954, a day before Bevan's resignation from the Shadow Cabinet on this very question, Attlee endorsed the Eden–Dulles agreement on the South-East Asia Treaty Organization and merely hinted at the desirability of having India join it. In reporting on the delegation's visit to Russia and Red China, Attlee stated, without equivocation, that he would like to see SEATO changed into an "all embracing organization with [Red] China in it too, just as we have the U.S.S.R. in U.N.O." [20] He concluded his report by fully endorsing Bevan's view that Chinese Communism is of a different variety than the Soviet brand and that the Red Chinese Communist leaders are kindly people with whom the West can do business, because "they apply their Communism with a good deal of elasticity." [21] Bevan and his supporters gave Attlee a warm round of applause. The adroit strategy of the astute Welshman was working better than he had every reason to expect. The trip of the official Labour Party delegation, during which Bevan was the acknowledged celebrity and the focus of attention, raised his prestige to new heights. He also managed to convince the Party leaders, including the trade union bosses, that if and when he were to be given proper consideration, he would stay within the bounds of Party discipline and loyalty. Attlee obviously felt that the consistent forbearance he had shown to Bevan was well justified.

Immediately upon his return, Bevan began to mobilize his forces for the showdown that was bound to come at the Annual Party Conference, scheduled to be held in Scarborough in October. While he knew that he had no chance to defeat Gaitskell for the treasurership, his hopes for the defeat of the National Executive's resolution on the addition of West German army units to NATO were bright, for a number of large trade unions had joined the Constituent Parties in opposing the Executive's stand.

The first battle at the conference concerned SEATO. A Constituent Labour Party introduced a resolution recording the Labour Party's opposition to any security pact in South-East Asia which would exclude any nation and which "has as its purpose the encirclement of China." [22] Jennie Lee warmly complimented Attlee for his "wise" report on Red China but asked him, "Clem, did I understand you rightly that you want us to support SEATO?" [23] She expressed firm opposition to SEATO because it excluded Red China, India, Indonesia, and Burma. The pact, she said, antagonized Nehru and increased Red Chinese fears of Western invasion. After a prolonged discussion, the Bevanite resolution lost by a vote of 2,570,000 to 3,669,000. A number of big unions defied their leaders and supported the dissidents.

On the second day of the conference the results of the balloting for the Executive Committee and the treasurership were announced. Gaitskell received 4,338,000 votes and Bevan got 2,032,000. Gaitskell's margin of victory was substantial, but Bevan made important inroads into the solid trade union bloc by getting the support of the Railwaymen and Shipworkers Unions. Bevan's brilliant lieutenant, Michael Foot, wrote after the conference: "Bevan's defeat is not the end of a career but the beginning of a campaign to inject a much needed dose of more active democracy into the constitution of the Labour Party. The party and the trade union machine sometimes become the enemy of democracy. . . . The fight to end this state of affairs in the Labour Party is now on." [24] One can doubt the validity of Foot's "democratization" issue, but he was right in putting the trade union leaders on notice that Bevan was determined to appeal over their heads and over their entrenched machines to the union members for support in the attainment of his goal—a position of top leadership in the Labour Party.

The resolution opposing "all proposals for German rearmament" [25] was introduced not by a Constituent Labour Party but by the powerful trade union of the Amalgamated Foundry Workers. R. W. Casasola, who introduced the motion, put the issue succinctly: "My union is opposed to arming Germany, East or West. Arms in the hands of Germans will only lead to war and a permanently divided Germany." [26] The opponents of German rearmament gave full expression to the deep distrust of the Germans whose ambitions to dominate Europe had led Britain to two world wars. Others stressed the incongruity of British Socialist support for the Christian Democratic Chancellor Adenauer and not of the West German Socialists. J. A. Birch, speaking on behalf of the Union of Shop Distributive and Allied Workers, stressed that the arming of West Germany would make any negotiations with Russia on free German elections difficult, if not impossible. "I believe," he said, "that the German Social Democrats and trade unionists have been absolutely right to stress the prior importance of reunification." [27] The debate was conducted in an atmosphere of tension and both the pro-Executive forces and the Bevanites, in defiance of the conference rules, interrupted the speakers with frequent heckling. Pandemonium broke loose during a speech of Desmond Donnelly, a young Labour M.P. who had become a supporter of German rearmament after a preconference visit to Russia, from which he returned convinced of Russia's aggressive intentions. He told the conference that opposition to German rearmament was wrong, and pointing his finger directly at Bevan said: ". . . some people will bear a heavy responsibility before history for their folly." [28] Bevanites howled, and Bevan told Donnelly to shut up. At that, Arthur Deakin rose and said: "You shut up!" The two glowered at each other and Deakin appealed to the chairman to protect the right of free speech at the conference. Herbert Morrison wound up the debate by pointing out that the Soviet Union had already rearmed East Germany and that Belgian, Dutch, and Norwegian Socialists wanted a German defense contribution to NATO. He concluded by pleading with the delegates "not to put us in a position whereby the Party is unduly fettered, which will result in injury and damage to us and will be inimical to the cause of peace and democracy throughout the world." [29]

The vote for the Executive's motion was 3,270,000 with 3,022,000 against. This was one of the closest votes on a major issue involving a position previously taken by the Executive in the history of Annual Conferences. The victory of the Executive was generally credited to Herbert Morrison, who through some ingenious behind-the-scene maneuvers succeeded in influencing the small Woodworkers Union (290,000 votes) to switch from opposition to the support of the Executive. The newspaper punsters immediately announced that the resolution squeezed through by a "wood shaving." If Bevan was deeply disappointed with the defeat which could have easily been his resounding victory and which could have propelled him to the Party's leadership, he did not show it. He lost on an issue which the *Manchester Guardian* termed a "gift of gods," but reporters were astounded to see him smiling with affability and confidence. He knew that the German vote was not a true test of his strength, because the coalition of left wingers, pacifists, crypto-Communists, and doctrinaire Socialists that constituted the anti-German vote did not support him on other issues, as the vote for the treasurership clearly demonstrated. In a clear-cut test of strength, on a motion for the suppression of American bomber bases in England, the Bevanites got only 1,822,000 votes against 6,400,000.

Bevan realized that his fight for control of the Labour movement had not yet reached a decisive stage. His next objective was still the big trade unions. In a speech to his followers he denounced Hugh Gaitskell, for whom he had an obvious personal dislike and whose cold and unemotional approach to Socialism rubbed him the wrong way. He put the union leaders on notice that he intended to get the support of the unions in spite of their opposition. "I know," he said, "the right kind of political leader for the Labour Party is a desiccated calculating machine who must not in any way permit himself to be swayed by indignation. . . . Power inside the movement no longer lies inside the Executive. I am going outside to meet it where it does lie." [30] Nye Bevan was still on his stubborn search for the source of power. Gaitskell too was put on notice that if he intended to become Attlee's successor by trampling over Bevan's lifetime ambition, he would have a fight on his hands. "I'll fight the blighter," he told his cohorts, "year after year, if necessary." [31] When informed of Bevan's threats, Arthur Deakin amiably commented, "Apparently in his disappointment Mr. Bevan lost his head." [32] Deakin was overoptimistic, as were many of Bevan's foes, who saw Scarborough as the end of Bevan's influence. The *Spectator* in its postconference editorial hopefully entitled "The End of Bevanism," dismissed the intellectual content of Bevanism as negligible and confidently predicted that Bevan would never be as powerful as he was before the German vote at the conference.[33] In the *New Statesman and Nation,* John Freeman argued against those who suggested that Bevan's defeats should cause the Labour Party's left to emancipate itself from its turbulent and widely hated and distrusted leader. He soberly pointed out that, "Mr. Bevan's is the only political voice in Britain, apart from Sir Winston's, which can command a hearing in almost any circumstances."[34]

The *Economist,* which disliked and distrusted Bevan but understood him best, provided a realistic and balanced appraisal of Bevan's fortunes following Scarborough. It pointed out that the vote on German rearmament was a cause for alarm because it showed that half of the Labour Party and a quarter of the politically-minded Britons were in the neutralist camp. "Those who pronounce Mr. Bevan's demise," the editorial continued, "forget how easily any demagogue of the left can find dupes. . . . His future tactics are clear; he will bid for the support of the unions' rank-and-file over the heads of their leaders—concentrating particularly on the 680,000 engineers and the 630,000 miners whose votes would together give him victory over Mr. Gaitskell at a future conference."[35]

The decisive stage of Bevan's bid for power was approaching. He was again gambling his entire political career, but he felt that since all other approaches and methods failed a direct challenge against the ruling Deakin–Gaitskell–Attlee–Morrison coalition could no longer be postponed.

~XIII~ The 1955 showdown— Bevan expelled from the Parliamentary Labor Party

IN THE early months of 1955, Aneurin Bevan played the dual roles of a humble backbencher and a leader of a powerful though unofficial faction of Bevanite M.P.'s with his customary skill and aplomb. He was free of the restraints imposed by membership in the Shadow Cabinet and the National Labour Party Executive and took full advantage of this freedom. He was, besides Churchill, the most avidly sought-after speaker in British politics, and his packed audiences were eager and enthusiastic. Bevan and his able lieutenants Foot, Crossman, and Mikardo concentrated on denouncing in speeches and articles, the official leadership of Attlee, Morrison, and Gaitskell as ineffective and bumbling. Attlee's nonpartisanship on foreign affairs and defense matters and his growing friendship with Churchill, his wartime comrade, irked and often exasperated the restless Welshman. Although he was deprived of any official Party post, Bevan's influence was strongly felt in the councils of the Labour Party.

The leaders continued to ignore Bevan, but they embraced Bevanism in an increasing measure. On February

23, 1955, the National Executive Committee adopted a resolution dealing with the American declaration that the United States armed forces would defend Formosa and the other offshore islands against any Red Chinese attack. The resolution stated that "the National Executive Committee urge the Government to make clear to the U. S. administration that it could not reckon on any military assistance from Britain in hostilities connected with the offshore islands and to exert their influence with the U.S.A. to obtain the withdrawal of Nationalist troops from those islands." [1]

The explosion came in the House of Commons on March 2, 1955, during a debate on the Government's White Paper on defense. Winston Churchill in opening the debate stressed that the possession of the H-bomb by Great Britain might induce the Soviet Union to negotiate with the West and abandon the policies of the cold war. He pointed out that Britain and America must have enough retaliatory military power to deter Soviet aggression. The speech was not among Churchill's memorable utterances in the House, but it received the thoughtful attention of members of both parties.

Aneurin Bevan, well prepared, took the floor to deliver one of the major and most skillful speeches of his long Parliamentary career. He denounced Churchill's alleged lack of imagination and mediocrity of thinking "concealed by the majesty of his language." [2] Bevan declared that the basic problem of the world—the maintenance of peace—cannot be achieved by military men or by scientists. "The scientists have spoken," he said, "we have had enough of science. It is time to have a little more wisdom." [3] He disputed Churchill's contention that Britain's possession of the H-bomb would make the Russians more eager to negotiate with the West. Bevan contended that the Soviets were ready to meet at a top-level conference but they were rebuffed by the British Government. Gleefully exploiting an opportunity to accuse the Government of taking orders from America, Bevan asked Churchill, "Why is it that he does not insist upon meetings with Russian leaders? . . . It may be that the right hon. Gentleman would like to do it, but that the United States will not permit him." [4]

Winston Churchill, inexplicably, interrupted Bevan and related that he was ready to meet Malenkov at a top-level conference and wanted to see President Eisenhower on the project, but had been "struck with complete paralysis." [5] After his recovery, Churchill told the House, he was not successful in persuading Eisenhower "to join in that process." [6]

Bevan immediately resumed his attack and triumphantly declared, "I think that the whole House is grateful to the right hon. Gentleman for his intervention and for the frankness he has displayed. *I am bound, to point out, however, that it is complete confirmation of what I have said*" [7] [italics mine].

Turning to speak on German rearmament Bevan noticed the absence from the House of Attlee and Morrison. Without a moment's hesitation he delivered a biting rebuke to his own Party leaders and told them: "I would like my hon. Friends to listen. We are very worried." [8] Attlee did not forget this rebuke and mentioned it a few weeks later during an attack on Bevan's lack of Party loyalty. Concluding his address, Bevan demanded a clear and unequivocal answer to this central question: ". . . if [Soviet] aggression would take place in Europe with conventional weapons, will America and Britain use nuclear weapons and thus invite the destruction of Great Britain. . . . The question is whether we intend to use nuclear weapons at once in the event of aggression of whatever type?" [9] Bevan defiantly declared that he would expect an answer to the question from the Government and also a policy declaration from the leaders of the Opposition. This was an unprecedented move which caused a storm in Parliament.

Harold Macmillan, the Defense Minister, declined to answer, explaining that he would prefer to answer after he heard the distinguished Leader of the Opposition. Macmillan was obviously hoping that Attlee would rescue him by ignoring Bevan's question and Attlee did precisely as the Government had hoped he would do. He began by complimenting Churchill for describing "with great power the position in the world today" [10] and launched a strong attack on Russia's aggressive intentions. Attlee fully endorsed the American doctrine of massive retaliation and stated: "They [the Russians] must also realize, and this is essential, that the free peoples are resolved to preserve their freedom and they have the means for instant retaliation and that they will use these means in the event of open aggression." [11]

Thus Attlee did not only ignore Bevan's stand and question, but hinted as strongly as he could that the Russians should not count on the British not using nuclear weapons in case of Russian aggression in Europe, even with conventional arms. The Government's spokesman, in winding up the debate, also declined to give a clear answer to Bevan, but merely reaffirmed Britain's determination to retaliate for any aggression with all means at her disposal.[12] He also expressed the Government's gratitude to Clement Attlee for the position he had taken. This was too much for Bevan to endure.

Angry and flushed, he stood up and, directly facing Attlee, asked him, "What we want to know is whether the use of the words to which I have referred in our Amendment associates us [the Labour Party] with the statement that we should use thermonuclear weapons in circumstances of hostilities, although they were not used against us." [13]

Attlee, pale and taken aback by this extraordinary treatment accorded to a Party Leader by a member of his own Party, more hurt than angry answered. "My right hon. Friend is asking me that question. I am answering this in the most general terms. I am not referring to anything in the White Paper, but to the general thesis with which I think my right hon. Friend agrees that deterrents by the possession of thermonuclear weapons are the best way of preventing another war." [14] Attlee courageously and patriotically refused to assure the Soviet leaders that they might commit an aggression with conventional weapons without fear of bringing about an atomic holocaust.

When the vote on the Labour amendment came, Bevan and sixty-one of his diehard followers abstained, but another surprise rocked the House when it became clear that several of his close and prominent collaborators had deserted him and supported the Party's official stand. Richard Crossman was one of those who decided publicly to break with his leader, at least on this important issue. He supported Bevan's demand for a top-level conference with Russia, but declared that those who had accepted the existence of NATO, including Bevan, ought to be consistent and be ready to accept the military consequences for Britain resulting from this membership.[15]

John Freeman, another prominent Bevanite, also agreed that it would have been folly for the Government and for the Opposition to announce that the hydrogen bomb would not be used, because the value of this fearsome weapon would have thus been lost. But Freeman made it clear that the Labour's left wing could not afford to repudiate Bevan's leadership. He wrote, "We should be innocent too, if we believed that despite the tragic events of the last few days, the Left can function effectively without Mr. Bevan. Inside

and outside the Labour Party he is the only distinctly Socialist voice in Britain, which carries authority all over the
world." [16]

Why did Bevan decide to challenge the Party's leadership
and risk his expulsion at that particular time? First, he was
genuinely distressed with the ineffective opposition of the
Labour Party and disgusted with the bipartisanship of Attlee and Morrison on foreign policy and defense. Second,
the H-bomb was tailormade for the rank and file campaign
on which he had to embark if he was to obtain a top position on the Party's hierarchy. Third, Bevan believed that
the Labour Party would lose the forthcoming elections
(which were to take place in May 1955) and his dramatic
break with the discredited leaders would allow him and his
supporters to step in, after the defeat, as the "saviors" of
Labour's cause. Fourth, the clash made it possible for Bevan
to dramatize himself and his views. And finally, he was tired
of playing the role of the humble backbencher. Bevan realized that he was taking a calculated risk but there is every
reason to suppose that he was convinced that Attlee and
Morrison and Gaitskell would not be able to muster enough
strength to expel him from the Party or make the expulsion
stick. The risk was even smaller because Bevan knew that
his constituents in Ebbw Vale would stand by him no matter what punishment the Party leaders would mete out to
him. As events have shown, he proved again that he knew
the mood and the temper of the Labour Party better than
his opponents.

The Shadow Cabinet, reportedly against Attlee's wishes,
recommended to the Parliamentary Labour Party that it
withdraw the whip from Bevan and report him to the
National Executive Committee. It was assumed that the
P.L.P. would recommend the supreme penalty, expulsion
from the Party. To strengthen its position with the rank and

file members and in recognition of the strength and popularity of Bevan's views, the Shadow Cabinet simultaneously adopted a resolution to introduce a motion in Parliament in favor of an immediate Big Four conference.

Bevan became overnight a *cause célèbre,* and all of Britain followed the case with bated breath. The newspapers were filled with reports and speculation and the Labour Party received a great deal of unsolicited advice from all quarters. The overwhelming weight of the advice was simple: "Kick him out, and the sooner the better." The *Spectator* called Bevan "the cancer in the Labour Party" and warned Attlee and Morrison that any retreat from Bevan's punishment would make the "Labour Leadership look contemptible and ridiculous." [17]

The *New Statesman and Nation* solemnly warned that expulsion of Bevan would result in a split in the Party because "the militant workers of the constituency parties and trade union branches would not meekly accept the decision of the block vote." [18] The Bevanite *Tribune* angrily came to the defense of its leader. Its editors correctly pointed out that sixty Labour members abstained with Bevan on the official Labour motion on defense and asked why Bevan was singled out for punishment. Answering its own question, the *Tribune* editorial bluntly charged that "a few Right-Wing leaders of the party, backed by elements in the Parliamentary Labour Party and on the General Council of the T.U.C., have long wished to silence him [Bevan]. They feared and fear more than ever today, the growing response to his appeal in the constituency Labour parties, in the trade unions and in the country as a whole . . . now they press for the kill." [19] Writing in the same issue of the *Tribune,* Bevan listed three major issues which, in his opinion, urgently required negotiations with the Soviet Union: the pacification of the Middle East, the status of Formosa and the admission of "New" China to the United Nations, and the future of Germany.[20]

Bevan's trial took place in the New Palace of Westminster, in Room 14, with about 290 members of the Parliamentary Labour Party present. Clement Attlee presented the Shadow Cabinet's case against Bevan. He cited his opposition in Parliament to the Party's policy on SEATO and his outburst during the defense debate on March 2. He demanded, although without great enthusiasm, that Bevan be expelled. There was no applause when Attlee sat down. Aneurin Bevan rose to offer his defense. He cited many instances of breaches of Party discipline in the past and recalled several cases when offenses against Attlee's authority went unpunished. He bluntly charged that his expulsion was demanded by the right-wing trade union bosses who were scared by his growing influence with the rank and file unionists. "Those who hold the money bags," he said, "demand my expulsion. They have given orders. They await a decision." [21] He affirmed his loyalty to the Labour Party. "I am now 57 years of age. I have given 45 years of my life to this party. My fundamental loyalties are still with it. I am not going out to form a new party." [22]

Attlee's obvious reluctance to press for drastic action, Bevan's strong defense, and the widespread demands for leniency influenced many Labour M.P.'s to seek a compromise solution. An amendment to substitute expulsion by censure was voted down by only eight votes—132 to 124. Impressed by Morrison and Gaitskell that a defeat of the motion for expulsion would be a shattering blow to the official Party leadership, Attlee finally stated that in case of an adverse vote he would resign as Party Leader and thus made the vote a direct choice between himself and Bevan. On this vote of confidence, which was actually forced upon Attlee by a woman M.P. who asked Attlee if he would resign if rebuffed by the P.L.P., the recommendation of the Shadow Cabinet was adopted by a slim majority of fourteen votes, 141 to 112. The victory of the anti-Bevan leaders was a Pyrrhic one. There was a general feeling that the Shadow Cabinet underestimated Bevan's strength and made a clumsy attempt to "get" him on trumped-up charges. The sense of fair play of many Britons, even those who heartily disliked Bevan, was outraged by the harsh punishment which did not suit the rather common offense of political unorthodoxy. As one historian pointed out, Bevan's "offense against Attlee was singled out for discipline even though it was appreciated that Bevan had spoken the sentiments of his followers and perhaps of some others as well." [23] The Bevanite section decided to exploit the division within the Parliamentary Labour Party to the fullest. The *Tribune,* instead of defending and pleading for Bevan, launched a strong attack on Bevan's foes. A fighting editorial said: "This week the Parliamentary Labour Party has made one of the most stupid and reckless decisions ever made by an adult political Party." [24] The editorial went on to assert that the decision to punish Bevan would have to be rescinded because of the storm of protest and indignation it aroused in the Constituent Labour Parties and among the rank and file membership of the trade unions.

The embattled Aneurin Bevan received support in a typically and uniquely British fashion from the Conservative Prime Minister and a Conservative Cabinet Member. Speaking at a political rally at Woodford, Winston Churchill stressed that the first duty of an M.P. is to his own judgment and conscience, his second duty is to his constituents, and only is it "in the third place that a man's duty to the party organization or program takes rank." In a direct reference to Bevan's case, Churchill continued: "Latitude and tolerance ought to be allowed to members of a party and leaders should prove their capacity to cope in the House of Commons and on the platform, with personal opponents, however misguided or ambitious they might happen to be." [25] J. A. Bevins, M.P. and Conservative Parliamentary Secretary to the Ministry of Works, stated in a widely quoted speech that Bevan should stay in the Labour Party to provide effective opposition leadership which, in his judgment, was a necessary part of the British political system. "I could make," Bevins concluded, "the same speeches as Gaitskell makes in the House of Commons, though perhaps not as well. Only the Bevanite section of the House of Commons can provide an effective opposition." [26]

Even the *Economist* asked, ". . . what possessed the Shadow Cabinet at their fatal meeting last week?" [27] While it reaffirmed its dislike and distrust of Bevan, the *Economist* expressed serious doubt whether Bevan was treated fairly by his colleagues. It said: "It is still possible to feel doubts about a party system that imposes such extreme penalty for offenses which are so difficult to define—and which, when defined, seem to be matters of personality and behavior rather than policy." [28] The editorial went further to advise the Labour leaders to compromise with Bevan or face a possible defeat at the Annual Conference. Clement Attlee heeded the advice and, following his own obvious distaste for the entire affair, himself pushed through the Executive, by a vote of fourteen to thirteen, a motion which called on Bevan to appear before an eight-man committee to give assurances of future good behavior.

Bevan appeared before the disciplinary committee and ingeniously succeeded in apologizing and scolding his foes for persecuting him for his political convictions. He stated that he had not intended to cause Attlee any embarrassment. "[But] if my actions or speech could lend themselves to the interpretation that such was my motive," he said, "then I am sincerely sorry and I apologize to Mr. Attlee for any pain I may have caused him. I ask for nothing more than the opportunity to serve our party under his leadership." [29] Having delivered this humble apology, Bevan proceeded to deliver a cautious rebuke to those who would restrict the right of members to hold honest differences of views and opinions, especially on the basic question of how "to apply the principles of Socialism to a particular situation." [30]

The Executive Committee accepted Bevan's apology and gave up the recommendation for his expulsion from the Party, but voted by a majority of sixteen to seven a strong resolution approving the withdrawal of the whip from him by the Parliamentary Labour Party. The National Executive also warned that it would take drastic action against violators of Party discipline. These resolutions were correctly appraised as face-saving devices; Aneurin Bevan had passed another crisis in his political life and surprisingly came out stronger and not weaker from the ordeal. The *Economist* made a correct diagnosis of the patient's political health when it said, "Mr. Bevan now seems better placed than ever before in the struggle for the Labour leadership which has always been his primary aim." [31] Bevan's lieutenants and followers were jubilant, and claimed a victory for their hero over the official leadership of the Labour Party. The *Tribune* correctly claimed that Morrison, Gaitskell, and the trade union leaders suffered a defeat and failed to expel or silence Bevan because of the tremendous outpouring of sympathy for the Welsh leader. The National Executive Committee backed down because

The protests throughout the constituency parties and from trade union branches have been widespread and instantaneous. . . . The Gallup Poll showed how heavy was the opposition among the active Labour workers and among the bulk of the Labour voters. Floods of letters have poured in to Mr. Attlee and Transport House not only from all over the country but from all over the world.[32]

Even if one discards the degree of exaggeration of the *Tribune,* it was clear that the Labour leaders backed down because they were uncertain whether the Labour Party Conference would uphold Bevan's expulsion.

Weary after weeks of strife and conflict, Aneurin Bevan needed the stimulation and the warmth of Tredegar's meeting halls and streets, where he knew that men and women would hail him as a conquering hero. He was not disappointed. Ebbw Vale once again gave him an enthusiastic welcome and Bevan made it clear that he was unbowed and unrepentant. He told his audience:

I solemnly declare that I am not prepared to buy a successful public life at the cost of a shameful silence about things I think should be heard. . . . I am not developing a persecution complex. . . . All I am asking from my movement is the same amount of toleration as I am ready to give. I don't want expulsion.[33]

Bevan was ready not to ask for the expulsion of the right wingers like Hugh Gaitskell and Arthur Deakin, provided that he was allowed to propagate his own doctrines. Even in the face of this unrepentant audacity, the leadership wrote a sorry epilogue to its debacle by restoring the whip to Bevan late in April.

The Labour Party lost the General Election in May 1957, when the Conservatives won a majority of sixty-seven seats. Aneurin Bevan remained discreetly but tellingly silent when his followers charged that the Party leaders caused the defeat by persecuting the popular Welsh hero. The Execu-

tive Committee did nothing to dispel these insinuations
when it appointed in September a devoted Bevanite, Harold
Wilson, to chair a committee to inquire into the reasons of
Labour's defeat. Wilson later issued a report which chival-
rously laid the primary blame on the faulty Party machinery, and in June, after the new Parliament convened,
Bevan was easily elected to the Shadow Cabinet together
with Harold Wilson. This time he was not the twelfth man
and was not alone. Bevan got a better seat on Labour's
front bench and was given frequent assignments to speak
in debates on behalf of the Party.

The partial victory over the official leadership convinced
Bevan that he must continue his efforts to get the support
of a substantial number of trade union members over the
heads of their hostile leaders. He was determined to put
his foes on notice that he would continue to fight for a top
Party post, and again announced his candidacy for the
treasurership of the Labour Party, in opposition to his bitterest foe and rival, Hugh Gaitskell. In an article called
"Why I am Standing for Treasurer," Bevan asserted that the
Labour Party lost the May General Election because it had
no clear and aggressive domestic and foreign Socialist
policy. He claimed that the great majority of the trade union
membership "is ready for a new forward thrust" [34] and
denounced the "bloc vote" system at Annual Conference
which assures the dominance of the big unions and stifles
the free expression of the rank and file members. In a rare
moment of self-appraisal, Bevan answered those who had
accused him of unbounded ambition. He wrote, "This is a
curious charge. I would have thought that ambition con-
sisted in coming to terms with the powerful and not in
challenging them at the very center of their power." He
admitted that his chances to beat Gaitskell were nil, but

asserted that the challenge itself was important because "the party will never regain its health until the stranglehold of bureaucracy is broken."[35]

The main subject of debate at the conference was the manufacture by Britain of hydrogen bombs. The conference was called upon to ratify the decision of the National Executive Committee taken on March 30, 1955, which reaffirmed the Labour Party's support for NATO as a vital deterrent to Soviet aggression, and declared that as long as there was a great disparity between the military power of Russia and that of the West "unilateral disarmament is folly."[36] On the controversial question of the hydrogen bomb, the Executive stated that since the United States and the Soviet Union had the H-bomb, the Labour movement considered that Great Britain should have it too, in order to assure Britain's influence for peace. Without equivocation the Executive concluded: "It was for that reason that the Labour Government decided on the manufacture of the atom bomb, and that we support the production of the hydrogen bomb in this country."[37]

The opposition to the Executive's stand was led by Konni Zilliacus, who moved a resolution which called the H-bomb manufacture by Britain "economically wasteful and militarily futile"[38] and urged British initiative in convening a top-level conference with Russia and Red China, with or without the United States, to achieve "peaceful co-existence."[9] Zilliacus' motion did not outrightly call for a ban on H-bomb manufacture, but demanded a study of the effects of hydrogen bomb tests. The debate was short and not very spirited. The top Bevanites did not take the floor and only two large unions, the Amalgamated Engineering Union and the Amalgamated Union of Foundry Workers, came out in opposition to the official Party policy. The resolution offered by Zilliacus was defeated by a vote of 4,330,000 to 1,995,000.

It was evident that Aneurin Bevan refused to make the H-bomb question the battle cry of the conference. He was once again in a period of his best behavior, hoping to convince Gaitskell, whose star was rapidly rising, and the big union bosses that they could do business with him. Such a change of tactics required a great deal of patience and he proved that he was capable of keeping his volatile character in check.

It was surely difficult for Bevan to restrain himself from giving a strong rebuttal to a programmatic speech of Hugh Gaitskell, in which Attlee's heir presumptive in effect gave up the ghost of the principle of nationalization as the Labour movement had known it for many decades. Gaitskell's view was the opposite of Bevan's famous doctrine of the necessary agony of public ownership. He bluntly told his comrades that the Labour Party's defeats in the general election in 1950, 1951, and 1955 came because "we failed in those years to get across our nationalization proposals to the people." [40] The incoming Labour Party leader told the conference that no further attempts at nationalization would be made unless a thorough study of a particular industry clearly demonstrated that public ownership would be of benefit to the industry, to the standard of living conditions of its workers, and to the general public. "We have to show," Gaitskell said, "that nationalization is related to economic security, we have to show that it is related to greater equality and to a new spirit in industry, that it is a necessity for economic planning." [41] To those who would say to him that by expressing these views he ceased to be a Socialist, Gaitskell said to stop the name-calling and to face the realities of Labour's defeats at the polls.

The official report of the 1954 Conference notes that Gaitskell's speech was accepted with "loud and prolonged applause." [42] The Labour Party made in domestic policy a decided swing to the right, and Aneurin Bevan apparently considered it futile to oppose it. He was getting older, and if he were to reach his life's ambition it would have to come soon. He was ready for a bargain and would renounce his radical views on domestic issues in exchange for an important post on the Shadow Cabinet dealing with foreign affairs.

ᨳXIV ᨳ   "The New Nye"

WHILE MUCH of his political philosophy and world outlook, known as Bevanism, was adopted by the Labour Party, Bevan himself was restrained to cooling his temper as an obscure member of the Shadow Cabinet. He was clearly becoming impatient with his lack of progress in the climb toward a top Party post. At fifty-eight, he saw the much younger Gaitskell advance to a position of leadership with the full support of Attlee, Morrison, and the trade union leaders. Bevan, in excellent health, was still full of bounce and energy, but his unruly hair was turning white. He was spending a great deal of time on his farm in Buckinghamshire raising flowers and pigs in the best tradition of distinguished British politicians. But the dream of leadership and the ambition to become Britain's Prime Minister or at least its Foreign Secretary, was as strong in him as ever.

Early in December 1955 Bevan got a chance to renew his bid for leadership. Clement Attlee, of whom Churchill unkindly said that he was modest "because he had a lot to be modest about," but who in reality was firmly believed to be the most suitable man to lead the Labour Party, finally resigned his post. Bevan immediately announced his candidacy for the vacant post. He fully realized that he had no chance to win, because Hugh Gaitskell's election was assured by the support of the official leadership of the Transport House. But Bevan again wanted to put the union bosses on notice that he was not giving up the fight and that sooner or later they would have to accept him into their inner circle. Gaitskell won the election with a clear majority over the combined votes of Bevan and Herbert Morrison, who made a pathetic but hopeless bid to gain the post due him on the basis of seniority and long and distinguished service to the Party. Deeply hurt, Morrison resigned as Deputy Leader on December 14. Bevan announced his candidacy, hoping that this time he would be unopposed. He was disappointed when the popular and generally acceptable James Griffith was prevailed upon to run against him. The election was close, but Griffith won. Aneurin Bevan was stung and angered by this second humiliating defeat suffered in a short period of time. He bitterly resented the implacable opposition of the trade union leaders, which continued in spite of Bevan's acknowledged effort to mend his ways and to comply with Party regularity.

Two days after his second defeat, Bevan threw away many of the assets and much of the good will he had been carefully accumulating and loosed an angry blast at the Labour Party's official leadership. In a fiery speech in Manchester he attacked those leaders whose Socialism stemmed from their studies in economics and not from moral fervor and working-class solidarity. This barb was clearly aimed at Gaitskell. Bevan further blasted the Party's bureaucracy for enforcing unnecessary discipline and discouraging honest differences of opinion. "I know," he added, "these are words that are going to get me into trouble, but I am not a Communist. I am a democratic socialist. . . . The trouble with the movement is that decisions are being reached on top and imposed on the bottom."[1] Strangely enough, these denunciations did not get Bevan into trouble, as he expected. On the contrary, he was shortly informed by Gaitskell of his appointment to the important post of Colonial Secretary on the Shadow Cabinet.

The reasons for this unexpected solicitude for Bevan were many and complex. Hugh Gaitskell intelligently reasoned that he needed the Welshman, in spite of their long-standing mutual personal dislike, to solidify his leadership and assure the support of the left wing. The new Labour Party leader was well aware of his lack of popular appeal to the masses of Labour's rank and file members and his limited oratorical prowess, and he wisely decided to supplement this lack with Nye Bevan's dynamic oratory and mass appeal. Above all, Gaitskell wanted to see the Labour Party's return to power after its repeated election defeats in the last eleven years. Such a victory, he was convinced, would come only after unity was restored to the Party and after Bevan's complete and wholehearted support was assured. It was generally agreed in the high councils of the Labour movement that Bevan's rifts with the leadership cost the Labour Party several General Elections.

Bevan too was ready for a peaceful accommodation with the leadership. He became of necessity reconciled to the idea that Hugh Gaitskell, while still a "desiccated adding machine," was the choice of the overwhelming majority of the Labour M.P.'s and the trade unions because his moderation and caution and lack of spectacular appeal were fully in keeping with the type of a leader traditionally preferred by the Labour Party. Bevan no doubt considered himself much better equipped than Gaitskell to lead Labour back to power, but the years of strife and battling brought him to a realization that he would never be admitted to the charmed circle of the official leadership on his own terms. He was called upon to prove that he could be an amiable colleague, respectful of Party discipline, and above all a

loyal member of Hugh Gaitskell's term. This being his best
chance to achieve, even if in part only, his life's ambition,
Bevan was ready to accept the challenge.

The reconciliation was also made possible by a very
propitious, from Nye Bevan's point of view, change in the
leadership of the Trades Union Congress. The unexpected
death of Arthur Deakin, who hated Bevan, brought Frank
Cousins to the powerful post of General Secretary of the
Transport and General Workers Union late in 1955. Had
Sir Arthur Deakin lived, Bevan's climb to power and leadership would have been tortuous, if not impossible. Frank
Cousins, on the other hand, was a personal friend of Bevan
and was considered a mild left winger. His background
was remarkably similar to Bevan's. He too was a miner's son
and had suffered poverty and deprivation in his younger
years.

Cousins was born in Bulwell, in Nottinghamshire, but
spent his childhood and early manhood in Doncaster, and
regarded himself a Yorkshireman. Like Bevan, he was
born to a large and poor family and went to the pit at the
age of eleven. At eighteen he began to drive colliery trucks
and later moved to long-distance haulage; at twenty-five,
like Bevan, he participated actively in the 1926 General
Strike and saw the bitterness and the suffering which he
never forgot. His father went on strike and his father-in-law,
a railway clerk, was victimized for seven months for defending the strikers—in public. In 1938 Frank Cousins became a
union organizer; he rapidly climbed to a position of importance in the Transport Union and became a section
secretary in the union's headquarters in London. Deakin
tolerated Cousins because of his ability, courage, and intelligence, but considered him a dangerous left winger.
Although to Deakin, who was obsessed with a fear of
Communism and Communist infiltration of the unions,

Frank Cousins' views might have sounded very radical,
Cousins could not be classed as a Bevanite. The *Observer*
(London) characterized Cousin's ideology as middle-road
Socialism. It wrote,

He wants a planned economy, but he wants a trade union movement sufficiently strong to be the chief determinant of wages.
. . . He is a socialist consciously, if at times slowly, working to
shape a society from which one day the private motive will have
been eliminated.[2]

Frank Cousins, who had a personal affection for Bevan,
was fully in agreement with Gaitskell's efforts to achieve a
high degree of Party unity. He reversed Deakin's policy
of cooperation of the trade unions with the Government
on holding the wage levels, and he needed the full, united
political support of the Labour Party for his new radical
stand. Cousins considered Bevan's cooperation essential.
The new triumvirate of Gaitskell, Cousins, and Bevan was
ready to lead the Labour Party to an election victory, but
Bevan had still to show that he would not get out of step
with his new allies. Many of his enemies were predicting
that the notorious rebel would soon show his true colors and
turn on Hugh Gaitskell and his leadership, and he had to
move fast to convince everybody that he was really turning
a new leaf in his political career.

The "New Nye," as he was soon referred to by the British
press, began his period of reformation by showing a large
degree of politeness and amiability in Parliamentary debates. Soon many Conservative and Labour members had
on occasion to rub their eyes to make sure that the man
speaking from the box was Nye Bevan.

During a debate in February 1956 on a Government bill
to reduce by more than half the subsidies for building
homes, Bevan, who was proud of his accomplishments in the

area of public housing, was mild and restrained in his attack. He scolded the Government for its reluctance to engage in a largescale building program to clear slums and provide homes for low-income families, but he was thoughtful and amiable. Duncan Sandys, the Minister of Housing and Local Government, graciously acknowledged Bevan's moderation. "I am sure," he said, "that we have all listened with enjoyment to the characteristic speech of the right hon. Gentleman the Member for Ebbw Vale. . . . The right hon. Member . . . yesterday referred to his own amiability in the course of the debate, and I should like to thank him for it." [3]

After assuming his task as Colonial Secretary in the Shadow Cabinet, Bevan in a short time drew the applause and approval of Gaitskell and the other Party leaders and of the great majority of the British press. As in the period of his tenure as Minister of Health and Housing, he used his agile intelligence with great sense of responsibility. His speeches on colonial affairs were well constructed, effective, and provided ample proof that Bevan was making a determined effort to study the conditions in British colonies and mandated territories thoroughly and objectively. Officials in the British Colonial Office were pleasantly surprised with Bevan's grasp of British colonial policies, and they soon realized that their fear of his well-known left-wing views was unfounded. Bevan did not agree with all the policies of the colonial officials, but he had no intention of contributing to the liquidation of the British colonial system and he showed a healthy respect for the basic interests of the British Empire. Once again, the ogre proved to be a reasonable and sensible opponent, and in a short time Bevan succeeded in gaining the grudging respect of Alan Lennox-Boyd, the Conservative Colonial Secretary.

In March 1956, Bevan participated, on behalf of the

British Labour Party, in a full-dress debate on the Cyprus issue. He offered a weak motion expressing regret that the negotiations with Cypriot leaders had broken down, and urging their resumption.[14] In a brilliant and lengthy analysis of the Cyprus problem, Bevan urged the Government to determine whether it wants "to have Cyprus as a base, or a base in Cyprus," [5] and act accordingly. He declared that the Government should grant the Cypriot population self-government with the understanding that the British would continue to have a military base on the island. Bevan unequivocally acknowledged that the British Government needed the Cyprus base to fulfill its NATO obligations and to protect the free flow of Middle Eastern oil to England and to Western Europe. He advocated that potential foes and allies alike be put on notice that Britain considered free access to the oil resources in the Middle East vital to its economic military and political survival. "The Soviet Union" he said,

has been given to understand, and, indeed, should understand, . . . that access to Middle-Eastern oil is an absolute essential for Western society. The United States, also, should understand that British access to Middle-Eastern oil is a British necessity as well as American, and that American oil interests ought not consider that it is a safe thing to play with British embarrassments in the Middle East in order to extend their own interests there.[6]

This statement was warmly cheered by all sections of the House, including the right-wing rebels of the Conservative Party.

Bevan disputed the Government's position—that it discontinued negotiations with Archbishop Makarios because it had evidence of his connections with Cypriot terrorists—by pointing out that British Governments in the past negoti-

ated with Nehru of India, Dr. Nkrumah of the Gold
Coast, and Ben Gurion of Israel in spite of their known
connections with underground independence groups and
organizations.

In February 1956 Aneurin Bevan was appointed by Lord
Chancellor Viscount Kilmuir a member of a round table
conference, consisting of experts from Parliament and the
House of Lords, to inquire into the status of Malta. He
worked on the commission in full harmony with the Conservative members and the representatives of the Colonial
Office. In a speech he made in Parliament, in the course of
the debate on the report of the conference, Bevan expressed
sympathy for the Government's position and declared that
he did not wish to add to its difficulties. He conceded a priori
that Malta, an important British naval base, could not yet be
granted full independence. "How are we to satisfy," he
said, "the national desires of Malta for status if we *cannot*
give Malta a complete self-government? In what other way
can we do it? This is the crux of the whole matter." [7] He
recommended the integration of Malta into the United
Kingdom, a step which would have assured the Maltese
population of direct representation in the British Parliament.

Bevan kept his temper and emotions in check even during the heated debates on the explosive Mau Mau rebellion
in Kenya. His was the calm voice of reasonableness. As
usual, he spoke on behalf of the Labour Party after a
thorough study and preparation. He knew Kenya's social,
agricultural, and political problems as well as any expert of
the Colonial Office, and in a reflective mood he pointed out
to Parliament that Britain was facing serious trouble in
many of its colonial territories, including Cyprus, Singa-
pore, Aden, Malta, and Kenya. He made it clear that he
did not advocate any radical solutions, certainly not a

British withdrawal, and he stressed that he did not blame Alan Lennox-Boyd, the Minister of Colonies. Bevan declared that the colonial troubles should not be construed as "a criticism of the holder of the existing office, nor am I making it a reflection upon his predecessors, on either side of the House; . . . I am not attacking the Colonial Office, nor any of the officials, who are, within their limits and powers, most courteous and attentive. . . ." [8] He expressed the "utmost abhorrence" of the crimes committed by the Mau Mau terrorists and acknowledged the necessity of suppressing the terror and restoring law and order, but he pleaded for humane treatment of prisoners and detainees and urged that the Government assure a greater representation for the natives in Kenya's legislative assembly.

In August 1956 Bevan expressed the feelings of a large segment of British public opinion, including many Conservatives, when he protested the arrest and exile of Archbishop Makarios of Cyprus. He decried the step as injurious to Britain's standing with the uncommitted nations of the world. The action, he said, was "a lovely present to Mao Tse-tung, to Khrushchev, to Colonel Nasser, and every one now attacking British Imperialism." [9] In a flash of temper reminiscent of the old Bevan, he cried out: "Good heavens, look at the Front Bench opposite. A bigger collection of guileless ignoramuses I have never seen in my life." [10] He gave a lefthanded compliment to Lennox-Boyd by telling him that in dealing with the homogeneous African population, his reputation was all right, "but when he has to do with plural communities, his reputation is becoming rotten." [11]

Utilizing the respect he was gaining by his brilliant performance as the Labour Party's spokesman on colonial affairs and assured by Gaitskell's neutrality, Bevan announced that he was once again a candidate for the post of

Treasurer of the Labour Party. It seemed for a time that
Bevan's candidacy would go unchallenged and that he
would be elected without opposition, but it soon became
clear that some of the big union leaders had not forgotten
Bevan's past transgressions and had decided to block his
election. While the powerful National Union of Mine
Workers and the National Union of Railwaymen announced
that they would back Bevan, the Amalgamated Engineering Union decided to nominate Charles Parnell, M.P., for
the job. The leaders of the Union of Shop Distributive and
Allied Workers were successful in preventing, by devious
parliamentary tactics, Bevan's endorsement, which was
strongly backed by the overwhelming majority of the rank
and file of the union.

The battle was joined when the largest of the big unions,
the Transport and General Workers, nominated George
Brown, M.P., a Bevan foe of long standing. Luckily for
Bevan, Frank Cousins, the boss of the T. & G. W., refrained
from an open endorsement of Brown. Had he done so,
Bevan's defeat at the forthcoming Labour Party conference
would have been almost certain. The anti-Bevan forces
mobilized their full strength in support of the candidacy of
George Brown, while the Bevanites worked hard to assure
the support of the Constituent Labour Parties and of the
unions. The election was clearly a toss-up, and no one was
able to predict the outcome with any certainty.

The Labour Conference, which opened on October 1,
1956, in Blackpool, met in an atmosphere of great solemnity
and tension caused by the ever growing danger of war
resulting from the Suez Canal crisis. The unilateral nationalization of the Canal by the Egyptian dictator evoked
a menacing reaction from the British Government under
Anthony Eden. Britain condemned Nasser for violating international treaties and obligations and warned him not to

interfere with the right of free passage through the Suez Canal. Eden was adamant in stating that the free passage of oil to England and to Western Europe must be assured at all costs. The threat of military intervention was present and clear.

The Labour Party, while not condoning Nasser's illegal acts, declared its unalterable opposition to the use of force against Egypt and demanded that Britain act through the United Nations and act in consonance with the United States. It became somewhat incongruous to hear the Labour spokesmen, and especially Aneurin Bevan, who spent years in denouncing the Conservatives for following American policies and lacking courage to go it alone, painting the dire consequences that would follow if Great Britain should part from the United States on the Suez issue. Rightly or wrongly, the Labour Party felt that it had the overwhelming support of the British people for its stand and decided to close ranks to force the Government's retreat. Labour strategists believed that the Suez question and the Party's record during the crisis would assure a Labour victory at the next General Election.

The best speech of the conference was given by the new leader, Hugh Gaitskell. It was indeed a masterful and brilliant speech delivered under difficult circumstances. Gaitskell had to prove to the country that the Labour Party, while opposing war on Egypt, was not unpatriotic and did not approve of Colonel Nasser's aggressive and illegal acts. He succeeded in making this point admirably. "While we condemn the way in which Colonel Nasser nationalized the Company," Gaitskell said, "while we recognize (and would be very foolish not to) the dangers of aggression in the Middle East, nevertheless what he did, did not, in our view, justify in any way the use of armed force against Egypt." [12] The Labour Party leader upheld the right of

Great Britain and the other users of the Canal to free passage, reasonable charges, and a share in the administration, but stressed that the fundamental issue "concerns the attitude which a British Government adopts to its obligations under the Charter of the United Nations." [13] At the close of his speech, Gaitskell made a stirring appeal for Party unity. "Now let us," he concluded, "be 100 per cent united on this tremendous issue. There is no ground for division. We are all in it on the same lines together. . . ." [14] Gaitskell's speech received a full two-minute standing ovation from all the delegates, and the *Economist* conceded that "Mr. Gaitskell handled the task of leadership, especially in the crucial opening debate on Suez, quite magnificently." [15]

In spite of Gaitskell's plea for unity, the battle for the treasurership continued unabated and the outcome was in doubt. George Brown suffered a grievous setback when his supporters failed to persuade Charles Parnell to withdraw. For the first time in many years the big unions were split on the election of a high Party official. Bevan had succeeded in cracking the solid front of the big union bosses. This success brought him the long-sought victory. Bevan was elected Treasurer by 3,029,000 votes, while George Brown received 2,755,000 and Charles Parnell got 644,000. When the results were announced, Aneurin Bevan received a tumultuous ovation. It was a moment of great triumph, coming only a little over a year after he was expelled from the Parliamentary Labour Party.

The victory was hard won and came as a result of tireless work, careful strategy, and a wise exploitation of favorable circumstances. The *New Statesman and Nation* wrote in a front-page editorial, gleefully but with a dose of regret, that "Mr. Bevan won his battle the hard way. None of his rivals or opponents conceded him anything. He won

against the block vote of the general workers' union. He won
against the gerrymander of the A.E.U. . . ." [16]

What were the principal factors in Bevan's victory? First
was the 90 per cent support he received from the Constituent Labour Parties. The years of careful attention to the
local Parties paid off handsomely. It was the constituencies
that, with the help of several big unions and a number of
small craft unions, put Bevan over. Second, Bevan received
a large number of votes, probably a million, from the
middle-of-the-road delegates who heeded Gaitskell's plea
for unity and were eager to heal the scars left by the
Bevanite rebellions in the past. These delegates were convinced that the Party needed Bevan's abilities and following
to win a majority in Parliament, and they hoped that the
hearty but aging rebel would settle down in a top responsible post. Third, the accession to power by Frank
Cousins, who publicly declared his friendship for Bevan
although he neither supported nor opposed his election,
broke the solid and crushing opposition to Bevan by the big
union bloc. Barbara Castle, a faithful Bevanite veteran,
related that after Bevan's election was announced, many delegates were heard to exclaim: "It could not have happened
in Arthur's day." [17] It was eminently true that had Sir
Arthur Deakin lived and been present at the Fifty-fifth Conference, Aneurin Bevan would have gone down to defeat.
Deakin would not have adopted a hands-off policy on
Bevan's candidacy, who in his eyes was a dangerous fellow
traveler.

The speech made by Frank Cousins gave an indication of
the mild trend to the left by the Labour Party; Cousins,
unlike Deakin, talked like an old-fashioned Socialist. "We
have to go to the doors," he told the conference, "and tell
the people our story, and it has to be a Socialist story.
. . . Some of the people I represent would not agree with

the critics who say that nationalization, for instance, does not work. Some of them would say that it does work, and it has worked well." [18] The leftward swing was also demonstrated in the election of R. W. Casasola who moved at Scarborough the anti-Executive resolution against German rearmament.

The reaction in the American press to Bevan's victory was again jittery, if not panicky. One magazine editorialized that if Bevan "ever came to power, the whole structure of the free world's defensive alliance against Communism would be shaken." [19] The wiser *Economist* saw it in another light, and prophetically foretold that "*Mr. Bevan is now going to allow himself to be absorbed, painlessly and profitably, into Mr. Gaitskell's party. . . . It is a party that urgently needs Mr. Bevan as a lieutenant.*" [20]

Strengthened by his victory at the conference, Bevan returned to his duties as Labour Party's spokesman on colonial affairs and on Egypt. He had a big job and a great challenge before him. Parliament was in an almost continuous session during the latter part of October and during November, debating the Anglo-French attack on Egypt and then the Hungarian revolt. The Labour Party, led by Gaitskell, put up a vigorous opposition to the armed action against Egypt. Hugh Gaitskell told Parliament that millions of Britishers were ashamed and shocked by the R.A.F. bombing raids on Egyptian airfields and demanded that Britain abide by the decisions of the United Nations and withdraw its expeditionary force from Egypt. "All I can say is," he told the House, "that in taking this decision the Government, in view of Her Majesty's Opposition, have committed an act of disastrous folly whose tragic consequences we shall regret for years." [21]

Surprisingly, Aneurin Bevan gave a calmer and more thoughtful speech than the leader of his Party, who was generally considered a right-wing moderate. The record also shows that unlike the speeches of other Labour Party Leaders, Bevan's speech was listened to by the entire House without interruptions and with obvious respect. The respect was well deserved. Aneurin Bevan showed that he was capable of talking and behaving in a manner befitting a British statesman. He began by telling the House that he did not relish the task of opposing the Government's policy on Egypt. "We would much prefer," he said, "that this situation had never arisen." [22] He expressed his sympathy for the hard-pressed and "distraught" ministers who "are in great difficulties and have been in them for a long time. . . ." [23]

In a generous and philosophical mood, Bevan declared that even the Labour Party should not put all the blame on the Government. "It would be," he stated, "a very grave mistake for us, even on this side of the House, to indict the existing Government as though they bear the exclusive responsibility for the existing state of affairs." [24] The long-suffering Anthony Eden and his colleagues must have indeed appreciated these thoughtful expressions of sympathy and understanding. This was truly a "new Nye," who sounded more like the Attlee of old, with an added dose of eloquence and excitement. Bevan proceeded to develop the theory that the stalemate in the balance of power between Russia and America made the use of force in international conflicts an utter act of folly. In accordance with his often expressed theory, Bevan expressed his conviction that "the Soviet Union itself is recognizing that it cannot hold down whole populations merely by terror and by police action. For myself, I find that an infinitely encouraging fact." [25] On November 4, four days after Bevan made this statement, the Red Army entered Hungary in large strength and crushed the rebellion of the Hungarian people. Bevan again had shown his complete misunderstanding of Soviet aggressive ruthlessness. Returning to the Suez issue, Bevan condemned Eden's policy of defying the United Nations and declared that destruction of the United Nations prestige and effectiveness would mean no hope for mankind's survival. While he conceded that no party had a "simple quick solution to these problems before us," [26] he ripped into Eden's ineptness in the presentation of the Government's case. "I have often listened to bad cases in this House," he said, "but rarely have I listened to them so badly put as I have heard them in the last few days." [27]

Bevan again gained the sympathy and the cheers of the Conservative right wingers by refusing to condemn the Government for taking in Egypt an action independent of the United States. To do so, he told the House, would be foolish in view of his past record. He did not mind the independence of the action but he blamed the Government for the action itself. Bevan concluded his brilliant address, which was listened to by the entire House in a tense silence, with a stirring appeal to the Government. He concluded:

We say to the Government, not in any spirit of partisanship— I say so, anyhow, and no one can accuse me of lack of partisanship—not in the spirit of partisanship but with a deep sense of sorrow that I attack the Government for this policy. . . . I do beg and pray of them to retrace their steps even now. . . . For God's sake, get out! [28]

R. A. Butler, Lord Privy Seal, acknowledged Bevan's statesmanlike contribution to the crucial debate. "We always enjoy," said Butler, "the right hon. Member for Ebbw Vale when he is in one of his philosophic moods and he certainly did not in any way derogate from the dignity of the debate. Nor, although we disagree with many points

that the right hon. Gentleman made, can we be unduly upset by the tone of his intervention early today." [29]

Relentlessly but responsibly, Bevan was pressing the
Government to order the withdrawal of British forces from
Egypt in compliance with the decisions of the United
Nations. On November 5 he assured the Government that
"some of us are trying to maintain an objective attitude on
this matter," [30] and on November 8 Bevan told Parliament:
"I myself am not going to say anything which will make it
more difficult for the Government and for Hon. Members
opposite to try to retrace their steps." [31] Even during a
tumultuous demonstration against the Government organized by the Labour Party on Trafalgar Square, which
resulted in some clashes with the police, Bevan, the
acknowledged head of the demonstration, did not allow
his demagogic instincts to get the better of him. He delivered a relatively calm speech that got him a reluctant
compliment from the *Economist,* which wrote, "It was for
Mr. Aneurin Bevan—the new Mr. Bevan who is at the
moment trying so hard to sound moderate—to feel the
mood, and he made an undeniably brilliant speech." [32]

When on December 3, 1956, Eden finally ordered the
withdrawal of the British Expeditionary Force from Egypt,
Parliament was anxiously if hopelessly debating the ruthless
suppression of the Hungarian revolution by the Soviet
armed forces. Bevan did not participate in the debate on
Hungary, which was held on the day after the Soviet intervention, Sunday, November 4. When he did take the
floor of Parliament, on November 8, he failed to come out
with a forthright condemnation of the Russians' brutality.
He assigned to Britain a part of the blame for Soviet aggression, claiming that Eden's use of force in Egypt encouraged
and strengthened the warlike faction in Russia. British use

of force in Egypt, Bevan claimed, was "an example of brutality" [33] to the Soviet rulers. Surprisingly, the House heard this dubious and quite irrelevant analogy between the Egyptian and the Hungarian situations without interruptions or protests. "I do not believe," Bevan said, "that it is possible to separate the events in Hungary from the events in Egypt." [34]

Addressing the House again several weeks later, Bevan softened his previous assertion that Eden was to blame for Khrushchev's atrocities in Hungary, as, according to him, Churchill was to be blamed for Stalin's excesses, and he conceded that "to what extent what we did, led them to do what they did will continue to be a matter of speculation." [35]

But he continued to assert that because of British action in Egypt Britain's reaction to Hungary "has been muted, if not mutilated." [36] While a great many Britons, including many Labour Party leaders, suffered no guilt complex and vigorously denounced the Russian crimes in Hungary, Bevan's conscience did not allow him to do so. Instead, he called for negotiations to get the Russians out of their "increasing embarrassment" because "the essence of diplomatic wisdom is to find it possible for them to do so as quickly as possible." [37] Bevan did not take the trouble to explain why it was diplomatic wisdom and not sheer gullibility or worse to help the Russians to forget the atrocious crimes they have committed. Again, he partly justified the Russian attack on Hungary by citing two unnecessary, in his view, provocations of the Soviet Union— the Baghdad Pact and the rearming of Western Germany. He concluded by proposing to negotiate with the Russians the establishment of a neutral belt of countries in Central Europe. Regardless of the merits of this proposal, the demand that Western statesmen sit down to a negotiating table with the Russians, voiced a few weeks after the Soviet intervention in Hungary, was a gratuitous insult to the memory of the young Hungarian patriots who died in the streets of Budapest.

In spite of his unspectacular record on Hungary, Bevan's star was shining brightly. His performance during the Egyptian crisis was widely acclaimed. "There are two important things to say about Mr. Bevan at this juncture," wrote the *Economist* with true British detachment:

First, he is so clearly one of the biggest men in the Labour movement that he ought to be given one of the biggest jobs in any Labour Government. Secondly, however, any Labour M.P. who thinks that Mr. Bevan will not some day re-open his personal feud with Mr. Gaitskell is almost certainly living in a fool's paradise.[38]

While recognizing Bevan's contributions and stature, the Parliamentary Labour Party made it clear that it wanted him as a lieutenant to Gaitskell and not as its Leader. In the elections to the Shadow Cabinet, held on November 29, 1956, Bevan ran third after Harold Wilson and Alfred Robens. Reassured that Bevan was not an immediate threat to his position and desirous of having an effective voice in Parliament on foreign affairs, Gaitskell appointed Bevan Foreign Secretary on the Shadow Cabinet.

Remarkably, this appointment did not cause as much surprise or resentment as could have been expected. It seems that a great many people did believe that Bevan's "new look" was a genuine and lasting transformation. The *Manchester Guardian* expressed the interesting theory that the Conservatives, many of whom were preaching anti-Americanism in recent years," tended to build up the reputation of Mr. Bevan." [39] The *Economist,* whose editors had followed Bevan's career with attention and great perception, stated that Bevan's past aberrations stemmed from his struggle for personal power. The influential Conservative and pro-American weekly had words of assurance for the country: "Mr. Bevan's appointment as shadow Foreign Secretary should not frighten the country . . . he has it in him to be a more thoughtful Ernest Bevin." [40]

Even the American *Time* magazine accepted the appointment as a logical sequence to his record as Shadow Colonial Secretary. "He handled the assignment," *Time* wrote, "with humanity, undefatigable curiosity and parliamentary skill, demonstrating what his able mind can do when he checks his flamboyant gift for invective and extravagant statements. . . . Many in the House believe that Bevan handled the Suez case against Eden more effectively than Gaitskell himself." [41]

Bevan's triumph came two years after he denounced Clement Attlee on SEATO, two years after he called Gaitskell a "desiccated calculating machine," eighteen months after he was expelled from the Parliamentary Labour Party and threatened with expulsion from the Party, and only ten months after he denounced the Labour Party's leadership as a travesty of democracy. It was a remarkable achievement.

~XV~ The tamed lion of British Labor

At the beginning of 1957, Aneurin Bevan, a hearty, vigorous and handsome man of sixty, was happy and confident. He was the official spokesman of the Labour Party for foreign affairs, a field which he loved best, second to Gaitskell in the Party's hierarchy, and given the diminishing fortunes of the Conservatives in the by-elections most probably Britain's next Foreign Secretary. But even now, after many years of almost incessant struggle for power, his position was not secure. He was again called upon to prove that he could represent the Labour Party in the important field of foreign policy with statesmanlike moderation. He was required to keep his temper in check as the responsible spokesman of Her Majesty's Opposition, and by all accounts he was impressing foes and friends alike by his ability to do justice to his new post.

Issues which only a short time before would have provided Bevan with ammunition for an angry denunciation of the Government were handled now in the traditional manner of the British Parliament. When in January 1957 the Hungarian Government arrested four British students on trumped-up charges of espionage, Bevan fully associated himself with the sentiments of the Foreign Secretary,

Selwyn Lloyd, who demanded the students' release. Bevan bitingly expressed the hope that "the Hungarian Government should exercise a little sense of humor in the matter. It seems to me," he concluded, "that such espionage activities belong not to serious international relations, but to a Mack Sennett comedy." [1]

Even on the explosive issue of the banning of H-bomb tests, Bevan acted in the manner of a responsible statesman, carefully avoiding the use of any oratorical tricks. After Great Britain tested its own hydrogen bomb in the Pacific on May 31, Bevan and Gaitskell pressed Prime Minister Macmillan for a pledge to negotiate an agreement with Russia and America to ban future tests. They insisted that such an agreement should not be tied to the general disarmament negotiations. When Macmillan demurred, Bevan calmly pointed to the testimony of many scientists on the dangers to mankind from nuclear and hydrogen tests and to the possibility that many deaths might be caused by atomic fall-out. When interrupted by a Conservative M.P., he scolded him for being bloodthirsty and asked,

Is it not, therefore desirable that there should be agreement to stop any further tests? . . . How many more by-elections is the party opposite going to lose before it realizes how strong is the feeling in the country? [2]

An experienced American correspondent and observer of the British scene reported that Bevan was getting the

suave accents of the elder statesman. . . . His star is on the ascendant [and] . . . old suspicions and animosity toward him in the Labour movement are weakening. This represents a triumph of ability and personality. . . . It is hard to think of him as nearing 60. He does not alter greatly. The face is chubby but not soft. In repose, it has some of the determination of Churchill's. The body is thick and strong, not fat. [3]

Bevan was rapidly gaining acceptance and respect, not only among his erstwhile foes in the Labour movement, but even in the ranks of the Conservatives. Because of his record during the Suez crisis, he became, surprisingly, the fair-haired boy of the Conservative right wing. He often said things about the Americans, and especially about John Foster Dulles, that they would have liked to have said themselves, but refrained for fear of censure by their Party leaders.

In April 1957 Bevan went on a prolonged visit to India. But this time his Indian friends, including Nehru and Krishna Menon, beheld a new "Nye." He was still respectful toward Indian neutralism, but demanded equal respect for the British point of view on crucial international affairs. He carefully avoided any criticism of the United States and did not hesitate to tell his Indian audiences that India's policy on Kashmir was wrong. He stressed that India must live in peace with Pakistan and ought to strive for a compromise solution of the Kashmir issue. On one occasion Bevan told Nehru that he should use his influence with Nasser and the Arabs to make them accept the existence of Israel as a political reality. The *Economist* heartily approved of the new "Nye" and reported that "his words seem to have had a healthy impact. . . . This kind of plain speaking, addressed to an important Asian audience by a speaker whose independence of judgment could hardly be challenged, can do nothing but good." [4]

The Parliamentary Labour Party welcomed Bevan's return from his long trip abroad with a sigh of relief. Gaitskell, it became obvious, was in dire need of the services of his lieutenant. By a general consensus of opinion, he was as yet not a strong leader. R. A. Butler mockingly said, "Anything Hugh can do, Nye can do better." [5] It was generally expected that Bevan, true to his lifelong ambition, would soon move to unseat Gaitskell. Commenting on the wild acclaim with which Bevan was greeted at a May 1 Labour Party demonstration, the *Economist* said, "The growing acclaim for Mr. Bevan, even in the most unlikely places, contrasts with the growing criticism of Gaitskell, especially in the most likely ones." [6] But the unpredictable Bevan did not move. For once he did not allow his emotions to get the upper hand over his sober judgment, which told him that any attempt to oust Gaitskell would arouse the hostility of the trade unions and of the majority of the Parliamentary Labour Party, which preferred an able but cautious and unspectacular leader.

In the summer of 1957 Bevan made a trip to Russia, Poland, and Germany. He had long talks with the Soviet leader Nikita Khrushchev and the boss of the Polish Communist Party, Wladyslav Gomulka. Bevan gave a report on his impressions and conversations during his trip at the meeting the *Tribune* traditionally held before the Annual Labour Conference. The trip confirmed his long-standing views on Russia and on the security of Western Europe. The West, he said, must bring about a settlement and a closer relation with Russia. These closer ties will gradually bring a relaxation of the Soviet dictatorship and more democratic freedoms for the Russian people. "Changes are taking place in Russia and Poland," said Bevan, "which, if they are permitted to work themselves out, will bring these nations into line with what we call free people of the world." [7] There will be no peace in the Middle East, Bevan asserted, unless Russia is made a partner to any agreement made toward the pacification of that area of the world. Bevan again called for the neutralization of a united Germany, and expressed fears that Adenauer's Government was getting increasingly under the influence of the same economic and financial forces which helped Hitler to power. The fact that Red China was still not in the United Nations was, according to Bevan, "a disaster for mankind." [8] He again had some advice for America: "What I would say to my American friends is this, if you are incensed by what you consider repugnant features of the Chinese and Russian regimes, the best thing to do is not stand aloof or send them to Coventry . . . but to bring them into closer relations with the rest of the world." [9] An American magazine commented on the speech: "Nye seemed to have seen much good, observed little evil and gained no wisdom. . . . The U. S. might find it more difficult to work with the kind of Laborite government Nye Bevan envisions." [10] The speech, however, pleased the assembled Bevanites. Their leader was in fine fettle. They of course had no inkling of the blow they were to suffer at his hands in a very short time. At the very moment when he was acknowledging the applause of his faithful followers, Bevan must have known that he, himself, paradoxically, had ceased to be a Bevanite.

The next day, when the Fifty-sixth Labour Party Annual Conference opened at Brighton, Aneurin Bevan helped to do away with the principle of nationalization, one of the sacred tenets of Bevanism. Staring impassively at the audience and avoiding the pleading glances of his long-time followers and admirers, he sat on the platform while Hugh Gaitskell called upon the delegates to substitute for nationalization a scheme calling for the acquisition of shares in large industrial companies instead of an outright take-over of the industries by any future Labour Government. Gaitskell repeated the pledge to renationalize the transport and steel industries, but asserted that the country would not approve any further extension of public ownership of industry. Insistence on the old Socialist principle of nationalization, he said, would cost Labour the next election.

The efforts of a few diehard Socialists, including Emanuel

Shinwell, to fight the new policy were in vain, because it became clear that Aneurin Bevan had joined the Gaitskell-Cousins coalition. Bevan did not stir even when Jennie Lee denounced the share-buying plan as a betrayal of Socialism. Shinwell, former Defense Minister in the Labour Government, pleaded with the conference not to "abandon the vital principle on which this party was founded." [11] The opposition also included the embittered and aging Herbert Morrison. It was indeed strange and a sign of changing times to see Herbert Morrison fighting to hold on to nationalization and Bevan oppose it. The vote, 5,309,000 for to 1,276,000 against, was a resounding victory for Gaitskell.[12] The Labour Party, including Bevan, was determined to close ranks toward the attainment of one central objective, Labour's return to power.

The Bevanites had hardly recovered from the disappointment of the nationalization debate when their ranks were jolted by a far more shocking event. On the basis of Bevan's past record, speeches, and writings, they had every reason to expect that their leader would give vigorous support to a resolution committing any Labour Government to renounce, unilaterally if necessary, the manufacture and the testing of nuclear weapons. Bevanites were shocked and angered when Bevan strode to the platform and, in a speech three-quarters of an hour long, urged the delegates to defeat the resolution. "To pass this motion," he said, "would mean that you will send the British Foreign Secretary naked into the conference chamber." [13] To abandon the H-bomb unilaterally, he further argued, would mean Britain's abdication of her position of power and influence in the world. His former followers listened to their former chief first in stunned silence, and then they heckled him mercilessly. There were cries of "shame," "nonsense," and "rubbish." One delegate cried out, "You've sold the pass," and another

shouted, "I'll carve him up if it's the last thing I do." [14]
Bevan flushed and, visibly uncomfortable, acknowledged
that many of his supporters seemed to feel that he sold them
down the river for the promise to become Britain's Foreign
Secretary. His hecklers cried, "Hear! Hear!" while Bevan
assured the conference that the charge was false and that
he arrived at his new position after a long, careful, and
"agonizing" appraisal of the international situation. It
was obviously a painful ordeal for the audience and the
speaker. With Bevan on his side, Gaitskell's well-oiled
machine, supported with some reluctance by Frank Cousins
and the big trade unions, had no difficulty in disposing of
the resolution by a crushing vote of 5,836,000 to 781,000.

This time Bevan had no difficulty in getting elected
Treasurer of the Labour Party—he was unopposed. But
the election to the National Executive showed already the
results of the disintegration of the Bevanite group. Sydney
Silverman, an unreconstructed Bevanite, was ousted and
Richard Crossman, who was considered a renegade by many
Bevanites, was re-elected. Actually, only three Bevanites
remained on the Executive—Barbara Castle, Ian Mikardo,
and Tom Driberg. Harold Wilson, who was elected by a
large majority, had long since abandoned much of the
Bevanite philosophy.

What made Bevan throw away the loyalty and the
support of his followers and sound the death knell to
Bevanism? The answer to this question is as complicated as
the man himself, but those who considered Bevan's performance at Brighton a complete break with his past plans
and convictions failed to analyze all aspects of his bizarre
political career. In the thirty years of constant political
warfare, Bevan kept a steady eye on the central goal—a
position of real power and real leadership in the Labour
Party. The leadership of the Bevanite group and Labour's

left wing and the philosophy which became known as Bevanism were not aims in themselves, but means toward the attainment of the main objective. Bevan had on several crucial occasions in his Labour Party work made clear that, if accommodated in full or in part, he would be willing to compromise or even to sacrifice. At the age of sixty, he came to the realization that within the peculiar power structure of the Labour Party, his only chance to fulfill his lifetime ambition was to get the support of the Party's official leadership and of the trade unions. Labour, Bevan knew, had a chance of returning to power only if and when complete inner harmony and unity were restored. He also reconciled himself to the idea that he had no chance to become the Labour Party's leader, because he was not the type of a leader historically preferred by the British Labour movement.

The advent of the atomic age and the manufacture of nuclear weapons by the Soviets and by the United States and Britain, Bevan was sure, presented the world with a choice of lasting peace, which depended upon a lasting coexistence settlement with the Soviets, or the complete destruction of mankind. Aneurin Bevan felt that he, as Great Britain's Foreign Secretary, could save mankind from the horrors of an atomic war. "Somewhere amid that misty Celtic fervor," wrote the *Economist,* "there is now a vision of himself as the man of the people who is to lead the world out of the nuclear shadow of mankind's destruction into peace." [15]

Even the *New Statesman and Nation* conceded that Bevan had no choice but to join Gaitskell and Cousins at Brighton. "The Labour Party," the *Statesman* wrote, "has the scent of electoral victory in its nostrils and, if Mr. Bevan is to share in the victory, he can no longer disassociate himself from winning it." [16]

Another student of Bevanism wrote that "He [Bevan] is now like Samson, shorn of his locks." He lost his following and he might even not become Foreign Secretary. "Mr. Gaitskell is quite tough enough to do just that, if Mr. Bevan should become a nuisance." [17] While it is true that Bevan could have found a better if less dramatic way to signify his break with the Bevanites, the *Statesman* and many others who have attempted to picture him as a helpless prisoner of the right wing and the unions were once again underestimating his abilities, his political acumen and drive and energy. They were also forgetting that in the turbulent days of its climb to power, the Labour Party and Gaitskell would be in dire need of Bevan's parliamentary experience and dynamism and skill. He was after all the ablest and most outstanding personality in the British Parliament, except on the rare occasions when Winston Churchill made his appearance at Westminster.

The *Times* had a simple explanation for Bevan's performance at Brighton. It ascribed Bevan's caution and moderation to the sobering thought of burden and responsibility that comes to a successful candidate for office on the morning after a hectic election. "He demonstrates," the *Times* wrote, "that the anticipation of responsibility as well as responsibility itself can pin a man down to realities." [18]

It soon became quite evident that many political analysts, both in England and in America, seriously misinterpreted Bevan's dramatic move at the Brighton Conference. For reasons that seemed compelling to him, Aneurin Bevan broke with the Bevanites; but he did not give up Bevanism, if this term represents a set of positions and views concerned primarily with British foreign policy. All of Bevan's rebellions against the Labour Party's leadership concerned issues of foreign policy, and there is enough evidence to support the contention that while Bevan agreed to fight for his view *inside* the Party councils and abide loyally by Party discipline, he had not changed his views on the major issues of Britain's foreign policy.

In October 1957 Bevan decided to visit the United States for a brief lecture tour. The visit lasted nineteen days and if it intended, as was widely heralded, to present to the United States public the new and reformed Nye, it must be judged a complete failure. British journalists writing for American publications, in anticipation of the visit, predicted that Aneurin Bevan, coming to the United States only a few weeks after the Brighton conference, would break down the distrust and hostility the American press and people so consistently displayed toward him. One wrote:

The Aneurin Bevan now visiting the United States is rather a different person from the man most Americans have come to feel is their inveterate enemy. . . . The mere thought of Mr. Bevan's fervent views on socialism has sent a shudder of apprehension through the heart of every true Republican. They can now go easy to bed.[19]

Another stated that:

Bevan's friends and enemies have recognized a profound change in him in recent months. . . . It is of more importance to Britain than it is to Bevan himself that his trip should be a success and that he should maintain in America the statesmanlike bearing he has shown during the past twelve months.[20]

Bevan did maintain a statesmanlike bearing, and he looked quite impressive on the speaker's platform in photographs taken with President Eisenhower and Secretary Dulles; but it is seriously doubtful whether his trip was a success. Americans, who were much more interested in his views than in his bearing, saw and heard not the new but the old Bevan, whose views on most international issues were diametrically opposed to the stated American foreign policy. An American magazine made a factual compilation of the views expressed by Bevan in his series of lectures, and his television and press conferences on major foreign policy issues, and concluded, "The man who will run British foreign policy if the Socialists return to power disagrees with practically everything the U. S. is doing in the world." [21] The list included the following summation of Bevan's views:

Forget ideas about the Communists wanting to conquer the world or starting a war, trust Nikita Khrushchev, sit down to a "summit" conference with Russia, accept the fact that the Communists are in the Middle East and negotiate with them to keep peace there, recognize the Chinese Reds and let them into the United Nations, abolish all barriers to "normal" trade with Red China, follow the Kremlin line on suspending H-bomb tests and accept "neutral" unified Germany.[2]

The magazine proceeded to cite chapter and verse from Bevan's utterances to substantiate the summary. On October 28 Bevan told the Economic Club in New York: "I have found nothing at all where I have been in China and Russia, to suggest this, that their leaders are now nurturing the idea of world revolution . . . the old, classical Communist idea that revolution thrives upon war no longer holds good, when war itself would be the end of all political systems." [23]

In a press conference in Los Angeles on November 7, Bevan said about Khrushchev: "I think that on the whole, he is a man that you could get on terms with." [24]

"The United States must not arm the West Germans and allow them to adopt a policy of neutrality. The Russians," Bevan said on a radio program on November 3, "couldn't conceivably be expected to accept a proposition of that sort, and therefore, the neutralization of a United Germany must be regarded as a pre-requisite." [25]

In contradiction to the position he took at Brighton, Bevan announced (probably on his own authority) that "If the Labour Government was in power in England, we would set an example by stopping the [H-bomb] tests and hope that the other nations would follow suit." [26]

The reaction to Bevan's speeches was bitterly critical. He was again getting a very bad press and his audiences were polite but obviously unhappy, especially since Bevan unaccountably chose to speak during his tour almost exclusively to the most conservative groups, including the Economic Club of New York and the New York Commerce and Industry Association. It was reported that he refused to accept any engagement before more liberal organizations. The United Press reported that several members of his audience in the plush Economic Club, hearing Bevan compare the "irregular" establishment of the United States to the Red Chinese grab of power, could not refrain themselves from audible protests.[27] One listener, Gordon W. Reed, chairman of the board of Texas Gulf Producing Company, told a columnist that "what is really biting Bevan is the success of the free enterprise or capitalist system. He is ruthless in his Socialist bias and he cannot forgive the United States for being a living contradiction of everything in which he believes." [28]

Victor Riesel, a widely read columnist, wrote bitingly, "That British Socialist, 'Nye' Bevan, who hopes he soon will be Britain's next Prime Minister, is a gentleman farmer who fancies pigs and Khrushchev. But he doesn't like President Eisenhower." [29]

One cannot escape the conclusion that while Bevan knew exactly how he could have made a good impression in America and made his visit a success, he deliberately decided to rub his hosts the wrong way. He often chose to adopt a slighting and condescending attitude which infuriated his listeners. Asked on a nationwide television program to comment on American nonrecognition of Red China, he heatedly answered, "You will not recognize China because you say its troops killed GI's and British boys and yet you have built Germany into a great power again, and insisted that we help. Where is the consistency in this?" [30]

As America was not impressed with Bevan, he was not impressed with the United States. He found the country prosperous but "shallow" and tawdry, and the people ridden by fear.[31] Bevan undoubtedly intended his tour of the United States to help convince the strongest British ally that he was not the irresponsible fellow-traveling rebel he was pictured to be for so many years by the American press. The reason why his "mission to America" failed cannot be put to his inability to impress the Americans. Bevan had a great deal of charm and innate persuasiveness, and he knew exactly what the American audiences and reporters wanted him to say. One is compelled to conclude, therefore, that his poor showing was the result of his sincere and serious disagreement with American foreign policy, or that his dislike for America was so deep that, at times, he formulated his views purposely in a fashion bound to irritate greatly his American listeners. Judging on the basis of Bevan's complex personality, both explanations are probably valid.

There was one occasion during his visit when Bevan made a serious attempt to impress the American public that he was a responsible statesman. During his appearance on the radio program *Face the Nation,* on November 3, Bevan declared that he was a strong supporter of NATO and, in contradiction to his record, that he never supported the idea of Britain becoming a neutralist "third force" mediating between Russia and America. He stated the United States military bases in Britain were there with the consent of the British Government and people and should remain to fulfill their role in the defense of the West. Bevan assured his listeners that if (he actually said "when") he becomes Britain's Foreign Secretary, he would strive for closer relations with the United States, and he expressed his delight that Queen Elizabeth's visit to the United States, which preceded his own, was an outstanding success. He repeated, although much more cautiously, his views on the neutralization of Germany, the recognition of Red China, the ban on nuclear weapons, and negotiations with Russia. On this program, faced by some of America's ablest reporters, Bevan was suave, brilliant, and effective. Bevan was disappointed with the results of his talks with President Eisenhower and Secretary of State Dulles. While he found Dulles, whom he met at a British Embassy dinner in Washington, personally agreeable and likeable,[32] he told British audiences that he found the official American attitude to be: "It's no use trusting the Russians. What's the use making treaties . . . in other words, it is an attitude of complete hopelessness."[33]

The failure of his visit to the United States apparently did not adversely affect Bevan's standing in the Labour Party. On the contrary, his stature and influence grew steadily. He succeeded in convincing Gaitskell of his loyalty, and for the first time in years the Labour Party presented a united front of opposition to the Macmillan Government, which was increasingly on the defensive. Aneurin Bevan was effective in needling the Government and Foreign Secretary Selwyn Lloyd for their reluctance to press for negotiations with Russia. Together with Gaitskell, he led the Labour attack on Macmillan's agreement to station atomic missile bases in Britain.

Rising to speak in the House of Commons in the debate on the results of the heads-of-government NATO meeting in Paris in December 1957, Bevan was greeted with a mas-

sive cheer. He delivered one of the best speeches he ever
made in the House of Commons. As one erstwhile hostile
paper said: "He was trying on the statesman's mantle—and
with success." [34] He forcefully and effectively ripped into
the Government and charged it was not making forceful use
of opportunities to bridge the gab between East and West.
He expressed his conviction that Khrushchev and Bulganin
wanted peace. "It seems to us," he said, "there exists between us and the Soviet Union a common interest to avoid
conflagration." [35] Bevan was cheered when he demanded
that United States planes discontinue flights over Britain
with loads of hydrogen bombs and summarized the Labour
Party's attitude on the stationing of missile bases in Britain
in one telling sentence, which brought the Opposition
benches to their feet. "We are prepared," he stated, "to
abrogate British sovereignty for an overriding purpose, but
we are not prepared to do it merely to add to the sovereign
power of another nation." [36] As he sat down, he received
the greatest ovation of his long Parliamentary career. He
was well on his way to become Britain's next Foreign Secretary.

❧XVI❧ Britain's Foreign Secretary?

THE DRAMATIC BREAK with his followers that Bevan made at the Brighton Labour Party Conference generally obscured the fact that in the course of several years much of his personal ideology and world outlook had become either widely accepted or at least respectable. By 1957 many of Bevan's positions on issues of foreign policy continued to be opposed, but many found support in respectable quarters and could no longer be brushed aside as the fuzzy thinking of a fellow traveler. It might be of value to list the major tenets of Bevanism and appraise the present degree of their acceptance in the Western world.

1. The Soviet Union, Bevan consistently preached, does not present a clear and serious threat of a military attack on the West. The Russian leaders realize the dangers of an atomic war and fear the retaliatory power of the West, and have therefore decided to engage the West in political, cultural, and economic competition. This position has been repeatedly confirmed by Nikita Khrushchev, who had told Western diplomats and correspondents that the Soviet Union would in a short time outproduce America in industrial and food production. The Soviet leaders have, with increas-

ing frequency, challenged America to compete with the Soviet Union in the realm of economics and culture.

Secretary of State John Foster Dulles acknowledged the fact that the Soviet threat shifted in emphasis from the military field to "economic warfare to gain control of newly independent and newly developed countries. . . . *Unless we wage successfully the political-economic war that is now being fought, Communist imperialism can win without even a gun being fired.*" [1]

Aneurin Bevan expressed the same ideas in the House of Commons, at Labour Party conferences in the pre-World War II period and in the years following the war, and restated them in his book, *In Place of Fear,* published in 1952. His was one of the first voices raised in the West urging massive economic aid to the underdeveloped countries in Asia, Africa, and the Middle East as the best deterrent to the spread of world Communism, and he warned that the West was bound to compete with the Soviets in the struggle for the allegiance of the uncommitted nations in Asia and Africa.

Bevan's position on the nature of the Soviet threat was supported by an eminent expert on Russia, historian and diplomat George F. Kennan. Kennan argued that the usual interpretation of Russian intentions "to overrun Western Europe, in particular by force of arms, as soon as military conditions might prove favorable" was false. "I personally feel," he wrote, "that this is a dangerously inaccurate view. . . . The hostility has been there . . . but the threat has not been an all-out military attack. It has been a combined political and military threat, but more political than military." [2]

Writing in 1957, George Kennan expressed complete agreement with views expressed by Aneurin Bevan many years before. Kennan writes:

I have never thought that the Soviet Government wanted a general war at any time since 1945. . . . I do not believe, in other words, that it was our possession of the atomic bomb which prevented the Russians from over-running Europe in 1948 or at any other time.[3]

Kennan states that if asked how to counter the Soviet threat, he would reply by pointing to the necessity of improving conditions in America and in other Western countries. We must eliminate "our own American failings . . . the things that we are ashamed of in our own eyes, or that worry us." [4]

It is remarkable that Aneurin Bevan appraised the Soviet threat in almost identical words in 1952. He wrote, "There is no evidence to show that the Soviet Union wants a trial of strength. . . . An effective answer to Russian aggression involves a re-examination of our attitude to the social problems in our own country." [5]

2. Bevan's was one of the first voices to express confidence that the development of the Soviet educational system, the emergence of large number of scientists, engineers, and highly skilled workers, would inevitably force the Soviet rulers to relax the dictatorship and give the Russian people more political, cultural, and economic freedom. This point of view, when expounded by Bevan, was neither popular nor acceptable. It became clear, however, that during the post-Stalin era Bevan's prophecy came true, at least in part. Responsible observers of the Soviet scene agree that Russian artists, musicians, poets, and writers enjoy today considerably more freedom than ever before.

Secretary Dulles would probably have been surprised to find how closely his view on this issue paralleled that of Aneurin Bevan. Speaking in January 1958, the American Secretary of State said, "Minds that are fine enough to deal with modern scientific and technical problems cannot be kept from coming to independent conclusions about other matters. The growth within the Soviet Union of a new intelligentsia is bound to affect Soviet policies." [6]

Bevan wrote in 1952 on the same subject:

The economic enfranchisement of the Soviet workers is proceeding and their political enfranchisement must follow . . . the totalitarian states are bound to fail, because you cannot educate a man to be intelligent inside the workshop and a fool outside the workshop. . . .[7]

Once you start educating the working class to use all the complicated machinery of a modern civilisation and it learns to read blueprints, it reads other things as well.[8]

George Kennan agrees with Dulles and Bevan when he writes, "By its [the Soviet Union's] admirable program of popular education . . . it has created a new educated class which is simply not prepared to accept the old devices of Communist thought control and is determined to do its thinking for itself." [9]

3. Negotiation with Russia, aiming at reaching a settlement with the Soviet Union which would end the cold war and lead to world disarmament, was one of the most important principles of Bevanism. Sensing the emotional desire of Britons to see a more peaceful world which would permit substantial British trade with Communist countries, Bevan often accused the United States of dragging its feet to the negotiating table. He demanded that the United States not engage in a crusade against international Communism, that it understand "that reaching an accommodation with the Communist countries is not the same thing as accommodating Communism." [10] Bevan was a determined opponent of the American policy of military containment. If the frontiers of Communism are to be frozen where they are now, he wrote, "it can be accomplished only by pacifying and stabilizing conditions in adjacent territory." [11] A

great many British statesmen and most American leaders
would flinch at this latter suggestion of Bevan's, which could
only mean an official Western sanction and approval of the
Soviet grab and subjugation of the countries of Eastern
Europe. But there are very few Western statesmen who
would oppose East–West negotiations aimed at the attainment of a state of affairs which Khrushchev is wont to describe as "peaceful coexistence." On the issue of negotiations with Russia, Bevan had the overwhelming support of
the British people and the leaders and populations of the
British Commonwealth. A Gallup Poll taken in December
1957 disclosed that 85 per cent of the British voters favored
East–West talks and 62 per cent believed that it was possible to reach a peaceful settlement of differences with Russia.[12] Lester Pearson, former Minister for External Affairs
of Canada, said in a speech accepting the Nobel Prize
Award:

No progress can be made if one side merely shouts "coexistence"
. . . while the other replies "no appeasement." Our policy and
diplomacy is becoming as rigid and defensive as the French warfare of forty years ago. . . . There ought to be frank, serious
and complete exchanges of views—especially between Moscow
and Washington—through diplomatic and political channels.[13]

Secretary Dulles had also endorsed the view that "there
should be, and will be, further neogtiations with the Soviet
Union."[14]

4. Bevan's views on the recognition of Red China and
the desirability of neutralization of Germany continued to
be strongly resisted in America, but found a large measure
of support in Britain and Western Europe. Bevan's attacks
on American policy in the Far East were supported not only
by the Labour Party but also by the right wing of the Conservatives. A well-informed American correspondent wrote

that "the American Secretary of State is pictured by the British Opposition and the rebels in the Conservative Party as hostile to negotiations with the Soviet Union, sterile in policy and the decisive influence on the making of British foreign policy." [15] A public opinion poll conducted in Britain disclosed that 51 per cent of the British population supported the admission of Red China to the United Nations and 21 per cent were opposed. In line with his more statesmanlike approach, Bevan now refrained from attacking Chiang Kai-shek, but urged a change in America's China policy, because "it is causing bad blood in British business circles as well as among those whom Americans would describe as radicals." [16] The United States, while continuing in its opposition to recognition of Red China, has nevertheless abandoned its policy of unleashing Chiang Kai-shek against the Chinese Red regime. "If we preach liberation," wrote a veteran American political writer,

we practice "containment." Chiang has been leashed, not unleashed. In December, 1954, we induced him to give a written guarantee not to attempt invasion, except with our prior approval. . . . Once we saw in Chiang our strongest Asian ally. Now we find him emperor of an oriental Elba and imagine ourselves responsible. Yet we fear to let him risk his Waterloo.[17]

5. Bevan had consistently opposed the rearmament of West Germany and had urged a German settlement, negotiated with Russia, which would restore German unity but assure and guarantee a neutralized and disarmed Germany. Many years before George Kennan delivered his sensational talks over the B.B.C. in England, in which he urged Soviet-American "disengagement" in Germany by simultaneous withdrawal of their respective military forces from Europe, Aneurin Bevan advocated the same policy. When asked for comment on Kennan's proposals, Bevan correctly answered,

"I have said that many years ago." Bevan and Jennie Lee had a deep distrust of Germany and had been vigorous opponents of the rearming of Western Germany. They had often in the years immediately following World War II expressed their dissatisfaction with the denazification process and the fear that the growing economic strength of Western Germany would in time bring the revival of German militarism and ultranationalism—which would once again become a menace to the security of Britain and of Europe. Bevan and his followers fought bitterly within the councils of the Labour Party for a policy of opposition to Adenauer's rearming of the West German Federal Republic as part of the NATO defense system, and they pleaded for support of the neutralist policies of the West German Socialist Party. The Bevanites threw all of their support to the decisive attempt made at the 1954 Labour Party conference to put the British Labour Movement on record as opposing German rearmament and Germany's military alliance with the West. Their slogan, "No Guns for the Huns," was indicative of their thinking. Bevan was firmly convinced that Germany would not be unified unless the Soviet Union was sure that the United German State would be disarmed and neutral. He told an American radio audience during his 1957 visit to the United States that he fully understood Russian fear of an armed Germany, and he asserted that it was foolish to arm West Germany when German leaders made no secret of their determination to regain the eastern provinces Germany lost to Poland, and which could be retaken only by the force of arms.

George Kennan expressed full agreement with Bevan's views when he stated:

Moscow is really being asked to abandon—as part of an agreement on German unification—the military and political bastion in Central Europe which it won by its military effort from 1941 to 1945, and to do this without any compensatory withdrawal of American armed power from the heart of the Continent. . . . So long, therefore, as it remains the Western position that the hands of a future all-German government must not be in any way tied in the matter of Germany's future military engagements, I see little hope for any removal of the division of Germany at all—nor, by the same token, of the removal of the division of Europe.[18]

As his views received wider acceptance, Aneurin Bevan began to look and to sound more and more like the "Right Honorable Aneurin Bevan," the principal spokesman for Her Majesty's Opposition on foreign affairs, and the next British Foreign Secretary in a Labour Government. Following the exit of Winston Churchill from active political life, Bevan was unquestionably the ablest parliamentarian and the best orator in the House of Commons. He could on occasion exchange the suave accents of an elder statesman for a biting, sarcastic, and perfectly aimed down-to-earth tongue lashing. The occasional slight stammer in his speech served only to accentuate his flowing and persuasive Welsh oratory.

Bevan's position within the Labour Party became prominent and secure. Although the right wing of the Labour Party did not forget nor forgive the rebel's past, and although his erstwhile left-wing followers and supporters were bitter in denouncing their former leader for selling them down the river in a "deal" with Gaitskell and the big trade unions, the bulk of the Party recognized and appreciated Bevan's capacity for leadership and his great oratorical and parliamentary skills. Among the Conservatives, Bevan continued to be disliked and feared but generally respected. Significantly, a number of right-wing Conservative politicians treated Bevan with open favor and sympathy because they shared and applauded his anti-American sentiments.[19] An American correspondent wrote, ". . . since he [Bevan] became the Labour Party's chief spokesman on foreign affairs, suggestions that he would make a good Prime Minister come more often from Tory than from Socialist politicians." After his election in 1959 as deputy leader of the Labour Party, Aneurin Bevan worked loyally with Hugh Gaitskell. As Gaitskell found himself under increasing pressure and criticism from the left wing for his compromising stand on the issue of nationalization and his opposition to Britain's unilateral nuclear disarmament, Bevan attempted to heal the breach and to find an acceptable compromise. It was asserted, after Bevan's death, that had he lived he might have restored unity in the Labour Party. Aware as he was of his powers of persuasion, and inordinately proud of his skills in negotiation, he would have surely made the attempt.

Bevan, whose main preoccupation in life was a constant search for the source of political power, must have become increasingly aware of the fact that the power to lead the nation, and the world, had eluded him. But until his grave illness, which came in December 1959, Bevan led a rewarding and busy life. He was happily married to Jennie Lee, whose constituents in the mining district of Cannock in Staffordshire were as faithful to her as the miners of Ebbw Vale were unwavering in their support of "Nye." The Bevans divided their time between an apartment in London and their country home in Buckinghamshire. They entertained many guests both in London and in their country home, and their circle of friends was varied, including artists, musicians, journalists, and political leaders of various shades of political opinion. Bevan had a penchant for striking close personal friendships with people representing diametrically opposed political philosophies. He included among his close friends the London correspondent of the Yugoslav official government newspaper *Borba* and the veteran London correspondent of the *Chicago Tribune*. As was his custom for many years, when in need of respite and invigoration Bevan would go to the valleys of South Wales where his faithful miners would shout themselves hoarse cheering their beloved "Nyrin."

Bevan mellowed with the years and with the frequent rebuffs to his political ambitions. But even in his later years of restraint and responsibility he was like a dormant volcano, ready to erupt at any moment. Few doubted that the explosion would come eventually, probably on the issue of nationalization, which Bevan considered central to his Socialist philosophy. While his public utterances on foreign issues became moderate and infrequent, Aneurin Bevan made no secret of his disapproval of the military emphasis in the North Atlantic Treaty Organization. Since he did not believe in the danger of Soviet armed aggression, he favored the strengthening of the United Nations and a greatly expanded program of economic help to the underdeveloped countries of Asia and Africa, where Bevan's prestige was high and where he had many friends. Bevan was distrustful of West Germany and wished to restrict its role in NATO, hoping that a neutral Germany would make possible a "disengagement" in Europe between the United States and the Soviet Union. He continued to believe that keeping Communist China out of the United Nations was a blunder and a tragedy, because it drove China into a close and unnatural alliance with Russia.

A proud Britisher who considered the British parliamentary system by far the best form of government yet devised by men, Bevan wanted Great Britain to take the political initiative to find a *modus vivendi* with the Soviet Union and end the cold war. He frankly doubted that America had the maturity and the wisdom to accomplish this task.

A Welshman, a rebel, and a radical, Bevan was not an oddity in British politics. On the contrary, he had a rightful place in the tolerant, flexible, and mature framework of British democracy. Bevan had deep roots in the rich political tradition of Great Britain. His radicalism was in the best tradition of the Levellers, the Chartists, the Socialists, and the pre-World War I Liberals. In an age of uniformity and dull conformity, his was a refreshing and stimulating personality.

Bibliography

GOVERNMENTAL PUBLICATIONS

British Labour Party Annual Conference Reports: 1934, 1935, 1947, 1948, 1950, 1952, 1953, 1954, 1955, 1956.

Debate in House of Commons (Pamphlet), British Information Services, New York, 1948.

Hansard's Parliamentary Debates (5th series), CCXLIV, CCXCV, CCXCVIII, CCCXV, CCCLXXXIV, CCCLXXXIII, CCCXCVIII, CCCLXVIII, CCCLXXXIII, CCCXLIII, CCCXCIX, CCCXCVIII, CDXCVI, CDXLVII, CDLIII, CDXCIV, CDXLVI, CDXIII, CDXXX, CDXXV, CDXLVI, CDLXIV, CDXCVI, D, DII, DIV, DVIII, DX, DXII, DXIV, DXV, DXXVI, DXXXVII, DXLVIII, DLIII, DL, DLVII, DLVIII, DLX, DLXII, DLXIII, DLXXI.

Health Services in Britain (Pamphlet), British Information Services, New York, 1948.

Report of the South Wales Regional Survey Committee, Ministry of Health, London, His Majesty's Stationery Office, 1921.

NEWSPAPERS

Cincinnati Enquirer
    October 29, 1957.
    Victor Riesel, "Likes Pigs and Reds," November 6, 1957.
Cincinnati Post
    Inez Robb, "Bevan Sings Old Songs," November 9, 1957.
The Miami Herald
    December 21, 1957.
Daily Herald (London)
    December 1, 1950.

Daily Worker (London)
   October 7, 1939.
   February 11, 1940.
New York Times
   May 25, 1940
   May 27, 1945.
   December 13, 1946.
   October 8, 1957.
   November 7, 1957.
   December 4, 1957.
Miami Herald
   December, 1957, p. 1.
The Observer (London)
   February, 1958, p. 5.
The Times (London)
   March 11, 1951.
   April 25, 1951.
   October 10, 1951.

PERIODICALS

America
   Editorial, "America Fears Bevan," October 13, 1956, p. 23.
The American Political Science Review
   Leon D. Epstein, "Cohesion of British Parliamentary Parties,"
      June, 1956, p. 373.
Antioch Review
   John P. Roche, "Crisis in British Socialism" (Winter, 1952–
      53), p. 391.
Commentary
   George Lichtheim, "Behind the Anti-Americanism of Mr.
      Bevan," July, 1952, pp. 16, 17.
Commonweal
   Geoffrey Ashe, "Bevan vs. Bevanism," July 4, 1952, p. 312.
Economist
   Editorial, January 17, 1948, p. 85.
   Leading Article, July 10, 1948, p. 48.

Leading Article, "Paying for Sickness," December 25, 1948, p. 1054.

Editorial, April 24, 1954, pp. 261, 262.

Editorial Notes, October 2, 1954, p. 23.

March 19, 1955, p. 973.

Leading Article, March 26, 1955, p. 1070.

April 9, 1955, p. 106.

October 6, 1956, p. 19.

October 15, 1956, p. 19.

November 10, 1956, p. 493.

November 17, 1956, p. 580.

December 2, 1956, p. 764.

April 20, 1957, p. 213.

May 4, 1957, p. 478.

October 15, 1957, p. 16.

Encyclopaedia Britannica, Vol. XXIII, 1956, p. 28.

Foreign Affairs

Aneurin Bevan, "Britain and America at Loggerheads" (October, 1957), p. 67.

The Foreign Policy Bulletin, Foreign Policy Association, New York, December 1, 1957, p. 42.

Journal of International Affairs, Columbia University

Élie Halévy, "Socialism and the Problem of Democratic Parliamentarism," July–August 1934, pp. 490–495.

Quincy Wright, "The Status of Communist China" (Autumn, 1957), p. 171.

Manchester Guardian Weekly

Salvador de Madariaga, "Russia and the West: An Open Letter to Mr. Bevan" (March 27, 1952), p. 12.

Jules Menken, review of A. Bevan, *In Place of Fear*, April 10, 1952, p. 11.

"Comment and Criticism" (October 2, 1952), p. 8.

"Comment and Criticism" (October 5, 1952), p. 8.

"Comment and Criticism" (October 16, 1952), p. 8.

"Review of Parliament" (March 4, 1953), p. 5.

"Review of Parliament" (April 23, 1953), p. 5.

"Review of Parliament" (May 28, 1953), p. 5.

Sir Walter Fletcher, M.P., "Trade with China after an Armistice" (July 23, 1953), p. 3.

Quoted from Manchester Guardian Weekly (August 6, 1953), p. 9.

"Comment and Criticism" (September 3, 1953), p. 9.

Quoted from Manchester Guardian Weekly (September 10, 1953), p. 3.

By Labour Correspondent, "A Constructive Week's Work at Margate" (October 8, 1953), p. 3.

November 29, 1956, p. 3.

December 26, 1957, p. 2.

Nation

January 27, 1951, p. 71 (Comments).

Howard K. Smith, "Bevan's Rebellion" (May 12, 1951), p. 437.

Andrew Roth, "The Rise of Bevan" (October 11, 1952), p. 317.

Aneurin Bevan, "Formula for Peace—A Plea to Americans" (April 18, 1953), pp. 324, 325.

Aneurin Bevan, "Journey to India" (May 16, 1953), pp. 415, 416.

Michael Foot, "The Meaning of Bevanism" (October 16, 1954), p. 323.

New Republic

Michael Curtis, "Back-Seat for Bevan" (October 19, 1953), p. 5.

Denis Healey, "Aneurin Bevan Does It Again" (May 3, 1954), p. 5.

Hugh Massingham, "Bevan—Where Are the Loves of Yesteryear?" (November 4, 1957), p. 8.

New Statesman and Nation

G. D. H. Cole, "After Edinburgh" (October 17, 1936), p. 581.

Richard H. S. Crossman, "Sir Stafford Cripps and the Younger Generation" (January 28, 1939), pp. 117–118.

Editorial (March 18, 1939), p. 412.

Editorial (May 13, 1944), p. 313.

Editorial (September 22, 1945), p. 185.

Editorial (March 5, 1952), p. 1.

Kingsley Martin, review of Aneurin Bevan, *In Place of Fear* (April 5, 1952), p. 392.

Unsigned, "Prospect for Morecambe" (July 14, 1952), p. 92.

Editorial, August 9, 1952, p. 114.

August 16, 1952, pp. 175, 176.

Unsigned, "What Happened at Morecambe" (October 4, 1952), p. 368.

Editorial (October 11, 1952), p. 405.

November 1, 1952, pp. 152, 512.

Editorial (December 6, 1952), p. 665.

Editorial (August 29, 1953), p. 221.

Editorial (September 12, 1953), p. 273.

Editorial (April 24, 1954), p. 517.

Unsigned leading article (May 15, 1954), p. 620.

Editorial (October 2, 1954), p. 377.

John Freeman, "After the Scarborough Conference" (October 9, 1954), p. 424.

John Freeman, "Labor and the H-Bomb" (March 12, 1955), pp. 344, 345.

Editorial (March 12, 1955), p. 341.

"Mr. Bevan's Broadside" (Unsigned) February 11, 1956, p. 140.

Editorial (October 6, 1956), p. 393.

Barbara Castle, "It Could Not Have Happened in Arthur's Day" (October 13, 1956), p. 441.

Editorial (October 12, 1957), p. 448.

New York Times Magazine

Vincent Brome, "Bevan and Churchill" (November 21, 1948), pp. 7, 78.

Everett Lawson, "If Not Attlee or Churchill, Who?" (July 24, 1949), p. 10.

Hugh Massingham, "Nye Bevan's One Rule—Fight" (July 13, 1952), p. 16.

Drew Middleton, "Nye Bevan's Biggest Gamble" (April 25, 1954), p. 14.

Drew Middleton, "How "Nye" Bevan Prepares His Bid" (April 14, 1957), p. 26.

John Beavan, "A New 'Nye' Comes for a Visit" (October 27, 1957), p. 80.

The New York Times Book Review

D. W. Brogan's Review of *In Place of Fear*, May 4, 1952, p. 1.

Political Science Quarterly

Lane Davis, "British Socialism and the Perils of Success" (December, 1954), p. 513.

The Observer (London)

February 9, 1958, p. 5.

Reader's Digest

Aneurin Bevan, "The Best Advice I Ever Had" (October, 1953), pp. 91, 92.

Walter S. Robertson, "The Case Against Red China" (December, 1957), pp. 223–225.

The Reporter

Barbara Vereker, "The Rebel of Ebbw Vale" (July 11, 1957), p. 26.

Saturday Evening Post

James P. O'Connell, "Can Britain's Reckless Radical Take Over?" (December 18, 1954), p. 82.

The Spectator

Editorial, "The Flight that Failed" (April 27, 1951), p. 544.

Sir Norman Angell, "Toryism and Freedom" (October 19, 1951), p. 499.

Robert Waithman, "Washington and Bevanism" (October 10, 1951), p. 497.

Robert Waithman, "Churchill–Truman" (January 4, 1952), p. 5.

Francis Williams, "Labor's Rifts" (August 8, 1952), p. 177.

Unsigned, "Mischief at Morecambe" (October 3, 1952), p. 461.

Lord Pakenham, "Morecambe in Retrospect" (October 10, 1952), p. 461.

Hugh Gaitskell, "Further Thoughts on Morecambe" (October 17, 1952), p. 494.

Rev. Mervyn Stockwood, "Attlee and Bevan" (October 31, 1952), p. 558.

Robert Touneley, "Two Views on China" (August 14, 1953), p. 165.

Francis Boyd, "Mr. Bevan's Search for Power" (October 2, 1953), p. 318.

Leading Article, "No Challenge to Britain" (October 2, 1953), p. 343

Leading Article, April 23, 1954, p. 479.

Editorial, October 1, 1954, p. 381

Editorial, March 11, 1955, p. 269.

Time

March 21, 1949, pp. 31–32.

March 17, 1952, p. 27.

March 24, 1952, p. 32.

October 5, 1953, p. 35.

January 11, 1954, p. 17.

May 3, 1954, p. 30

July 19, 1954, p. 24.

October 11, 1954, pp. 33, 34, 42.

March 28, 1955, p. 33

December 10, 1956, pp. 26–27.

October 14, 1957, pp. 35, 36.

The Times (London) Weekly Review

Editorial (March 11, 1951), p. 1.

Editorial (April 25, 1951), pp. 5, 6.

Editorial (April 25, 1951), p. 1.

Editorial (October 10, 1951), p. 6.

October 10, 1957, p. 6.

Tribune

January 3, 1941, p. 9.

January 10, 1941, p. 9.

February 7, 1941, p. 2.

February 28, 1941, p. 1.

March 21, 1941, p. 9.

April 18, 1941, p. 13.

May 2, 1941, p. 12.

July 4, 1941, p. 13.

July 18, 1941, p. 12.

September 5, 1941, p. 12.

October 10, 1941, p. 12.

October 17, 1941, p. 12.

October 24, 1941, p. 13.

February 11, 1944, p. 6.

March 17, 1944, p. 6.

October 20, 1944, p. 8.

November 10, 1944, p. 6.

December 1, 1944, p. 6.

December 15, 1944, pp. 1–2.

May 5, 1945, p. 4.

May 4, 1951, p. 3.

October 5, 1951, p. 2.

March 11, 1955, pp. 1, 6.

March 18, 1955, p. 1.

April 1, 1955, pp. 1, 2

The Welsh Review (*Cardiff*)

Gwyn Jones, Editorial (March, 1944), p. 5.

Aneirin Aptalfan, "Welsh Folk Verse" (December, 1944), p. 264.

Sir Frederick Rees, "Address to Convocation of the University of Ceylon" (September, 1945), p. 285.

Joseph Herman, "A Welsh Mining Village" (June, 1946), pp. 135–137.

W. Idris Jones, "The Future Pattern of Welsh Industry" (Autumn, 1946), p. 209.

U. S. News & World Report

November 22, 1957, p. 118.

BOOKS

Allen, Harry Cranbrook. *Great Britain and the United States: A History of Anglo-American Relations* (*1783–1952*). New York: St. Martin's Press, 1955.

Attlee, Clement A. *As It Happened.* New York: The Viking Press, 1954.

Bevan, Aneurin. *In Place of Fear*. New York: Simon and Schuster, 1952.

Bevin, Ernest. *The Balance Sheet of the Future*. New York: R. M. McBride and Co., 1941.

Black, C. E. and Helmreich, E. C. *Twentieth Century Europe*. New York: Alfred A. Knopf, 1950.

Carr, Philip. *The English Are Like That*. New York: Charles Scribner's Sons, 1941.

Cole, G. D. H. *The People's Front*. London: Victor Gollancz Ltd., 1937.

Corbett, Percy Elwood. *Britain: Partner for Peace*. New York: Harcourt, Brace and Co., 1956.

Cowles, Virginia Spencer. *Winston Churchill: The Era and the Man*. New York: Grosset and Dunlap, 1953.

Dalton, Hugh. *Call Back Yesterday*. London: F. Muller, 1953.

Deane, Herbert A. *The Political Ideas of Harold J. Laski*. New York: Columbia University Press, 1955.

DeJouvenel, Bertrand. *Problems of Socialist England*. London: The Batchworth Press, 1949.

Epstein, D. Leon. *Britain—Uneasy Ally*. Chicago: University of Chicago Press, 1954.

Estorick, Eric. *Stafford Cripps*. New York: The John Day Co., 1949.

Evans, David. *Labor's Strife in South Wales*. Cardiff: Educational Publishing Co. Ltd., 1911.

Fitzsimons, A. Matthew. *The Foreign Policy of the British Labour Government, 1945–1951*. South Bend: Notre Dame University, 1953.

Halévy, Élie. *The World Crisis of 1914–1918*. Oxford: The Clarendon Press, 1930.

———. *A History of the English People Epilogue, 1895–1905*, Vol. I. New York: Barnes and Noble, 1929.

Halifax, Lord. *Fullness of Days*. New York: Dodd, Mead and Co., 1957.

Hunter, Leslie. *The Road to Brighton Pier*. London: Arthur Barker Ltd., 1959.

John, Arthur Henry. *The Industrial Development of South Wales, 1750–1850.* Cardiff: University of Wales Press, 1950.

Jones, Evan J. *Some Contributions to the Economic History of Wales.* London: P. S. King and Son, 1928.

Jones, Idris D. *Modern Welsh History from 1485 to the Present Day.* London: G. Bell and Sons, Ltd., 1934.

Jones, Thomas. *Lloyd George.* Cambridge, Massachusetts: Harvard University Press, 1951.

Kennan, George F. *Russia, The Atom and the West.* New York: Harper and Brothers, 1958.

Laski, Harold J. *Marx and Today.* London: Victor Gollancz Ltd. and the Fabian Society, 1943.

Laski, Harold J. *Where Do We Go From Here?* New York: The Viking Press, 1940.

Lee, Jennie. *This Great Journey.* New York: Farrar and Rinehart, Inc., 1942.

Low, David. *Low's Autobiography.* New York: Simon and Schuster, 1957.

Matthews, Herbert and Nancie. *Assignment to Austerity.* Indianapolis: Bobbs-Merrill Co., 1950.

McKenzie, Robert T. *British Political Parties.* New York: St. Martin's Press, Inc., 1955.

Mowat, Charles L. *Britain Between the Wars: 1918–1940.* Chicago: The University of Chicago Press, 1955.

Ogrizek, Doré, Editor. *Great Britain—England, Scotland and Wales.* New York: Whittlesey House, 1949.

Owen, Frank. *Tempestuous Journey—Lloyd George: His Life and Times.* New York: McGraw-Hill Book Co., Inc., 1955.

Pelling, Henry M. *America and The British Left—From Bright to Bevan.* London: Adam and Charles Black, 1956.

Reynolds, James. *Sovereign Britain.* New York: G. P. Putnam's Sons, 1955.

Schuman, Frederick L. *International Politics.* New York: McGraw-Hill Co., 1948.

Schuyler, R. L. *Some Modern Historians of Britain.* New York: The Dryden Press, 1951.

Spender, John Alfred. *A Short History of Our Times.* New York: Frederick A. Stokes, 1934.

Strauss, Patricia. *Bevin and Co.* New York: G. P. Putnam and Sons, 1941.

Thomson, Malcolm. *David Lloyd George.* London: Hutchinson, 1948.

Truman, Harry S. *Years of Trial and Hope.* New York: Doubleday and Co., 1956.

Watkins, Ernest. *The Cautious Revolution.* New York: Farrar, Strauss and Co., 1950.

Williams, David. *A History of Modern Wales.* London: Murray, 1950.

Williams, Francis. *Socialist Britain.* New York: The Viking Press, 1949.

————. *Fifty Years' March—The Rise of the Labour Party.* London: Odhams Press Ltd., 1949.

Wilson, H. H. and Glickman, Harvey. *The Problem of Internal Security in Great Britain in 1948–1953.* New York: Random House, 1954.

Windrich, Elaine. *British Labour's Foreign Policy.* Stanford: Stanford University Press, 1952.

Notes

Chapter II

[1] Malcolm Thomson, *David Lloyd George* (London: Hutchinson, 1948), p. 39.

[2] David Williams, *A History of Modern Wales* (London: Murray, 1950), p. 9.

[3] Sir Frederick Rees, "Address to Convocation of the University of Ceylon," *The Welsh Review* (Cardiff), September, 1945, p. 285.

[4] Williams, *op. cit.*, p. 12.

[5] Rees, *op. cit.*, p. 289.

[6] Gwyn Jones, Editorial, *The Welsh Review*, March, 1944, p. 5.

[7] Arthur Henry John, *The Industrial Development of South Wales, 1750–1850* (Cardiff: University of Wales Press, 1950), p. 1.

[8] W. Idris Jones, "The Future Pattern of Welsh Industry," *The Welsh Review*, Autumn, 1946, p. 209.

[9] Williams, *op. cit.*, pp. 187–189.

[10] *Encyclopaedia Britannica*, XXIII (1956), 28. It is estimated that even now Wales produces 85 per cent of Britain's sheet metal and 99 per cent of her tin plate.

[11] John, *op. cit.*, p. 166.

[12] Williams, *op. cit.*, p. 229.

[13] Evan J. Jones, *Some Contributions to the Economic History of Wales* (London: P. S. King and Sons, 1927), p. 18.

[14] *Ibid.*, p. 184.

[15] Williams, *op. cit.*, p. 231.

[16] *Ibid.*, p. 240.

[17] Élie Halévy points out that while 90,000 out of 139,000 South Wales miners went on strike, "not a single act of violence was committed by the miners." The Government, however, at the request of the owners, sent troops into the district to intimidate the strikers. Élie Halévy, *A History of the English People, Epilogue, 1895–1915*, Vol. II (New York: Harcourt Brace, 1924), p. 214.

Chapter III

[1] Williams, *A History of Modern Wales*, p. 267.
[2] Thomas Jones, *Lloyd George* (London: Oxford University Press, 1951), p. 4.
[3] W. Idris Jones, *Modern Welsh History* (London: G. Bell and Sons Ltd., 1934), p. 252.
[4] T. Jones, *op. cit.*, p. 4.
[5] Frank Owen, *Tempestuous Journey—Lloyd George; His Life and Times* (New York: McGraw-Hill Inc., 1955), p. 54.
[6] *Tribune* (London), October 20, 1944, p. 8.
[7] *Welsh Review*, Autumn, 1946, p. 174.
[8] Sir Harold Idris Jones, "The Literary Tradition of Wales," *The Welsh Review*, Winter, 1947, p. 234.
[9] Dóré Ogriżek (ed.), *Great Britain, England, Scotland and Wales* (New York: McGraw-Hill, 1949), pp. 351–352.
[10] Welsh Folk Verses, translated by Aneirin Aptalfan, *The Welsh Review*, December, 1944, p. 264.

Chapter IV

[1] *Report of the South Wales Regional Survey Committee*, Ministry of Health (London, 1921).
[2] *Ibid.*, p. 10.
[3] *Ibid.*, p. 10.
[4] *Ibid.*, p. 11.
[5] *Ibid.*, p. 14.
[6] *Ibid.*, p. 14.
[7] Josef Herman, "A Welsh Mining Village," *The Welsh Review*, June, 1946, pp. 135–137.
[8] Aneurin Bevan, *In Place of Fear* (New York: Simon & Schuster, 1952), p. 25.
[9] Aneurin Bevan, "The Best Advice I Ever Had," *Reader's Digest*, October, 1953, p. 91.
[10] *Ibid.*
[11] *Ibid.*
[12] *Ibid.*, p. 92.
[13] *Ibid.*
[14] Bevan, *In Place of Fear*, p. 20.

[15] *Ibid.*

[16] *Ibid.*, p. 24.

[17] *Ibid.*, p. 26 [italics mine].

[18] John Alfred Spender, *A Short History of Our Times* (New York: Frederick A. Stokes, 1934), p. 292.

[19] David Low, *Low's Biography* (New York: Simon & Schuster, 1957), p. 170.

[20] Bevan, *In Place of Fear*, p. 27.

[21] *Ibid.*

[22] Patricia Strauss, *Bevin and Co.* (New York: G. P. Putnam, 1941), p. 81.

[23] Francis Williams, *Fifty Years' March, the Rise of the Labour Party* (London: Odhams Ltd., 1949), p. 327.

[24] Drew Middleton, "Nye Bevan's Biggest Gamble," *New York Times Magazine*, April 25, 1954, p. 14.

[25] Low, *op. cit.*, p. 102.

[26] Bevan, *Reader's Digest*, p. 92.

[27] *Ibid.*

[28] Owen, *Tempestuous Journey*, p. 714.

[29] *Ibid.*, pp. 714–715.

[30] *Ibid.*, p. 715.

[31] Great Britain, *Hansard's Parliamentary Debates* (5th series) (Commons). Vol. CCXLIV (1930), col. 1758. Hereinafter referred to as *Hansard.*

[32] Hugh Dalton, *Call Back Yesterday* (London: Frederick Muller Ltd., 1953), pp. 273–278.

[33] *Ibid.*, p. 297.

[34] Clement Attlee, *As It Happened* (New York: Viking, 1954), p. 111.

[35] Charles L. Mowat, *Britain Between the Wars: 1918–1940* (Chicago: University of Chicago Press, 1955), p. 361.

[36] *Hansard*, Vol. CCLXCV (1934), col. 1305.

[37] *Ibid.*, Vol. CCCXV (1935), col. 1768.

[38] Francis Williams, *Socialist Britain* (New York: Viking, 1949), p. 58.

[39] *Hansard*, Vol. CCCXV (1936), col. 878.

Chapter V

[1] Strauss, *Bevan and Co.*, p. 190.

[2] *Report*, 34th Annual Labour Party Conference (London, 1934), p. 13.

[3] *Ibid.*, p. 139.

[4] *Ibid.*, p. 141.

[5] It should be remembered in the United Front Movement, Sir Stafford Cripps was the acknowledged leader, and the younger and less known Bevan one of his distinguished followers.

[6] G. D. H. Cole, "After Edinburgh," *The New Statesman and Nation,* October 17, 1936, p. 581.

[7] G. D. H. Cole, *The People's Front* (London: Gollancz, 1937), p. 23.

[8] Eric Estorick, *Stafford Cripps* (New York: John Day, 1949), p. 135.

[9] John Roche, "Crisis in British Socialism," *Antioch Review,* Winter, 1952–53, p. 391.

[10] Estorick, *op. cit.,* p. 137.

[11] *Ibid.,* p. 138.

[12] Churchill knew that Cripps was not a Communist or a fellow-traveler but a deeply religious Socialist, who, in addition to political activity, devoted a great deal of his time to the affairs of the St. Matthew Church in London.

[13] "An Appeal to the Movement by the Labour Party Executive Committee," Appendix in Cole, *The People's Front,* p. 353.

[14] "Unity Manifesto," Appendix in Cole, *The People's Front,* p. 357.

[15] The Labour Party Annual *Report,* 1935 (London, 1935), p. 158.

[16] Cole, *The People's Front,* p. 298.

[17] "Unity Manifesto," *ibid.,* p. 35.

[18] Estorick, *op. cit.,* p. 143.

[19] Richard H. S. Crossman, "Sir Stafford Cripps and the Younger Generation," *New Statesman and Nation,* January 28, 1939, p. 118.

[20] *Ibid.*

[21] Editorial, *New Statesman and Nation,* March 18, 1933, p. 412.

[22] Dalton, *Call Back Yesterday,* p. 292.

Chapter VI

[1] Attlee, *As It Happened,* p. 160.

[2] Estorick, *Stafford Cripps,* p. 212.

[3] Ernest Bevin, *The Balance Sheet of the Future* (New York: McBride', 1941), p. 51.

[4] Phillip Carr, *The English Are Like That* (New York: Charles Scribner, 1941), p. 50.

[5] *Hansard,* Vol. CCCLXXIV (1941), col. 1980.

[6] *Ibid.,* Vol. CCCXCVIII (1944), col. 1483.

[7] *Ibid.*, Vol. CCCLXXXIII (1942), col. 241.

[8] Harry S. Truman, *Years of Trial and Hope* (New York: Doubleday, 1956), p. 410.

[9] *Hansard,* Vol. D, col. 1518.

[10] *Ibid.*, Vol. DXXII, col. 608.

[11] *Daily Worker* (London), October 7, 1939.

[12] *Ibid.*, February 11, 1940.

[13] *Hansard,* Vol. CCCLXVIII (1941), cols. 467–475.

[14] *Ibid.*, Vol. CCCLXVIII (1941), col. 516.

[15] *Tribune* (London), January 3, 1941, p. 9.

[16] *Ibid.*

[17] *Ibid.*

[18] *Ibid.*, February 7, 1941, p. 2.

[19] *Ibid.*, p. 1.

[20] Aneurin Bevan, "All Is Not Well," *Tribune* (London), February 28, 1941, p. 1.

[21] Aneurin Bevan, "M.P.'s Tongues Must Be Loosed," *Tribune* (London), March 21, 1941, p. 9.

[22] *Tribune* (London), April 18, 1941, p. 13.

[23] Aneurin Bevan, "Now Is Our Chance to Strike," *Tribune* (London), July 4, 1941, p. 13.

[24] *Hansard,* Vol. CCCLXXIV (1941), col. 1977.

[25] *Ibid.*, col. 1982.

[26] *Ibid.*, col. 1997.

[27] Aneurin Bevan, "Complacency Will Not Win the War," *Tribune* (London), September 5, 1941, p. 12.

[28] Aneurin Bevan, "The People Demand Action," *Tribune* (London), October 10, 1941, p. 12.

[29] *Ibid.*, p. 13.

[30] *Tribune* (London), October 17, 1941, p. 12.

[31] *Tribune* (London), October 24, 1941, p. 13.

[32] Aneurin Bevan "Hope and New Strength," *Tribune* (London), May 2, 1941, p. 12.

[33] Aneurin Bevan, "Meaning of the Alliance," *Tribune* (London), July 18, 1941, p. 12.

[34] *Hansard,* Vol. CCCLXXXIII (1942), col. 246.

[35] *Ibid.*, col. 249.

[36] *Ibid.*, col. 249.

[37] *Ibid.*, col. 261.

[38] *Ibid.*, Vol. CCCXLIII (1943), col. 245.

[39] *Ibid.*, col. 302.

[40] *Ibid.*, Vol. CCCXCIX (1944), col. 1065.

[41] *Ibid.*, col. 1072.

[42] *Ibid.*, col. 1118.

[43] Editorial in *New Statesman and Nation,* May 13, 1944, p. 313.

[44] *Ibid.,* p. 2.

[45] *Hansard* Vol. CCXCVIII (1944), col. 1485.

[46] Aneurin Bevan, "Labour and Coalition," *Tribune* (London), December 11, 1944, p. 6.

[47] *Ibid.,* p. 7

[48] Aneurin Bevan, "A Labour Plan to Beat the Tories," *Tribune* (London), February 11, 1944, p. 6.

[49] *Tribune* (London), March 17, 1944, p. 6.

[50] Aneurin Bevan, "The Parties' Line-Up in Parliament," *Tribune* (London), December 1, 1944, p. 7.

[51] *Ibid.*

[52] *Ibid.,* p. 8.

[53] *New York Times,* May 25, 1945, p. 4.

[54] *Ibid.*

[55] Vincent Brome, "Bevan and Churchill," *New York Times Magazine,* November 21, 1948, p. 78.

[56] *Ibid.*

[57] *Ibid.,* p. 79.

[58] John Beavan, "A New 'Nye' Comes for a Visit," *New York Times Magazine,* October, 1957, p. 80.

[59] Hugh Massingham, "Nye Bevan's One Rule, Fight," *New York Times Magazine,* July 13, 1952, p. 16.

[60] *Hansard* Vol. CDXCVI, col. 987.

Chapter VII

[1] *New York Times,* May 25, 1945, p. 4.

[2] Frederick L. Schumann, *International Politics* (New York: McGraw-Hill 1948), p. 855.

[3] F. Williams, *Socialist Britain.*

[4] Schumann, *op. cit.,* p. 855.

[5] Roche, "Crisis in British Socialism," *Antioch Review,* Winter, 1952–53, p. 388.

[6] Quoted by Herbert and Nancy Matthews, *Assignment to Austerity* (New York: Bobbs, Merrill, 1950), p. 221.

[7] Attlee, *As It Happened,* p. 215.

[8] F. Williams, *op. cit.,* p. 125.

[9] *Ibid.*

[10] Roche, *op. cit.,* p. 393.

[11] *New York Times,* December 13, 1946, p. 27.

[12] Bevan, *In Place of Fear,* p. 93.

294 *Aneurin Bevan: Cautious Rebel*

[13] *Ibid.*, p. 79.
[14] *Ibid.*, p. 81.
[15] *Ibid.*
[16] *Ibid.*
[17] *Ibid.*, p. 92.
[18] *Ibid.*
[19] Ernest Watkins, *The Cautious Revolution* (New York: Farrer, Staus, 1950), p. 221.
[20] *Hansard*, Vol. CDXLVII (1948), col. 42.
[21] *Ibid.*, col. 47.
[22] *Ibid.*, col. 36. See: Editorial, *Economist*, January 17, 1948: ". . . Mr. Bevan has become suspect in the eyes of the profession because he has become identified as the leader of the extreme Socialists in the Government" (p. 85).
[23] *Health Services in Britain* (New York, 1948) (pamphlet).
[24] *Ibid.*, p. 7.
[25] *Time*, March 21, 1949, p. 32.
[26] C. E. Black and E. C. Helmrich, *Twentieth Century Europe* (New York: Alfred A. Knopf, 1950), p. 779.
[27] "Paying for Sickness," *Economist*, December 25, 1948, p. 1054.
[28] *Ibid.*
[29] Quoted in *New York Times Magazine*, November 21, 1948, p. 79.
[30] Brome, "Bevan and Churchill," *New York Times Magazine*, November 21, 1948, p. 7.
[31] *Economist*, July 10, 1948, p. 48.
[32] *Ibid.*
[33] Everett Lawson, "If Not Attlee or Churchill, Who?" *New York Times Magazine*, July 24, 1949, p. 10.
[34] See for example *Time*, March 21, 1949, pp. 31–32.
[35] *Hansard*, Vol. CDLIV (1948), col. 196.
[36] *Hansard*, Vol. CDLIV (1948), col. 196.
[37] In 1958, Heathcoat Amory, the Conservative Minister of Health, estimated the cost of the Health Service during the coming fiscal year at £740,000,000 ($2,072,000,000), *New York Times*, February 19, 1958, p. 4.
[38] Bevan, *op. cit.*, p. 88.
[39] Watkins, *op. cit.*, p. 194.
[40] F. Williams, *op. cit.*, p. 126.
[41] *Report*, 46th Annual Labour Party Conference (London: Transport House, 1947), p. 191.
[42] Watkins, *op. cit.*, p. 196.
[43] *Report*, 46th Annual Labour Party Conference, p. 191.
[44] *Ibid.*
[45] *Ibid.*

[46] Watkins, *op. cit.*, p. 203.

[47] *Hansard*, Vol. CDLIII (1949), col. 1317.

[48] *Ibid.*, col. 1318.

[49] Watkins, *op. cit.*, p. 204.

[50] *Hansard*, Vol. CDXCIV (1952), col. 2261.

[51] *Report*, 49th Annual Labour Party Conference, (London: Transport House, 1950), p. 162.

[52] *Ibid.*

Chapter VIII

[1] *Report*, 49th Annual Labour Party Conference, p. 114.

[2] *Ibid.*, p. 115 [italics mine].

[3] Harold Laski, *Marx and Today* (London: Victor Gollancz and the Fabian Society, 1943), p. 7.

[4] *Report*, 49th Annual Labour Party Conference, p. 132.

[5] Lane Davis, "British Socialism and the Perils of Success," *Political Science Quarterly*, December, 1954, p. 513.

[6] *Hansard*, Vol. CDXIII (1945), col. 312.

[7] *Ibid.*, Vol. CDXLVI (1948), col. 550.

[8] M. A. Fitzsimmons, *The Foreign Policy of the British Labour Government 1945–51* (South Bend: Notre Dame University Press, 1953), p. 27.

[9] *Ibid.*, p. 28.

[10] Editorial, *New Statesman and Nation*, September 22, 1945, p. 185.

[11] *Hansard*, Vol. CDXXV (1946), col. 1835.

[12] *Ibid.*, Vol. CDXXX (1946), col. 386.

[13] Fitzsimmons, *op. cit.*, p. 54.

[14] Henry M. Pelling, America and the British Left from Bright to Bevan (London: Adam and Charles Black, 1956), p. 151.

[15] Bevin was lauded for this action by the *Times Weekly Review* (London) on March 11, 1951, the day Bevin relinquished the post of Foreign Secretary because of ill health.

[16] *Debate in the House of Commons, British Foreign Affairs*, British Information Service (New York, February, 1948), pp. 9–13.

[17] *Ibid.*, p. 21.

[18] *Ibid.*, p. 22.

[19] *Report*, 47th Annual Labour Party Conference (London, 1948), p. 197.

[20] *Hansard*, Vol. CDXLVI (1948), col. 562.

[21] *British Foreign Affairs* (pamphlet), p. 43.

[22] *Ibid.*

[23] *Ibid.*, p. 12.

[24] *Hansard,* Vol. CDLXIV (1949), col. 2076.

[25] *Ibid.*, col. 2077.

[26] *Face the Nation* (Radio Program,) Washington, D. C., November 3,1957.

[27] *Hansard,* Vol. D (1952), col. 1511.

[28] *Ibid.*, col. 1512.

[29] Ernest Bevin told the Fiftieth Annual Conference that the decision to resist Korean agression was taken by the entire Cabinet. See *Report,* 49th Annual Labour Party Conference (London, 1950), p. 148.

[30] Elaine Windrich, *British Labour's Foreign Policy* (Palo Alto: Stanford University Press 1952), p. 216.

[31] Text of letter in *Daily Herald,* December 1, 1950, p. 1. Among signers were such well-known Bevanites as Ian Mikardo, Jennie Lee, and Tom Driberg.

[32] Truman, *Years of Trial and Hope,* p. 396.

[33] *Ibid.*

[34] *Ibid.*, p. 402. Bevan espoused the same point of view during his visit to the United States in October 1957. He stated in a speech reported by the United Press in the Cincinnati *Post* of October 30, 1957, that the United States should recognize China and added, "We must break down these barriers so they, the Communists, can become familiar with our ways of life and then the waves of Communism will be rolled back."

[35] *Ibid.*, p. 505. This is a remarkable statement because it is in essence identical with the position taken by Aneurin Bevan when he abruptly resigned his position in the Cabinet in April, 1957.

[36] *Report,* 49th Annual Labour Party Conference, p. 150.

[37] *Times Weekly Review* (London), October 10, 1951, p. 6.

[38] Attlee, *As It Happened,* p. 289.

[39] Robert T. McKenzie, *British Political Parties* (London: Macmillan, 1955), p. 527.

[40] *Times Weekly Review* (London), April 25, 1951, p. 5.

[41] *Hansard,* Vol. CDLXXXVII, cols. 34–43.

[42] See Nikita Khrushchev's speech at the fortieth Anniversary of the Bolshevik Revolution, *New York Times,* November 7, 1957, p. 10.

[43] *Hansard,* Vol. CDLXXXVII, col. 41.

[44] *Ibid.*, col. 43.

[45] Howard K. Smith, "Bevan's Rebellion," *The Nation,* May 12, 1951, p. 487.

[46] *Times Weekly Review* (London), April 25, 1951, p. 6.

[47] *Ibid.*, April 25, 1951, p. 1.

[48] Editorial "The Flight That Failed," *Spectator*, April 27, 1951, p. 544.

[49] Attlee, *op. cit.*, p. 289.

[50] Editorial, *Times Weekly Review* (London), April 25, 1951, p. 1.

[51] Attlee, *op. cit.*, p. 289 [italics mine].

[52] *Hansard*, Vol. DIV (1952), col. 1524.

[53] *Report*, 49th Annual Labour Party Conference, p. 130.

[54] *Nation*, January 27, 1951, p. 71.

[55] Smith, *Nation*, May, 1951, p. 438.

[56] *Ibid.*

[57] *Tribune* (London), May 4, 1951, p. 3.

[58] *Face the Nation*, November 3, 1957.

[59] *Tribune* (London), October 5, 1951, p. 2.

[60] *Times* (London), October 3, 1951, p. 9.

[61] Norman Angel, "Toryism and Freedom," *Spectator*, October 19, 1951, p. 499.

Chapter IX

[1] Jules Menken, Review of *In Place of Fear*, *Manchester Guardian Weekly*, April 10, 1952, p. 11.

[2] George Lichtheim, "Behind the Anti-Americanism of Mr. Bevan," *Commentary*, July, 1952, p. 16.

[3] Kingsley Martin, Review of *In Place of Fear*, *New Statesman and Nation*, April 5, 1952, p. 392.

[4] Menken, *op. cit.*

[5] H. and N. Matthews, *Assignment to Austerity*, p. 231.

[6] Lichtheim, *op. cit.*, p. 17.

[7] F. Williams, *Socialist Britain*, p. 114.

[8] Rev. Mervyn Stockwood, "Attlee and Bevan," *Spectator*, October 31, 1952, p. 558.

[9] Hugh Massingham, "Nye Bevan's One Rule, Fight," *New York Times Magazine*, July 13, 1952, p. 16.

[10] Francis Boyd, "Mr. Bevan's Search for Power," *Spectator*, October 1953, p. 318.

[11] *Ibid.*

[12] See Salvador de Madariaga, "Russia and the West: An Open Letter to Mr. Bevan," *Manchester Guardian Weekly*, 1952, p. 12.

[13] Bevan, *In Place of Fear*, p. 135.

[14] Bevan developed this point of view in a speech made in Jarrow in 1952. Quoted by Madariaga, *op. cit.*, p. 12.

[15] Bevan, *op. cit.*, p. 131.

[16] *Hansard,* Vol. D. (1952), col. 1521.

[17] Bevan, *op. cit.,* p. 147.

[18] *Report,* 50th Annual Labour Party Conference (London, 1951), p. 121.

[19] Bevan, *op. cit.,* p. 139.

[20] *Ibid.,* p. 43.

[21] *Ibid.*

[22] *Ibid.,* pp. 17–18.

[23] *Ibid.,* p. 148.

[24] *Ibid.,* p. 149.

[25] *Ibid.,* p. 43.

[26] *Report,* 49th Annual Labour Party Conference (London, 1950), p. 132.

[27] *Ibid.,* p. 18.

[28] Martin, *New Statesman and Nation,* April 5, 1952, p. 392.

[29] *Hansard,* Vol. DVIII (1952), col. 1870.

[30] *Ibid.,* Vol. DXIV (1953), col. 1592.

[31] Bevan, *op. cit.,* p. 130.

[32] *Hansard,* Vol. DVIII (1952), col. 1873.

[33] *Ibid.,* Vol. CDXCVI (1952), col. 993.

[34] *Ibid.,* Vol. DXXII (1953), col. 609.

[35] Bevan, *op. cit.,* p. 1.

[36] *Ibid.,* p. 6.

[37] *Ibid.,* p. 31.

[38] *Ibid.,* p. 2.

[39] *Ibid.,* p. 105.

[40] *Ibid.,* p. 22.

[41] *Ibid.,* p. 23. Élie Halévy said in 1934, "The Labor Leaders are men whose doctrine requires them to make the State stronger, and whose good British instinct is to make the State as weak as possible. . . . I am afraid that rather than socialistic in spirit they are whiggish, eager to protect the individual against the State, not to make the State strong against the capitalists. . . . I tell you frankly that I shudder at the thought of the Labor Party ever having a real majority not for the sake of Capitalism, but for the sake of Socialism." See Élie Halévy, "Socialism and the Problem of Democratic Parliamentarism," *International Affairs,* July–August, 1934, 490–495.

[42] *Hansard,* Vol. DVIII (1952), col. 1820.

[43] Bevan, *op. cit.,* p. 125.

[44] *Ibid.,* pp. 179–180.

[45] *Ibid.,* p. 125.

[46] *Ibid.,* p. 89.

[47] *Ibid.,* p. 103.

[48] *Report,* 51st Annual Labour Party Conference (London: Transport House, 1952), p. 82.

[49] *Ibid.,* p. 83.

[50] Massingham, *New York Times Magazine,* July 13, 1952, p. 16.

[51] *Ibid.*

[52] Bevan, *op. cit.,* p. 127.

[53] Massingham, *op. cit.,* p. 16.

[54] Bevan, *op. cit.,* p. 19.

[55] *Ibid.,* p. 30.

[56] *Ibid.,* p. 132.

[57] D. W. Brogan, Review of *In Place of Fear, New York Times Book Review,* May 4, 1952, p. 28.

[58] *Ibid.*

[59] Bevan's speech at Durham, quoted in *Time,* March 24, 1952, p. 32.

[60] Bevan, *In Place of Fear,* pp. 129–130.

[61] *Report,* 51st Annual Labour Party Conference, p. 82.

[62] *New York Times,* November 25, 1957, p. 2.

[63] *Ibid.,* p. 2.

[64] *Report,* 51st Annual Labour Party Conference, p. 83.

[65] *Foreign Policy Bulletin,* December, 1957, p. 17.

[66] *Ibid.*

[67] *Report,* 51st Annual Labour Party Conference, p. 108.

[68] *Ibid.,* p. 89.

[69] *Ibid.,* p. 153.

[70] *Hansard,* Vol. CDXCVI (1952), col. 979.

[71] Madariaga, *op. cit.,* p. 12.

[72] *Ibid.*

[73] *Ibid.*

[74] Bevan, *op. cit.,* p. 142.

[75] *Ibid.,* p. 134.

[76] *Ibid.,* pp. 150–151.

[77] *Report,* 52nd Annual Labour Party Conference (London, 1953), p. 151.

[78] Richard Towneley, "Two Views of China," *Spectator,* August 14, 1953, p. 165.

[79] *Ibid.,* p. 165.

[80] *Labour's Foreign Policy* (London: National Executive Committee, 1952), p. 8 (pamphlet).

[81] *Report,* 52nd Annual Labour Party Conference. p. 153.

[82] *Hansard,* Vol. DII (1952), col. 2266.

[83] *Ibid.,* col. 2270.

[84] *Report,* 50th Annual Labour Party Conference, p. 121.

[85] *Hansard*, Vol. CDXCVI (1952), col. 989.

[86] Editorial, *The Manchester Guardian Weekly*, August 6, 1953, p. 9.

[87] *New York Times*, December 4, 1957, p. 16.

Chapter X

[1] *Report*, 50th Annual Labour Party Conference, (London: Transport House, 1951), p. 122.

[2] Francis Williams, "Labor's Rifts," *Spectator*, August 8, 1952, p. 177.

[3] Michael Foot, "Mr. Bevan Remains," *Nation*, April 16, 1952, p. 325.

[4] Robert Waithman, "Churchill–Truman," *Spectator*, January 4, 1952, p. 5.

[5] *Time*, March 17, 1952, p. 27.

[6] *Time*, March 24, 1952, p. 32.

[7] Editorial, *Spectator*, March 14, 1952, p. 313.

[8] Geoffrey Ashe, "Bevan vs. Bevanism," *Commonweal* July 4, 1952, p. 312.

[9] "Prospect for Morecambe," *New Statesman and Nation*, July 14, 1952, p. 92.

[10] Churchill was guilty of breaking the same rule when he disclosed Morrison's commitment to the United States on British support in case of a Red Chinese attack from Manchurian bases.

[11] *Hansard*, Vol. DIV (1952), col. 1526.

[12] Editorial, *New Statesman and Nation*, August 16, 1952, pp. 175–176.

[13] *Report*, 51st Annual Labour Party Conference (London, 1952), p. 113.

[14] *Ibid.*, pp. 114–115.

[15] *New Statesman and Nation*, August 16, 1952, p. 175.

[16] *Report*, 51st Annual Labour Party Conference, p. 99.

[17] Deakin's threat was not an idle one. The National Executive Committee reported in its 1953 report that in 1952 the Trade Unions provided £126,000 in affiliation fees, while the Constituency Labour Parties contributed £27,000 in the same fees. In addition, T.U.C. contributed another £150,000 from its political funds for the expenses of Socialist propaganda and the maintenance of party machinery. See R. T. McKenzie, *British Political Parties* pp. 594–597.

[18] *Report*, 51st Annual Labour Party Conference, p. 78.

[19] *Ibid.*, p. 117.

[20] *Ibid.*, p. 118.
[21] *Ibid.*, p. 142.
[22] *Ibid.*, p. 147.
[23] *Ibid.*, p. 149.
[24] *Ibid.*, p. 153.
[25] *Ibid.*, p. 123.
[26] *Ibid.*, p. 83.
[27] *Ibid.*, p. 127.
[28] *Ibid.*
[29] "Comment and Criticism," *Manchester Guardian Weekly*, October 2, 1952, p. 8.
[30] *Ibid.*
[31] "Mischief at Morecambe," *Spectator*, October 3, 1952, p. 415.
[32] "What Happened at Morecambe?" *New Statesman and Nation*, October 4, 1952, p. 368.
[33] "Comment and Criticism," *Manchester Guardian Weekly*, October 5, 1952, p. 8.
[34] Hugh Gaitskell, "Further Thoughts on Morecambe," *Spectator*, October 17, 1952, p. 494.
[35] Lord Pakenham, "Morecambe in Retrospect," *Spectator*, October 10, 1952, p. 461.
[36] *Ibid.*
[37] Andrew Roth, "The Rise of Bevan," *Nation*, October 11, 1952, p. 317.
[38] Editorial, *New Statesman and Nation*, October 11, 1952, p. 405.
[39] *Manchester Guardian Weekly*, October 16, 1952, p. 8.
[40] *Manchester Guardian Weekly*, October 23, 1953, p. 5.
[41] *New Statesman and Nation*, November 1, 1952, p. 152.
[42] *Ibid.*, p. 512.
[43] *Hansard*, Vol. DVIII (1952), col. 1792.
[44] *Ibid.*, col. 1799.
[45] *Ibid.*, col. 1804.
[46] Editorial, *New Statesman and Nation*, December 6, 1952, p. 393.

Chapter XI

[1] *Hansard*, Vol. DX (1953), col. 201.
[2] *Ibid.*, Vol. DXII (1953), col. 2075.
[3] *Ibid.*, Vol. DXV (1953), col. 1066.
[4] *Ibid.*, col. 1077.
[5] Sir Walter Fletcher M.P., "Trade with China After an Armistice," *Manchester Guardian* Weekly, July 23, 1953, p. 3.

[6] Robert Waithman, "Washington and Bevanism," *Spectator,* October 19, 1951, p. 497.

[7] *Hansard,* Vol. DXV (May 12, 1953), col. 1085.

[8] *Ibid.,* cols. 1090, 1091 [italics mine].

[9] *Ibid.,* col. 1086.

[10] *Ibid.*

[11] "Review of Parliament," *Manchester Guardian Weekly,* May 28, 1953, p. 5.

[12] *Ibid.,* March 5, 1953, p. 5.

[13] *Hansard,* Vol. DXV (1953), col. 322.

[14] Aneurin Bevan, "Journey to India," *Nation,* May 16, 1953, p. 415.

[15] *Ibid.,* p. 416.

[16] Aneurin Bevan, "Formula for   Peace—A Plea to Americans," *Nation,* April 18, 1953, p. 324.

[17] *Ibid.,* p. 325.

[18] *Ibid.*

[19] Bevan, "Formula for Peace," *Nation,* April 18, 1953, p. 325.

[20] *Ibid.*

[21] *Ibid.*

[22] "Review of Parliament," *Manchester Guardian Weekly,* April 23, 1953, p. 5.

[23] *Hansard,* Vol. DXIV (1953), vol. 751.

[24] *Ibid.,* Vol. DXV (1953), col. 1071.

[25] Editorial, *New Statesman and Nation,* August 29, 1953, p. 221.

[26] "No Challenge to Britain," *Spectator,* October 2, 1953, p. 343.

[27] "Comment and Criticism," *Manchester Guardian Weekly,* September 10, 1953, p. 9.

[28] *Challenge to Britain* in the *Report,* 52nd Annual Labour Party Conference (London, 1953), p. 62.

[29] *Ibid.,* p. 64.

[30] *Ibid.*

[31] *Ibid.,* p. 65.

[32] *Spectator,* October 2, 1953, p. 343.

[33] *Manchester Guardian Weekly,* September 3, 1953, p. 9.

[34] *New Statesman and Nation,* September 12, 1953, p. 273.

[35] *Manchester Guardian Weekly,* September 10, 1953, p. 3.

[36] McKenzie, *British Political Parties,* p. 501.

[37] *Ibid.,* p. 426.

[38] *Time,* October 5, 1953, p. 35.

[39] *Report,* 52nd Annual Labour Party Conference, pp. 149–150.

[40] *Ibid.,* p. 150.

[41] *Ibid.*

[42] *Ibid.,* p. 151.

[43] *Ibid.*

[44] Michael Curtis, "Back-Seat for Bevan," *New Republic*, October 19, 1953, p. 5.

[45] *Report*, 52nd Annual Conference, p. 90.

[46] Labour Correspondent, "A Constructive Week's Work at Margate," *Manchester Guardian Weekly*, October 8, 1953, p. 3.

[47] Quoted by Bevan in his speech in Commons, *Hansard*, Vol. DXXII (1953), cols. 608–609.

[48] *Ibid.*, col. 609.

[49] *Ibid.*, cols. 601–611.

[50] *Ibid.*, col. 638.

Chapter XII

[1] *Time*, January 11, 1954, p. 17.

[2] *Hansard*, Vol. DXXVI (1954), col. 969.

[3] *Ibid.*, col. 920.

[4] *Ibid.*, col. 971.

[5] *Time*, May 3, 1954, p. 30.

[6] *Spectator*, April 23, 1954, p. 479.

[7] *Ibid.*

[8] Denis Healey, "Aneurin Bevan Does It Again," *New Republic*, May 3, 1954, p. 5.

[9] Editorial, *Economist*, April 24, 1954, p. 261.

[10] *Ibid.*, p. 262.

[11] Editorial, *New Statesman and Nation*, April 24, 1954, p. 517.

[12] *New Statesman and Nation*, May 15, 1954, p. 620.

[13] Editorial, *New Statesman and Nation*, October 2, 1954, p. 377.

[14] Michael Foot, "The Meaning of Bevanism," *Nation*, October 16, 1954, p. 322.

[15] *Time*, July 19, 1954, p. 24.

[16] James P. O'Connell, "Can Britain's Reckless Radical Take Over?" *Saturday Evening Post*, December 18, 1954, p. 82.

[17] *Report*, 53rd Annual Labour Party Conference (London, 1954), p. 71.

[18] *Ibid.*

[19] *Ibid.*

[20] *Ibid.*, p. 72.

[21] *Ibid.*

[22] *Ibid.*, p. 76.

[23] *Ibid.*, p. 77

[24] Foot, *Nation*, October, 1954, p. 323.

[25] *Report*, 53rd Annual Labour Party Conference, p. 323.

[26] *Ibid.,* p. 94.
[27] *Ibid.,* p. 96.
[28] *Ibid.,* p. 104.
[29] *Ibid.,* p. 108.
[30] *Time,* October 11, 1954, p. 42.
[31] *Ibid.*
[32] *Ibid.*
[33] Editorial, *Spectator,* October 1, 1954, p. 381.
[34] John Freeman, "After the Scarborough Conference," *New Statesman and Nation,* October 9, 1954, p. 424.
[35] Editorial Notes, *Economist,* October 2, 1954, p. 23.

Chapter XIII

[1] *Report,* 54th Annual Labour Party Conference (London: Transport House, 1955), p. 25.
[2] *Hansard,* Vol. DXXXVII (1955) col. 2113.
[3] *Ibid.,* col. 2114.
[4] *Ibid.,* col. 2115.
[5] *Ibid.,* col. 2116.
[6] *Ibid.*
[7] *Ibid.*
[8] *Ibid.,* col. 2117.
[9] *Ibid.,* col. 2120.
[10] *Ibid.,* col. 2110.
[11] *Ibid.,* col. 2170.
[12] It should be noted that Bevan's question was not finally and decisively answered (affirmatively) until the publication of the Government's White Paper on Defense on February 13, 1958.
[13] *Hansard,* Vol. DXXXVII (1955), col. 2176.
[14] *Ibid.*
[15] John Freeman, "Labor and the H-Bomb," *New Statesman and Nation,* March 12, 1955, p. 344.
[16] *Ibid.,* p. 345.
[17] Editorial, *Spectator,* March 11, 1955, p. 269.
[18] Editorial, *New Statesman and Nation,* March 12, 1955, p. 341.
[19] Editorial, *Tribune* (London), March 11, 1955, p. 1.
[20] Aneurin Bevan, "Churchill Confesses," *Tribune* (London), March 11, 1955, p. 3.
[21] *Time,* March 14, 1955, p. 33.
[22] *Ibid.,* p. 34.

[23] Leon D. Epstein, "Cohesion of British Parliamentary Parties," *American Political Science Review*, June, 1956, p. 373.

[24] Editorial, *Tribune* (London), March 18, 1955, p. 1.

[25] *Tribune* (London), April 1, 1955, p. 2.

[26] Editorial, *Tribune* (London), April 1, 1955, p. 2.

[27] *Economist*, March 19, 1955, p. 973.

[28] *Ibid.*, p. 374.

[29] Text of Statement, *Tribune* (London), April 1, 1955, p. 1.

[30] *Ibid.*, p. 1.

[31] *Economist*, March 26, 1955, p. 1070.

[32] *Tribune* (London), April 1, 1955, p. 1.

[33] *Economist*, April 9, 1955, p. 106.

[34] Aneurin Bevan, "Why I Am Standing for Treasurer," *Tribune* (London), October 7, 1955, p. 1.

[35] *Ibid.*, p. 2.

[36] *Report*, 54th Annual Labour Party Conference, p. 25.

[37] *Ibid.*

[38] *Ibid.*, p. 141.

[39] *Ibid.*

[40] *Ibid.*, p. 174.

[41] *Ibid.*, p. 175.

[42] *Ibid.*

Chapter XIV

[1] "Mr. Bevan's Broadside," *New Statesman and Nation,* February 11, 1956, p. 140.

[2] *The Observer* (London), February 9, 1958, p. 5.

[3] *Hansard*, Vol. DXLVIII (1956), col. 2475.

[4] *Ibid.*, Vol. DL (1956), col. 387.

[5] *Ibid.*, col. 291.

[6] *Ibid.*, col. 400.

[7] *Hansard*, Vol. DL (1956), col. 1798 [italics mine].

[8] *Hansard*, Vol. DLIII (1956), cols. 1194–1195.

[9] *Hansard*, Vol. DLVII (1956), col. 1473.

[10] *Ibid.*, col. 1474.

[11] *Ibid.*, col. 1488.

[12] *Report*, 55th Annual Labour Party Conference (London: Transport House, 1956), p. 77.

[13] *Ibid.*, p. 76.

[14] *Ibid.*, p. 78.

[15] *Economist*, October 6, 1956, p. 19.

[16] Editorial, *New Statesman and Nation*, October 6, 1956, p. 393.

[17] Barbara Castle, "It Could Not Have Happened in Arthur's Day," *New Statesman and Nation*, October 13, 1956, p. 441.

[18] *Report*, 55th Annual Labour Party Conference (London, 1956), p. 81.

[19] Editorial, "America Fears Bevan," *America*, October 13, 1956, p. 23.

[20] *Economist*, October 6, 1956, p. 20 [italics mine].

[21] *Hansard*, Vol. DLVIII (1956), col. 1454.

[22] *Ibid.*, col. 1707.

[23] *Ibid.*, col. 1708.

[24] *Ibid.*

[25] *Ibid.*, col. 1709.

[26] *Ibid.*, col. 1710.

[27] *Ibid.*

[28] *Hansard*, Vol. DLVIII (1956), cols. 1715–1716.

[29] *Ibid.*, col. 1717.

[30] *Ibid.*, col. 1965.

[31] *Hansard*, Vol. DLX, cols. 392–393.

[32] *Economist*, November 10, 1956, p. 493.

[33] *Hansard*, Vol. DLX (1956), col. 392.

[34] *Ibid.*, col. 391.

[35] *Ibid.*, Vol. DLXII (1956), col. 1401.

[36] *Ibid.*, col. 1402.

[37] *Ibid.*, col. 1405.

[38] *Economist*, November 17, 1956, p. 580.

[39] *Manchester Guardian Weekly*, November 29, 1956, p. 3.

[40] *Economist*, December 2, 1956, p. 764.

[41] *Time*, December 10, 1956, p. 27.

Chapter XV

[1] *Hansard*, Vol. DLXIII (1957), cols. 673–674.

[2] *Ibid.*, Vol. DLXXI (1957), col. 1081.

[3] Drew Middleton, "How 'Nye' Bevan Prepares His Bid," *New York Times Magazine*, April 14, 1957, p. 26.

[4] *Economist*, April 20, 1957, p. 213.

[5] Barbara Vereker, "The Rebel of Ebbw Vale," *The Reporter*, July 11, 1957, p. 26.

[6] *Economist*, May 4, 1957, p. 478.

[7] *Time*, October 14, 1957, p. 35.

[8] *Ibid.*
[9] *Ibid.*
[10] *Ibid.,* pp. 35–36.
[11] *New York Times,* October 3, 1957, p. 10.
[12] *Ibid.*
[13] *Economist,* October 15, 1957, p. 16.
[14] Hugh Massingham, "Bevan—Where Are the Loves of Yesteryear?" *New Republic,* November 4, 1957, p. 8.
[15] *Economist,* October 15, 1957, p. 16.
[16] *New Statesman and Nation,* October 12, 1957, p. 448.
[17] Massingham, *New Republic,* November 4, 1957, p. 8.
[18] *The Times Weekly Review* (London), October 10, 1957, p. 6.
[19] Massingham, *New Republic,* November 4, 1957, p. 7.
[20] Beavan, *New York Times Magazine,* October 27, 1957, p. 80.
[21] *U. S. News & World Report,* November 9, 1959, p. 118.
[22] *Ibid.*
[23] *Ibid.*
[24] *Ibid.*
[25] *Ibid.,* p. 120.
[26] *Ibid.*
[27] *Cincinnati Post,* October 30, 1957, p. 3.
[28] Inez Robb, "Bevan Sings Old Song," *The Cincinnati Post,* November 9, 1957, p. 12.
[29] Victor Riesel, "Likes Pigs and Reds," *Cincinnati Enquirer,* November 6, 1957, p. 8.
[30] *Cincinnati Enquirer,* October 29, 1957, p. 11.
[31] *New York Times,* November 25, 1957, p. 2.
[32] *Foreign Policy Bulletin,* Foreign Policy Association, New York, December 1, 1957, p. 42.
[33] Associated Press dispatch, *The Miami Herald,* December 21, 1957, p. 1.
[34] *The Manchester Guardian Weekly,* December 26, 1957, p. 2.
[35] *The Miami Herald,* December 21, 1957, p. 1.
[36] *The Manchester Guardian Weekly,* December 26, 1957, p. 2.

Chapter XVI

[1] Text of address by John Foster Dulles before the National Press Club, *New York Times,* January 17, 1958, p. 4 [italics mine].
[2] George F. Kennan, *Russia, The Atom and the West* (New York, 1957), p. 17.
[3] *Ibid.,* p. 52.

[4] *Ibid.*, p. 13.

[5] Bevan, *In Place of Fear*, pp. 131 and 135.

[6] Dulles, *New York Times*, January 17, 1958, p. 4.

[7] Bevan, *op. cit.*, p. 148.

[8] *Report*, 51st Annual Conference, p. 132.

[9] Kennan, *op. cit.*, p. 7.

[10] Aneurin Bevan, "Britain and American at Loggerheads," *Foreign Affairs*, October, 1957, p. 67.

[11] *Ibid.*, p. 67.

[12] *U. S. News & World Report*, December 17, 1957, p. 26.

[13] *Time*, December 23, 1957, p. 21.

[14] Dulles, *New York Times*, January 17, 1958, p. 4.

[15] Drew Middleton, "The Anti-U. S. Sentiment," *New York Times*, December 15, 1957, p. 9.

[16] Bevan, *Foreign Affairs*, October, 1957, p. 63.

[17] C. L. Sulzberger, "A Three-Handed Game of Chinese Checkers," *New York Times*, October 4, 1957, p. 20.

[18] Kennan, *op. cit.*, p. 39.

[19] Drew Middleton, *New York Times Magazine*, April 14, 1957, p. 26.

Index

Abraham, William, organizes miners, 21

Adenauer, Chancellor, rearmament with West Germany, 158

Amalgamated Association of Miners, organized, 21

America, Bevan on the United States, 138–142; U. S. policy on China, 144–146, 148; U. S. policies on Korea, 154; Bevan attacks U. S. on Yalu River bombings, 156–157; alliance with America, 159, 162–164; anti-Americanism, 178–181; press alarmed by Bevan's victory, 244

Amery, Julian, supports Bevan, 128

Anglican Church of Wales, history and policies, 23–25

Attlee, Clement, eulogizes Bevan, 12; on Bevan, 44, 49; enters Coalition Government, 57, 60; attacked by Bevan, 62–65, 68, 69, 74; appoints Bevan Health Minister; 82–84; supports Bevin's foreign policy, 101–104; confers with Truman on Korea, 111–113; on Bevan's resignation, 116–118, 120, 125, 137, 145; on recognition of Red China, 147, 149; supports Churchill's defense program, 151–154; demands sanctions on Bevan, 155–156; supports British rearmament, 161–163, 167; demands disbanding of Bevanites, 170–173; presses for China seat in U. N., 176; supports Churchill on foreign policy, 184; supports Bevan's views on China and negotiations with Soviets, 193; supports Government on Egypt, 197; visits China with Bevan, 207–208; supports H-bomb for Britain, 218; presents case against Bevan, 222; retires, 231

Baldwin, Stanley, depressed areas, 45; attacked on Italy, 54

Bevan, Aneurin, eulogies on death, 11–12; cool on Welsh nationalism, 27–28; Welsh characteristics, 29; youth in South Wales, 33; education and union activity, 34–36; participates in General Strike, 37–38; elected to Parliament, 39; fights MacDonald on unemployment and miners' bills,